D1561276

GOD, FAMILY, COUNTRY

GOD, FAMILY, COUNTRY

A MEMOIR

CRAIG MORGAN

WITH JIM DEFELICE

**BLACK
STONE**
PUBLISHING

Copyright © 2022 by Tripple Shoes Productions, Inc.
Published in 2022 by Blackstone Publishing
Cover and book design by Kathryn Galloway English
Permissions and credits listed at the end of this book

Printed in the United States of America

First edition: 2022
ISBN 978-1-6650-5868-1
Biography & Autobiography / Personal Memoirs

Version 1

CIP data for this book is available
from the Library of Congress

Blackstone Publishing
31 Mistletoe Rd.
Ashland, OR 97520

www.BlackstonePublishing.com

With great thanks to my Lord and savior,
and to my wife and family

AUTHOR'S NOTE:

The stories I've shared in this book are true, but they are based on my memory. The dialogue contained in this book is not meant to represent verbatim quotes of what was said, but rather a summary of the conversations as I remember them.

TABLE OF CONTENTS

PROLOGUE:
FACING THE MUSIC

It's a little past four in the afternoon, three hours and change before I walk onstage. The boys loaded our equipment out of the tractor trailer a couple of hours ago; we set up the stage with some help from the local crew and then worked through the sound check until everything was sorted.

I've played in bigger places, but I'd be hard-pressed to think of one prettier, my Grand Ole Opry excluded. The theater is a gem from the 1920s, built for movies and vaudeville, with sweeping lines, elaborate wallpaper, and a painted ceiling with clouds that float across the surface. It's not so much a place of grandeur as one of poetry, the kind of setting that elevates what a performer does. It's also small-town in the best sense of those words: preserved by locals, funded for the most part by folks who come out to see acts from big to small and everything in between.

Performing at the Grand Ole Opry

I reckon I'm on the big side of the ledger. What that mostly means is that after a bunch of hit singles and millions of albums and seemingly infinite downloads, the pressure is on me to perform. These folks coming out tonight will spend good money to be

3

entertained—thrilled, moved, assured, inspired—and as great as my band is, I'm the one the audience is counting on. I have to take them where they want to be. For a few hours, at least.

I've been doing it now for—well, a long time. I'm grateful for that. A lot of people in this business, most performers, don't have the privilege of being on the stage so long, let alone the number of hits I've had. I have a deep sense of gratitude every day I get to stand on the stage. I can't hardly believe I do this for a freaking living. When I see all those people lining up, I get emotional sometimes. Because I still believe I don't deserve it.

Grand Event Center, Oklahoma, 2021

But I'm not only a singer. My music doesn't define me. I'm not saying that it's not important or that I wouldn't miss it awful if it suddenly disappeared; I'm just saying there's more to me than that.

Like hunting. Fishing. Motorcycle racing. Being a dad and the best husband I can manage.

And a soldier.

I was a soldier for some of the best years of my life. It was hard, dangerous, occasionally crazy, but those years were tremendous. Heck, every so often, I think maybe I should go back, even if the army thinks I'm a little old to be jumping out of planes into the middle of a war zone or chasing drug-running rebels in a jungle.

Sure was fun, though.

I've had a lot of special experiences and opportunities, but at heart I don't think of myself as someone special. I'm just like most of the folks who I'll be playing for tonight: raised in a small town, weaned on a hundred odd jobs, happy to have settled down with their sweetheart, but still looking for a little fun and not opposed to cutting loose every so often when the workday's done. I love doing shows like this, where the venue is small enough to interact with the entire crowd. It's like a conversation. It's hard to do at the huge festivals and fairs that make up a decent part of my touring schedule, so I have to take advantage of places like this whenever possible.

Right now, though, I need time to prepare. Not so much to corral my thoughts as to concentrate my energy. To go all in on the show. So I walk to the back of my bus, close the door, lie back on my bed, and think.

It was a long road to get here. I'm not talking about the eight hours through the snowstorm we came up through, though that wasn't much fun. The road I've traveled in my life has stretched from Nashville to Texas, Korea to Panama, from impromptu sing-alongs to the great heights of country music. It took me down a street in Iraq where terrorists tried to blow me up, and to a stage not far away where a few hundred soldiers reminded me why I'm so proud to be an American. It's taken me undercover to pits of filth where children are peddled for sex, and delivered me to a black-tie reception where a president kidded me about my shaving style.

It's taken me to fame and a bit of fortune. But it's also taken me to the saddest place on earth, that desolate hole you're crushed into when your child dies unexpectedly. It's been a road with grief, but also intense triumph and love.

Celebration. Service. Reckoning with God. Struggling to figure out how to be a man in a world where everything is changing and the ground just won't stay solid for too long.

So much on this road has been out of my hands. I've done so much without thinking. A lot of it has been the right stuff, but I can't take credit for having thought it all out: you rush into a building on fire to drag a couple of kids to safety, not because someone's going to write it up in a newspaper and call you a hero, but because there just is no other thing to do in that moment.

You write a song about your son's passing not because you want to make a hit record or even relieve your grief, but because there just is no other way of living that morning until you get that song out of your head and onto the strings of your guitar.

That's my life—a long road through a good country, with a whole lot of stops along the way.

Why country music?

I like a wide range of music, and some people, God bless them, think that with my voice I could sing a wide range of music.

I appreciate that as a compliment, but I prefer country.

Why?

Probably because I grew up in it, same reason I was a Baptist for so long. I love country music better than any other genre because, for me, it tends to tell a story better. And I think the majority of the stories are more relatable than you might hear in some of the other genres. Country is middle-class America's music, and the middle class is the majority of our nation.

But really, I'm a country boy. I live the country lifestyle. So that's what I write and sing. I still live in the woods down a chip-and-seal road. I still take my own garbage to the dump. I could pee off my front porch and nobody could see me.

Except my wife, who would object.

Seriously, country is the lifestyle of taking care of yourself and your own and your people and helping your neighbor. To me, that's the country lifestyle. When you walk into a store, they know you.

Canton Palace Theatre, Ohio, 2020

Now, though, before the show, I lie back on the bed in the back of the bus and think of my wife, Karen, and how lucky I've been to have found her. I think about my kids—all of them blessings, even when they were trials, of which there were a few. I think of my dad, still a role model well into his golden years. I think about God, and the many mysteries of faith and religion.

My mind wanders across my long road, back and forth … bits and pieces of music come in my head, bits of songs I haven't written yet, pieces of something just out of reach.

I just think … until my road manager knocks on the door.

"It's time."

And like that, I'm all focused. There is no road behind, only ahead. There is nothing but the show, nothing but tonight, and those people I'm talking to with my music. I get up, and by the time my hand hits the door, I'm ready to do one of the many things I was born to do: sing.

Sometimes, though, things go a little differently.

Like this, say:

2006, IRAQ

Terrorists in Iraq were ratcheting up their war against US personnel and Iraqi citizens alike, attacking throughout the country. I had a hit album out—and a request to go to Iraq and perform for some of the troops with an organization called Stars for Stripes. I love doing my bit for the troops. For me, it's more than entertaining—it's almost like old home week. A lot of times I get to meet men and women I served with, including some of the generals who have moved up the ranks since I left.

And occasionally I'll do a little something for the government on the side—we'll tease that notion for later on.

Just being around soldiers again feels comfortable. I served in the army eleven years, with a few more on active reserves. I saw combat in Panama and the jungles of Costa Rica, earning Combat Parachute Wings—a badge of honor for anyone who has gone Airborne. Most of the time I was a forward observer trained to operate behind the lines in dangerous situations scouting the enemy and directing fire. I had a chance to work not only with the regular army, but with the high-speed folks from Special Forces, SEALs, Rangers, and "other government agencies" which shall not be named. A big challenge, but as rewarding as all get-out.

Those days were long gone in 2006 when my band and I landed in Baghdad. Things seemed calm enough as we boarded some Humvees and headed to the city. Next to me in the back seat was my good friend and band leader, Mike Rogers. He was both excited and tired—tired because it was a long flight, and excited because, well, we were in a war zone, and he'd never been before.

We were a few miles from the airport, in a convoy of military vehicles, when a couple of things happened all at once. An Iraqi stepped into the road ahead. The Hummers in front of us stopped. We stopped. I reflexively grabbed a rifle—

The man in the street had a vest.

Explosive vest.

Bam, bam—one of the soldiers ahead shot the man instants before he could detonate himself.

"Go," I growled. "Go! Go!"

Golden rule of travel in dangerous places: You do not linger, you don't stop. You travel at warp speed.

Meanwhile, my head was on a swivel, sighting down the road, looking to see the mujahideen's support team—or more likely, the next two or three bombers who'd be part of the ambush.

We got moving pretty fast, rushing on toward the base. I gave back the rifle—I'd pinched it from one of the soldiers escorting us, grabbing it before he even knew what was happening, I guess.

Mike looked at me in disbelief.

"What's up?" I asked, or something to that effect.

"You're eating M&M's."

I was. I can't remember if I offered him one or not.

Mike was amazed. To this day, he can't believe that, through that whole excitement, I apparently kept popping candy in my mouth.

Once a soldier, always a soldier, I guess. Whether you're going into combat or singing to a bunch of guys and gals who are.

It's not unusual for Old Glory to make an appearance at my concerts.

ONE:
OF ROYAL BLOOD

If you know my music, you almost certainly know me as Craig Morgan. But I was actually born Craig Morgan *Greer.* Craig Morgan came along many years later.

On the advice of Garth Brooks. But that's a story for later.

As far as I knew growing up, our family history was nothing special. We were regular, ordinary people—I certainly was, and am to this day. But the Greers—and the many varieties of our name, including and especially Grierson—can trace our history to Scotland. And while I can't exactly claim to be descended from Scottish kings, I can say I come from a long line of nobles and warriors, not all of them pleasant folk.

In fact, one was apparently so mean the locals wouldn't let him be buried next to them—something I only found out a few years ago, thanks to a Christmas present from my wife, Karen. She unlocked my family's entire past. Until then I thought I was just the son of an easygoing carpenter and country musician, the grandson of a hard-working farmer, a simple Tennessee man.

It began with a subscription to Ancestry.com, where you can look up your family's history. Honestly, though I was interested, I had too much going on to devote any time to it. But Karen dug into the project, working through all sorts of records, tracing the family back several generations to Scotland. She's that kind of person—when she's doing something, she doesn't let go. And don't stand in her way.

Her research revealed that the Griersons had been quite a power at one time. That alone was surprising—I hadn't even known that we came from Scotland. It didn't take all that long for her to get to the point where she needed to look at the records in Scotland to find anything else. She worked out that the Griersons had been the lords of Lag in the general area of Dumfries, which is near the River Nith and not that far from the England-Scotland border. To see records that far back, you have to go in person.

So, I said, why not? We flew over and began poking around in the past. We visited the National Records of Scotland in Edinburgh, but only descendants are allowed to go through the records. After proving myself worthy, I was admitted to the "hall"—a massive building in the center of town. Surrendering all possible writing implements and putting on a pair of white gloves, I was led to the collection of books and ledgers documenting everything from births to deaths of many of Scotland's families. There, under the careful gaze of armed guards, I began looking through the old handwritten records.

The archivists take their job to preserve the records seriously: I nearly caused an international incident when I picked up a book whose page I wanted to get copied and walked toward the machine to do it myself.

I've had automatic weapons pointed at me before, but never in a library. We worked it out peacefully.

The Griersons (spelled in a number of ways and possibly related to Gregor, another important clan) were kin to the kings and queens of both Scotland and England—the lineage kind of blurs. But hey, if enough people ahead of us were to die . . . I might be in line to rule Britain, or at least Scotland.

The Griersons' area of Scotland played a very big role in the history of the British Isles, with both the English and Scottish realms fighting against each other over the centuries. You'd have had to be a pretty strong noble to hold land in that area during times of conflict. Even more interesting, the Griersons were one of the few tribes in Scotland that had a female as the head of the clan.

It was pretty cool checking out the old records, but to get a real feel for my family's past we rented a car and toured the area. While Griersons have gone on to Ireland, America, and many other places around the world, a number of descendants live in that part of Scotland still, and we were able to find a village where a lot of their original homes remain. These are structures, some of them, that go all the way back to the 1500s and 1600s.

One of my Grierson ancestors lived in this home in Scotland seven centuries ago, as the crest above the door attests.

Wearing the Grierson tartan

Driving around the village gave me an eerie sense of history. I went up to the door of one ancient house and knocked, introducing myself as a descendant of the Griersons and explaining why I'd come.

To my surprise, the old gentleman who answered the door whisked me in. It turned out it was his birthday, and he was having a little party. More amazing, he was a history professor, and knew all about the house's past and its connection with the Griersons. We got refreshments and a lesson on our past, all unplanned, in the space of a couple of hours.

Eventually we found our way to an even older place, one of the castles of Lag, the seat of the Griersons.

It was for sale.

The great thing about the property was that it came with titles.

If you owned it, at least in theory, you would have the title that went with it. I'm not sure if I would've been a baron or an earl or just a lord, but you'd still have to call me *Sir*.

Please welcome to the stage, Baron Craig Morgan, the Scottish king of country music . . .

I considered buying it—well, briefly. Maybe it would have made me Scottish royalty, but the place needed a ton of work. And the paperwork looked pretty involved. All things considered, it was probably a good thing that I dropped the idea. I think Karen was disappointed, though. I consider her a princess if not a baroness, but this would have made it official.

We stopped in a local tea shop, and when the lady running the place heard what we were up to, she called up a friend and got us directions to a cemetery where some of the Griersons were buried. We found the burial place in a field not that far away, and after climbing over an eight-foot wall, I stood above the large marble grave of Gilbert Grierson. Historians credit Gilbert with securing the clan's fortunes—not so much through military feats, though he undoubtedly was an adept Scots warrior, but by marriage to a member of the royal family. Sometimes it's not whom you defeat but who you're related to that counts.

I found some tiny slivers that had been chipped off from the gravestone and took them back for my kids, a tangible connection to the past.

While we were doing that, a fellow who lived across the way came over to chat. He invited us into his house, which dated back several centuries. He had a whole collection of drawings that different Griersons had done of places around Lag. We had tea and crumpets while we talked about the past.

Among the tales we heard on our visit was one about Robert Grierson, infamous locally for his persecution of Protestants who were opposed to the Scottish king. He's said to have put them into barrels that were studded with nails, and then rolled them down the hills—not exactly a pleasant trip. Robert was so hated in death that the locals refused to let him be buried in the local cemetery, which explained the separate burial site.

Here's the kicker on my Scottish ancestry. According to a DNA test I took with my wife, I'm about 50 percent Scottish. She's like 67 percent. And she didn't even know she had Scottish blood until the test.

Kings and queens don't feature in the Greer family's more recent history, but then neither do torture or religious wars.

I was born in Nashville, the oldest of four kids: two boys, Joey and me, and two girls, Susan and Regina. I lived and hung out in the towns west of the city, Kingston Springs and out toward Dickson, for most of my life until I joined the army. My father, Jack, was one of six boys—no girls—and they were a close-knit family, all living in the general area. One or more would be at my grandfather's most weekends. There were a lot of kids—each of his sons had at least four, and one had seven. So we were an army when we got together, and we got together a lot. There'd be a reunion of the entire clan maybe once a year, complete with a pig roast. I believe some distant cousins would also bring along some moonshine.

Not that the kids were allowed to have any. Officially, anyway.

I remember spending a big chunk of summers on the farm my grandad Emmet, whom we called "Poppy," ran. I don't believe my grandfather owned the property itself; he was more likely the manager, but of course that means nothing to a kid. It was Poppy's as far as we were concerned. As it happens, one of the farms today is now a large cemetery; my mom, Betty, is buried there.

Me at age two

On weekends and over the summer, all us kids would run around, play hide-and-seek in the barn. We'd spend a lot of time helping in Poppy's garden. That was a massive thing, big enough to feed the entire clan. Snap peas like candy, vegetables so fresh your mouth watered just looking at them—that's a garden.

One year there were upward of three thousand tomato plants and we all went to work picking them. You're going to really love or really hate tomatoes after that. I love 'em, as long as they're plump and fresh.

But I haven't found one as good as those we picked that summer on Poppy's farm. I don't expect I ever will.

I can still see Poppy surveying our work, peering through or maybe over his thick Coke-bottle glasses, thumbs hitched in his overalls. I don't remember him not in overalls. I suspect he had at least two pair—a work pair and a Sunday best.

I'm told Poppy was stern through most of his life, but as he grew older, he must have mellowed quite a bit. He had a heck of a sense of humor. One year he had me spreading fertilizer when I heard the call of nature and started for a spot behind the barn just private enough to get things done without having to go back to the house.

"Where are you goin', Craig?" he asked. "That fertilizer won't make everything grow."

I didn't totally get the joke for a few years.

I loved my grandmother Thema, but my mom told me stories that made it clear Grandmother was all about her boys—my dad and uncles. She was a bit gruff with their women. Everyone got along, but Grandmother could be real funny about certain things. Like cooking in the kitchen: everything had to be made the way Grandmother wanted. Didn't matter what the daughters-in-law wanted. If Poppy was king of the fief, she was queen.

Those were the days when men did "men things," and women did "women things." A bit different than today. The women would all get dinner ready, and then the men would eat. Just the men. After that, it was the kids' turn. I think the ladies had to settle for what was left. Luckily, there was always more than enough.

I'm not saying it was right, just that was the way it was. Things have changed, thankfully.

When you're the oldest kid in the family, you get to learn leadership skills on the job. Or how to be babysitter—a lot of times, the same thing. Mom and Dad would leave to go to work in the mornings, and I'd get my brother and sisters to the bus stop for school, then home again in the evenings. My sister Susan—we called her Pebbles, though I'm not exactly clear how that came about—got me in trouble all the time. We'd argue, and it was my fault, being older and a guy. If something broke, it was always me that broke it.

Or so the others might claim.

Joey, my brother, was a little demon and a daredevil. He'd climb on anything, including the roof. He got stuck on the peak of a barn when he was six; I had to distract him while my dad climbed up to grab him.

Twenty feet high, and he told my father, "Catch me, Daddy."

My father managed to get up there and grab him before he impersonated Superman.

We didn't live fancy. Christmas was one present apiece for most of my childhood. Money might have been tight, but if we were poor, I didn't know it. Daddy was an excellent woodworker, cabinetmaker, and all-around carpenter. He and my mom would get a house, fix it up, and then sell it, which meant we moved around a bit. They were flipping houses before it was a thing. He still has that touch—at seventy, he bought a house, tore the roof off, and rebuilt the thing just about from scratch. He swears that's his last home, but a handy guy like that, you never can tell.

While my father made his living as a carpenter and woodworker, he was also a musician. He and his brothers were in a band, and they had more than a bit of success.

Let's get him to tell the story:

> *Three of my older brothers—Gilbert, Willie, and Shorty— started playing in bars back when I was still young. They had a fella playing bass for them, but he wasn't regular. So they decided I ought to join them.*
>
> *By that time I was in my early twenties, after I'd been married a bit and we'd had Craig. I was just dumb enough to say, why not?*
>
> *I'd gotten an old Sears bass and taught myself the basics. Come to think of it, I had another bass, an Ampeg, which would have been a sight better than the Sears. I'd choose one or the other depending on where we were playing. A decent bar, I'd bring*

the good one. A hangout—a place where things were likely to be interesting, say—I'd bring the Sears.

You see, as bass player, you often had the job of dealing with drunks. The bass guitar came in pretty handy for pushing 'em offstage, or at least off yourself.

We gradually worked our way up to the point where I only brought the good bass out. We even wore suits and bow ties. We called ourselves CML—"Country Music Lovers." Because that's what we loved, and that's what we played.

Country Music Lovers in the 1960s: my dad, Jack; Uncle Gilbert; Uncle Willie; Uncle Gene

My father would bring me to some of the better venues. I remember one called the Jingo Jamboree. It was there that I made my professional debut. I must've been between eight and ten years old. My dad and my uncles had me come on and sing "Raindrops Keep Fallin' on My Head," the Burt Bacharach and Hal David song. Not sure why—

"People liked a kid singing," says my father. "You were about to get a bit of applause."

He's right about that—I did get a good hand. They had me sing at a few other shows. Not a lot, and not enough to get me thinking about a professional career. It wasn't until years later that I gave any real thought to performing in front of audiences.

The Jingo Jamboree is long gone now, and I don't remember too much about the place, though I do remember getting into some sort of trouble there and being banished to the car.

"You were probably runnin'," interrupts Dad.

Can't argue with that.

Dad did this thing with his fingers when you were cutting up out of place. It was kind of like flipping a marble, but you were the marble. I think my lip still hurts from the time he popped me because I picked up a fork while we were still praying before dinner.

But back to my dad and his music:

CML played whatever country music was popular at the time. We did it off and on for quite a while; we were still playing around a bit after Craig came back from the army.

We had some chances to go professional, but it was tough to make a living. We had to think about the family. If we made a hundred bucks on a show, it would be something. We could probably have done it if we didn't have kids, or wives. But that wasn't the case.

There was an old rock quarry fitted out like a giant performance space underground. It was large enough you could have three different bands, each playing a different style of music. In the middle was a restaurant.

The space got filled in a few years back—not because of us, by the way.

There was another place, more of a bar, called the Capri. It started out good, but slid down to bad somewhere along the way. Some rough customers.

One night this old guy came up to us and said he wanted to sing.

He started out, and then for some reason known only to him, he turned around and kicked Willie's drum.

"Don't do that," said Uncle Willie.

The old guy did it again.

"I told you, don't kick my drum."

Well, he did it a third time. Willie got up and gave him a poke with a drumstick so hard the fella flew off the stage.

We went into another song and never saw that guy again.

One night we were on our way to Jingo Jamboree, and we stopped at Gilbert's, because it was on the way.

"I got something I want you to try," he said. He poured me a glass of this liquid he said was wine—wine made from watermelon.

I drank the whole glass.

If you ever have the chance to do that, don't.

I don't remember what songs or which guitar I played that night. It might not even have been a guitar.

Their band changed around a bit as they went on. My father ended up as the front man and acoustic player. Uncle Shorty—Gene to the world—was on the electric lead guitar. Uncle Willie was the outgoing, loud-mouth, funny guy on the drums. And Uncle Gilbert, before he died, played bass and sang backup as well.

Thinking about it, everyone in the family can sing, including my brothers and sisters, though they haven't gone out commercially like I did. Good voices and the ability to carry a tune run in the family.

My mom's family wasn't as tight as Dad's. She had three brothers, one older, then her, then two brothers younger than her. One of them joined the army and played guitar a lot; he was a bit of a black sheep, but I liked hanging around him and picked up a few things on how to play the guitar. I don't remember all that much of mom's father, Hardy—Peppaw to us. What I do remember has the smell of drink around it, so maybe those memories are best left untouched.

Both of my mom's parents died when I was still pretty young. When I think of my grandmother, I remember how regal she always looked. Her name was Mabel, but we called her "Mudder." That doesn't describe her in any way, except that it must have come from one of the kids not being able to say "mother" and somehow stuck.

She was the opposite of what you think of when you see the word on paper. "Ladylike" or "majestic" would be a better description. Her hair would always be fixed just so. She could stand on her concrete porch in rural Smyrna, Tennessee, and have the air of a glamorous socialite. She'd probably be twirling a cigarette, as everyone did in those days.

According to my mom, my grandmother bought a record player for me when I was about six, and would bring over records when she'd visit, picking songs that we'd heard on the radio. As the story goes, I would learn the words and the tune within three times of hearing it.

That's my *mom's* story. I don't quite remember, but I know better than to contradict my mom. No, sir. Never doing that.

My mother, Betty Sue, in the 1970s

My momma, Betty Sue, inherited some of her mother's regal air. She was one of those women who could go and have tea with the First Lady on Friday and mix in with the locals at a community dance the next night. She had a way of being with people no matter who they were.

Momma was the epitome of a mother. She put her children's welfare and well-being before anything and everything, including her own happiness. She had a heart of gold, Momma did. She was the person who'd be driving down the road, see someone walking in the rain, and stop to pick them up. Didn't have to know them. She didn't care what they looked like, what color their skin was, or even where they were going. She was going to get them there, because it was the neighborly thing to do.

But don't mess with her kids. This woman grabbed me one time for something or other, and Momma commenced to whoopin' her like she was a grown man.

Mom loved us, but she didn't take no guff. If she caught you cutting up, she was liable to smack you if you were close enough. If you weren't, she might toss something at you.

And don't smart off. I believe at least one of my sisters was chased around the house with a broom after saying something Mother deemed disrespectful—and Sis was a grown woman, pregnant besides.

Mom was the one who really raised us, which was pretty normal in those days. Dad worked a lot. Mom had a job, too, but when she got off work, she'd get into the kitchen and thirty minutes later had a big meal made. I've never seen another woman who could go into a half-empty kitchen cabinet, pull something out from the back, and a half hour later have a meal that not only tasted good, but was good for you as well.

But like I said before, she had rules. And she could rumble. As a kid, you absolutely showed her respect, no matter how old you were. After I enlisted, she drove me to the reception center. I don't remember how it happened, but something I said must have come out wrong, because even though she was driving and I was in the back seat, she turned around and went to slap me.

I caught her hand midswing.

"Momma, I'm too old for you to hit me—"

The words weren't out of my mouth when her other hand came across my unguarded face.

"You ain't never gonna be too old for me to hit you," she said.

Most kids tremble when their mother says, "Wait 'til your father comes home." I exhaled in relief. My father's punishments were never as stern as my mother's. Once or twice he even pretended he was going to fix me with a strap, but all he did was strike the bed. Behind a closed door, of course, so Mother wouldn't know.

That bed sure did take a beating.

Mostly, I was a good kid, and didn't need all that much correcting. I didn't do drugs. I didn't drink; I didn't do any of those things. I skateboarded in the street on some homemade ramps; that was the extent of my purposeful lawbreaking, if you want to call it that. I went to church—though to be honest, that was more because of the girls I wanted to date than my interest in religion.

No, the times I got into trouble were rare. But when I did, it was a doozy. And mostly, it was because of my cousin, Guy Eddie.

GUY EDDIE

Guy Eddie was Uncle Willie's son. He was like the big brother I never had, being the oldest in the family. A little older than me, a little more daring (at least back then), and above all, the inspiration for a multitude of adventures, misadventures, and mishaps. He wasn't evil by any means, but he sure wouldn't be confused with the stereotypical Boy Scout.

Except that he was always prepared . . . for mischief.

Like the time he told me there was an old car left for junk off the side of a nearby bluff. This interested me quite a bit, because I was fixing up a junker that needed a good set of wheels and passable tires. By the way, I was fourteen or fifteen, not old enough to legally drive yet, but that wasn't much of a factor to Guy. Or to myself, I must confess.

It developed that Guy knew the location of this car because he had pushed it off the bluff himself. That didn't deter either one of us. So when Guy promised he'd drive me over and help me get the wheels, I said let's go.

We went over, fetched the wheels and the tires. Things were going real well until the police showed up at the house.

"Where'd you get those tires, son?"

"There was a car off the cliff," I explained.

"Did you push it off?"

"No, sir."

He had a few more questions. My answers got shorter and shorter. Finally, he got to the point:

"Do you know the car was reported stolen?"

I had to give the wheels and tires back. As to who had taken the car in the first place . . . it remains a mystery.

Then there was the time when I was a freshman in high school and Guy Eddie persuaded me to come along with him to his auto mechanics shop. Back in the day, many high schools had classes like auto mechanics, along with wood and metal working, printing—useful things to learn, even if you weren't going into the trade. Guy Eddie pointed out a vehicle parked near the building.

"We just fixed the brakes on that," he told me. "But somebody's gotta test them. You want to do it?"

"What do I have to do?"

"Just go real fast down the lane here, then when you come about even to the front of the building, hit the brakes."

I followed his instructions to the letter—which resulted in a tire-squealing, smoke-churning power skid right in front of the building . . . and the principal, vice principal, and auto mechanics teacher, who were standing there.

Bad.

Worse was the fact that it was the principal's car, and it hadn't actually been in for work at all.

A paddling loomed. The atmosphere in the principal's office went from ominous to downright disastrous when someone suggested my mother be called.

An electric chair would have been less nerve-racking than the seat I waited in. Finally, Mother arrived.

"What happened?" she demanded.

I gave her the whole story.

"I'll deal with Craig at home," she told the men. "You get Guy Eddie down here and give him a paddling."

I don't remember if those were her exact words. I wouldn't be surprised if they were quite a bit harsher. But I do know Guy got the paddle. My own punishment has blurred into the fog of punishments past, neither light nor harsh enough to stand out from the pack.

Guy Eddie did have a way with vehicles, and he wasn't always getting me into trouble. We had a Friday night ritual in town where all the young guys would take their cars to the local mall and kind of parade around the lot, hanging out before heading to other adventures. Guy arranged for me to buy a Ford Torino, then helped me fix it up. It was a pretty car all around, but the motor was a thing of beauty, a 351 Cleveland high dome piston with solid lifts and an endless amount of horsepower.

Oh my God, what a car.

We'd drive it around the lot a few times, park, and go into the nearby arcade to invest a few quarters in *Donkey Kong* and the like.

Guy was a natural-born mechanic. You could have him listen to an engine idle over the phone and he'd figure out what was wrong with it. He'd say, "You sound like you've got a valve sticking, or your carburetor is clogged up." That would be followed by the suggestion that you bring it over for a look. And sure enough, he'd be right. Better, he could fix it, probably with his eyes closed.

He and I went into business together while I was still in high school, thanks to his great ability with cars. Here was the idea: Anyone that has a lot of vehicles needs a lot of service on those vehicles. Simple things—checking and replacing oil, wipers, coolant—can start to become expensive, not only because you have a lot of vehicles, but because you lose their use for a good part of a day or maybe even more.

What if, instead of having to drive to a service station, or more likely three or four of them, the mechanic came to you?

I asked the question, and we answered it: *Company Car Care.*

My father was working for a company making booths, tables, and counters for commercial operations like restaurants and places like hospitals that had cafés and whatnot. The business had accounts all over the area, and to get to them, they needed vehicles. Dad's company was the first of our accounts, and probably the biggest, but we got busier and busier as word spread of the service. Soon enough, we were making bank and living large.

At least we were until the taxman came around. Turns out that, even if you're under eighteen, you still have to pay Uncle Sam if you own a profitable business.

Apparently, we were very profitable, at least to judge by the numbers the IRS threw around. What saved us was our ages—I guess even the taxman has a soft spot for enterprising teenagers. Or maybe those in charge of our account just liked cars. I don't remember what the bill was, but I do know we paid it, and quietly went out of business.

There are many Guy Eddie stories, like throwing bicycles off a high spot to see what would happen when they hit a train.

Crushed 'em bad, as you'd imagine.

And many firsts—first time I got drunk, thanks to a can of spiked Sprite. That experience stuck with me most of my life. I like the occasional drink, and I even helped create my own wine, but most of my drinking is moderate—not always easy to accomplish in my profession.

So, in that way, Guy Eddie had a good influence on my life. Maybe he was a Boy Scout after all.

ADRENALINE & SERVICE

Round about the summer of my junior year in high school, my parents started having marital trouble. My dad took a temporary job in Texas, and I went along to work with him over the summer. What I didn't know then was that my parents were moving toward a divorce; that would happen a bit later, when I was out of the house.

That age, a boy's interests get focused on certain things, mostly involving girls. My mind focused on one in particular. I wanted to get her to return the favor, but I didn't have much to offer. I was living with my father without the usual attractions—to a teen's mind—of a fancy car and a lot of pocket change. About all I had with me was an old guitar which I'd been thinking about learning to play.

I put it to use, and started writing songs for her. It was the very first time I'd written anything musical. I don't remember the songs now, and that may be a good thing. But they did the trick, at least for that summer.

Back in Tennessee, graduation came around, and it was time to make something of my life. I'd joined the fire department as a volunteer and really liked it—despite my experience on my very first call, when I fell into a freshly dug septic pit on the way to the alarm. Angling toward law enforcement or emergency services, that sort of thing, I registered for police science and law enforcement studies at Nashville State Technical Institute in Nashville.

To pay my way, I got a job as an EMT. They took me on even though I wasn't legally old enough to drive the ambulance. I did have my medical certification, though, which may have made me the youngest EMT in the state. It also meant I answered all manner of calls, usually at least two a shift. I still remember the very first one I answered: car accident, girl in the front seat hit the windshield. Her face was embedded in the glass.

Not the worst thing I've seen in my life now, but it hit hard then and stuck with me. We had to cut up the windshield and transport it still attached so the surgeons could safely remove the glass at the hospital.

There were other calls that were pretty gruesome. Burn victims were the worst. There was a guy who died trapped in a car fire, arm halfway out the window: His skin flaked off in my hands when I tried to get him out. I'll never get the smell of burning flesh out of my mind. It's got a sweet stench that turns your stomach over and around.

But there were other moments. Not happy, exactly, but . . . interesting. Imagine you're an eighteen-year-old fella and a good-looking young woman hops into the back of the ambulance and starts taking off her clothes.

Then starts taking off yours.

If you're me, you hustle up the restraints—for her and yourself. And think about what might have been years later.

I'll be honest. The ambulance pay helped me through college, but the adrenaline of the calls kept me going. Even so, I reached a point where the books and the adrenaline weren't enough.

I wanted to help other people. I wanted to do that by serving my country. Oh, yeah, that sounds a bit corny, but it's true and there's no sense trying to find fancy words to describe it or make it sound high and mighty. It's something you know in your heart and your soul, with no need to dress it up.

It's just the way God made you. Or at least me.

I was also ready for a change and wanted to do something different than the rest of my family had. I love my dad, but every young man has to stretch his own legs and get out of the shadow a father casts.

I thought I'd join the service, find myself after a couple of years, and move on.

As for why I chose the army—well now, that's a slightly different story.

I tell people this: *The marines were too hard. The navy was too soft. I wasn't smart enough for the air force. The army was all that was left.*

There was a little more to it, I guess. Uncle Willie had been in the army, and he had a few stories that made it sound pretty good. There was also successful advertising: The army had a motto at the time— *Be all you can be.* I loved that idea. Test myself, find myself. And help my country at the same time.

Service was in my DNA, but those blueprints in my genes hadn't managed to map themselves out into a tangible plan for me. I thought I could join the army and . . . serve. Be all I could be. Whatever that was.

Here's how naive I was: I went down to the local recruiter and told him my story. He gave his spiel, and then asked if I wanted to be in Airborne.

"Hell, yes," I answered.

Maybe a touch more politely, with a "sir" or two thrown in.

He smiled and started working on the papers. Only later did I realize that "airborne" didn't mean I'd be flying planes or helicopters.

Airborne meant you jumped out of them.

Kind of a different thing. But it turned out I loved the hell out of it anyway.

TWO:
GUNG HO

A DESIRE TO JUMP

I mentioned earlier that my mom put me in my place on my way to report for the army. Maybe because of her, I breezed through basic, learning how to be a reasonably competent private.

Basic training is just that—get your foot in the door, learn how to salute and follow orders, understand how squaring away your cot in the morning leads to good things in the afternoon. It's after basic that the army starts putting soldiers into their niche. Some of this is up to the recruit, who gets to list the general assignment he or she may want. Most of it, though, is up to the army, which has certain personnel needs and is not shy about pursuing them.

In my case, my general desires lined up with the army's needs. Once I found out what "airborne" meant, that is.

I wanted to jump out of airplanes, and the army wanted to let me. I wanted to be in a combat or fighting job, not behind the lines in support or supply. They wanted to let me do that too. All I had to do was prove I could.

The army started training me for a job civilians might call a scout, or even a commando, but is generally termed a long-range observer by militaries around the world, including ours. In my specific case, I would be tasked to assist artillery units targeting the enemy.

Cannons helped us win our independence from Great Britain, and artillery has been an important part of American warfighting ever since.

The big guns can't be effective if you don't know where their targets are. Figuring that out is the job of the forward observer.

One of the jobs, I should say. There's a lot more to the observer's role. Technology has greatly changed artillery and everything connected to it over the last few decades, to say nothing of the two-plus centuries since our founding. Back when I joined and still today, the army assigns the task to Army Joint Fire Support Specialists, officially Military Occupation Specialty 13F, or 13-Fox, as we tended to refer to the job.

My additional qualification as "airborne" meant I could work directly with Airborne units, parachuting into an area where they were going to attack. I was the eyes and occasional ears for artillery (and later air) units that would support paratroopers in battle.

To explain a little for those who aren't familiar with the military: The army primarily fights on the ground, and travels that way as well. But certain units go by air—"airborne" or to use a common civilian term, paratroopers. Not counting special units like the Rangers, the army has traditionally had two paratrooper divisions, the 82nd and 101st Airborne. The 82nd still jumps into battles using parachutes from planes and helicopters. Starting in the late 1960s, the 101st began specializing in air assault—essentially traveling and attacking by helicopters, stepping off directly onto the ground or descending by rope. The division does utilize troops trained to do parachute jumps for certain tasks and in certain situations, but its primary mission consists of air assault.

The combat troops in both units operate the same way "regular" army divisions do once they hit the ground. And that means that they fight with artillery like the rest of the army.

Over the course of my service in the military, I would be trained to identify enemy targets and communicate their whereabouts. Some of those targets might be located several miles behind enemy lines; to target them effectively, I'd have to get as close as possible. I also had to be in position to supply intelligence to the unit commanders, who could use it to plan their tactics.

To do all this, I was taught how to jump out of aircraft and operate behind enemy lines with a very small team, or even on my own if necessary. Besides artillery, I learned about radios, laser targeting devices, aircraft capabilities, and a range of light weapons. The army would eventually expect me to be able to slink through hostile territory without being detected, guide bombs or missiles launched from aircraft onto a spot or "grid" measured in meters if not centimeters, and return to friendly lines when the fighting was done.

There are a truckload of dangerous jobs in the army, and I'm not here to say one is more dangerous, or even more important, than the others. But on the battlefield, if you're a soldier facing the enemy, and you see some guy in a different colored uniform than yours talking on a radio, you're going to aim at that guy first. Because no matter what his friends are firing at you, the people on the other end of that radio have something ten times worse.

I was that guy with the radio. Later on, I was his boss next to him, which might even have been worse. It was a very high-risk job.

Exactly my kind of thing.

For the record, we're not commandoes—that's a specific kind of unit in military terms, closest in our army to the Ranger Regiment—but we're trained and perform jobs along roughly the same lines.

I loved every moment, right from the start. Even those moments that, to use a technical term, sucked horse puddles.

Not that I knew all of this as a would-be private starting out in basic. You follow orders and you keep your head down—that much I knew when I arrived. I could shoot reasonably well, and I figured I wouldn't mind the physical stuff, from marching to pushing through the obstacle course. I was in reasonable shape and, being young and full of myself like most recruits, figured I could take whatever the army dished my way.

Things started off easy. We got off the bus, got a new uniform, got a haircut—they did ten at a time, buzz cutting whatever we had. We got a nice welcoming speech and saw nothing but smiles from everyone we met. We boarded the bus again, found our seats, and waited for the last person to board. This turned out to be a drill sergeant who was undoubtedly descended from a grizzly bear.

"Gentlemen, welcome to hell," was all he said.

Hell was an exaggeration, but basic wasn't pleasant. Not that it was designed to be.

Yeah, I got put in my place. But that wasn't a bad thing.

My training group included a platoon of us who had signed up for Airborne. I don't think it's my imagination that the drill instructors ran us a little harder, pushed us a little further, trying to get us ready to be members of an elite unit. Early training wasn't torture, but it was a shock to the system, a real change from civilian to military life—little sleep, tight schedules, running instead of walking, learning all the time.

I've never met a soldier who had an *easy* drill sergeant, so I'm not going to brag that mine was the hardest SOB that ever walked the earth. But this was his favorite line, uttered often during PT and marches, with a generous amount of four-letter words sprinkled in: "I don't care if you die, because I'm not going to be here after this class. Y'all are my last class. So if you die, it will not affect my record. I am going to Hawaii."

He did his damnedest to make those first few words come true. My leg muscles are tightening up just thinking about him.

PT may stand for physical training, but in the early days of basic, "prolonged torture" is a more apt definition.

I had no trouble following orders. As I'd predicted, the physical stuff, though tiring, tended to come easy, and on the gun range I excelled. I quickly mastered the "army way" and shot expert pretty much from the get-go. But no matter how squared away you are, drill sergeants will find something to get you on. Mine nailed me on stubble.

Stubble visible only to him, but he was the only one who mattered.

One morning at formation, my sergeant leaned the brim of his hat hard against my forehead and asked if I had shaved. He spoke so loudly my eardrums trembled.

Then again, so did the rest of me.

"No, Drill Sergeant," I replied truthfully.

Now, the fact is, a peach has thicker whiskers than I did at that moment. Even so, I was instructed to go back inside, get my shaving kit, and return.

I did so. Quickly. Had I been sprinting in the Olympics, I would have gotten the gold.

The drill instructor took my razor and ran it a few times over the concrete sidewalk. He then handed it back to me and told me to shave. Without water, soap, or cream. When I was done, my face looked and felt like I'd run twenty-four-grit sandpaper over it. From that point on, I shaved every day.

Gradually, the army molded me into a soldier. In my program, basic training and advanced infantry training were held back-to-back at Fort Sill, Oklahoma. It was the first time I'd been that far away from home, but you're too busy as a new recruit to focus on how much you miss your family. At some point they made me a squad leader—I can't remember now if it was because I did something good, or if maybe it was an extra task to keep me in line. Maybe a little of both. I was older than many of the other guys, with a year and a bunch of life experience under my belt. In the eyes of an instructor, those could be good or bad things.

Whatever. I certainly wasn't the best recruit in the army, but I was pretty far from the worst as well.

Basic Training, Fort Sill, Oklahoma, 1985; I'm on the bottom row, far right.

I did pick up a few things that aren't part of the standard army curriculum. Smoking, for example.

Back when I was young—maybe six or a touch older—I'd picked up a cigarette butt my mom's mom had left on her concrete porch. My dad saw me take a puff. As punishment, he made me eat the cigarette.

That was a lesson I learned real well. I avoided cigarettes the way turkeys avoid hunters . . . until I got to the army. In basic, I saw that if you stopped and had a cigarette during the few breaks our drill sergeants would give us, you didn't get "volunteered" for extra duty during the break. I may have been naive, but I wasn't dumb. I picked up the habit for a while, losing it later when there was no need to grab a smoke to get out of busy work.

Here's a lesson I learned in basic that did stay with me, not only through the army, but later on: It's not about you, it's about the team, the people around you, the country. God, Family, Country.

Basic gets you into the army way of doing things; infantry training orients you toward fighting in a war. Past that, things begin to get interesting, and specific. You learn what it is you're supposed to be doing in the army. In my case, it was jumping out of planes.

I mentioned that I didn't know what airborne units did in the military when I first signed up. I guess the first time I realized not only what "airborne" meant but that there was a little bit of danger involved happened during my airborne physical. They may have some high-tech lab tests, scans, and gadgets nowadays to make sure you're healthy enough to risk killing yourself by falling a few thousand feet, but when I signed up, the physical primarily consisted of a doctor giving you a good going-over.

I did OK, I guess, until we got to the drop arm test. The doc had me stand in front of him and hold my arms out, elbows into my side.

"Make a fist, palms up."

"OK."

"Turn your wrist up."

"Got it."

"Turn them down."

"Roger."

"All the way down."

"Working on it, sir."

"Down!"

I was supposed to be able to turn my hands completely flat at whatever angle that works out to. For some reason, I could just barely twist them, ending far short of whatever measure they were using.

The nurse looked on dubiously.

"Ah, he'll be all right," said the doctor. "That's from hauling too many bales of hay. He'll be fine."

Not to say that I'd never baled any hay, but I doubt that was the cause. I went away with some very mixed feelings—on the one hand, I felt like I had skated past a tough requirement. On the other hand, I wondered what in heck I had escaped to.

I remember everything about my first real parachute at Fort Benning—except the important parts.

I remember feeling nauseous in the plane. I also remember the humongous migraine I had before jumping, one of a string of monster headaches I got as a young man. They diminished and then vanished as I aged, but that day my head pounded so badly I could barely see.

And I remember the thump when I touched down.

Everything in between is lost to me. I know I went out, and I know the chute must have opened, because I'm here. But as far as the details go, your guess is as good as mine.

I honestly don't think fear caused the headache or erased the memory. We'd practiced so much, and I was so keyed up that there was no room to be scared. Or I should say, the only thing I was scared of, and I would bet this was true for everyone else in the plane, was screwing up.

You learn to jump with a static line, meaning that the parachute is automatically opened for you after you've fallen a certain distance from the aircraft. You get the hell out, wait, wait, wait—*tug*! Chute opens, check the canopy, risers, etc. Enjoy the ride.

Headache or not, as soon as I landed, all I could think of was doing it again. The next time was a hell of a lot easier—no headache, and I already knew I loved it.

I even grew to love night jumps, which can be an acquired taste, even for paratroopers. For one thing, they're a little trickier than day jumps. The basics are the same. As you approach the ground, get your feet together, knees a little bent. You're aiming to hit the earth on the balls of your feet and roll, falling in a controlled manner with five points of contact in the proper order—balls of your feet, calf, thigh, buttocks, side. That's a dynamite PLF, or Parachute Landing Fall.

When you're doing that during the day, you have plenty of height references, different cues to use as you get ready to land. Not so much on a night jump. The one really big cue is the thump of your pack hitting the ground. The bag carrying your gear dangles from your body below and hits the dirt a moment or two before you do.

That's what people say. What they don't mention, though, is that when you're landing with a large group of other people, everyone has a pack. So there are a lot of thumps.

Was that mine? Was that one? Was that—

I closed my eyes and hoped for the best. I hit, rolled, got up . . . and wanted to do it again.

It was in Airborne school at Benning where my military and songwriting ambitions first met each other.

Compared to basic training, Airborne school gives soldiers a lot more downtime. Typically, there are soldiers of different ranks, and often members of other branches as well, so things are a little more relaxed. Everyone present has volunteered to be there and has some inkling of what to expect. They're also highly motivated and understand that what they're doing is inherently dangerous. The training itself is intense, but the atmosphere following the sessions when you're done eases up a bit.

It's not a vacation by a long shot, but you do have time to breathe, maybe read a book, or take a few moments to do something other than drill and march. In my case, having free time meant that I had a few moments to strum on my guitar. Strumming on my guitar led naturally to making up a song. The two things seem to sit together in my brain. It's like walking—your feet move together without you thinking much about it.

Being that we were in Airborne school, the words that started popping into my head had to do with paratroopers and parachuting. I began fiddling around one night and came up with a few verses about Test Platoon and Red King, the first enlisted paratrooper. King was a member of the 501st Infantry Regiment when a number of its members were selected to become the army's first Airborne troops in 1940, before the US entry into World War II. He said later that he got the honor of making the country's first combat training jump when the man ahead of him in the "stick" balked at the door. He went on to make jumps during D-Day and Operation Market Garden, two of the largest and most dangerous Allied air assaults of the war. Ever since, he was a legend and inspiration.

The day after I'd played some of the song for my friends, one of the instructors came up to me and demanded to know where I'd heard the song. I explained I'd heard it in my head. I also explained that it wasn't really a song yet, just a few lines and such I was noodling on.

"Pick up your guitar and follow me," said the black hat, immediately turning on his heel.

I double-timed behind him to what we called the White House— the office of the school's commanding general.

The platoon was scheduled to have a big banquet coinciding with our graduation. A number of early paratroopers were being invited by our commander, Colonel Leonard Scott. Aside from being an awesome commander and a stellar paratrooper, the colonel had begun writing novels on the side. He'd recently published *Charlie Mike*, a fictional story now recognized as a classic tale of the Vietnam War.

I knew about the event. I'd been asked to sing cadence (helping pace parade march) during the ceremonies. This, though, was a lot different. I explained the situation as carefully as I could: I'd be happy to sing the song, but it wasn't finished, and if—

I was quickly informed that no ifs, ands, or buts were acceptable. I would finish the song. And sing it at the banquet.

"Sir! Yes, sir!"

From then on, I was rushed through lessons and exercises—I think I did five tower jumps a day, two-and-a-half times the norm. (Tower jumps are done off, well, towers, to give you the feel for falling through the air. They've been used since World War II to familiarize newcomers to the art of parachuting.) When I was finished with my assignments, I double-timed over to the White House with my guitar and worked out the rest of the song in a little room set aside just for me.

Not too much pressure, right? Jumping out of planes now seemed like a breeze.

I got the song together in time to rehearse with the 82nd Airborne Choir, which came in for the ceremony.

We were a hit. I believe there's a recording of the performance on a cassette in the Airborne Museum. Someday I'll work up the courage to have a listen.

When you graduate Airborne school, you get to wear a set of wings symbolizing that you are a paratrooper. Many guys have their mom or dad or both pin them on. My parents couldn't come to graduation, but I had the next best thing: Red King and Colonel Scott pinned me. Not too many people can say that.

By the way, these are considered "blood wings"—unless the pinner is your mom, he or she pounds them in hard enough to draw blood. You wear the scars as proudly as you wear the wings themselves.

COMPASSIONATE ASSIGNMENT

Now airborne-qualified, I saw Ranger training as the next step in my army career. I was assigned to RIP, or Ranger Indoctrination Program at Fort Benning. RIP has since been replaced by the Ranger Assessment and Selection Program (RASP), but I suspect the overall aims are similar. It was basically a transitional phase to get you ready for Ranger training and a gateway to the Ranger Regiment (or battalion, depending on which year we're talking about). It is a very intense school, as is the regiment, which would have been perfect for me. (Completing the full Ranger training course does not make you a member of the regiment, which has its own organization and command structure. Whether you are a member of the regiment or not, though, successfully completing Ranger training means you have acquired advanced fighting skills, qualifying you for a number of dangerous jobs, and generally helps your career.)

My instructors worked me like a dog from day one. I'm not sure why I was singled out. Maybe they thought I was an up-and-comer who would respond by becoming a stellar leader; that's not an uncommon strategy.

Maybe they thought I was too full of myself and had to be taken down a notch. Or maybe the lead instructor was just tough on me because we happened to have the same last name, though we weren't related.

Whatever. I always found myself at the back of the line. Literally.

At the time, in order to get into the chow hall and get your meal, you had to recite the Ranger Creed:

RECOGNIZING that I volunteered as a Ranger, fully knowing the hazards of my chosen profession, I will always endeavor to uphold the prestige, honor, and high esprit de corps of the Rangers.

ACKNOWLEDGING the fact that a Ranger is a more elite soldier who arrives at the cutting edge of battle by land, sea, or air, I accept the fact that as a Ranger my country expects me to move further, faster and fight harder than any other soldier.

NEVER shall I fail my comrades. I will always keep myself mentally alert, physically strong and morally straight and I will shoulder more than my share of the task whatever it may be, one hundred percent and then some.

GALLANTLY will I show the world that I am a specially selected and well-trained soldier. My courtesy to superior officers, neatness of dress and care of equipment shall set the example for others to follow.

ENERGETICALLY will I meet the enemies of my country. I shall defeat them on the field of battle for I am better trained and will fight with all my might. Surrender is not a Ranger word. I will never leave a fallen comrade to fall into the hands of the enemy and under no circumstances will I ever embarrass my country.

READILY will I display the intestinal fortitude required to fight on to the Ranger objective and complete the mission though I be the lone survivor.

Rangers Lead the Way!

For some reason, I always stumbled over the first few lines, sometimes even the first few words.

"I am an American—"

"Back to the end of the line, Greer."

"Recognizing, uh—"

"Back of the line, Greer."

Darned if I could ever get the whole thing out on first try. I always ate last.

That wasn't the half of it. We'd line up to run Heartbreak Hill—a particularly good slope at Benning, well-known to all would-be Rangers, I'm sure—and my instructor would point me to the back of the line. I'd gradually start passing people, only to have the instructor send me back to the end again.

Not every instructor had it in for me, and I have to say that, personal differences aside, they were all studs. Some were living legends, and those who weren't should have been. I remember a parachute jump where the smell of a cigar wafted through the cargo hold as we lined up to walk off. The jumpmaster overseeing the operation had a lit stogie in the corner of his mouth as he looked us over in front of the open ramp. No safety line, but a good cigar.

Nowadays they won't let you near the plane with a cigarette let alone a cigar, but things were a bit freer back then. I don't remember if he went out with us on that flight, but I'm sure he would have smoked the whole way down if he did.

I only lasted at RIP for three weeks—not because I was having trouble with the course, but because I was having trouble with my marriage.

My early days in the military overlapped a complicated phase of my personal life. My parents were getting divorced, and I was figuring out what I was going to do with my life. And, in the time between high school and joining the army, I'd gotten married.

Our romance had begun the year after I graduated high school. Besides going to college and working as an EMT, I helped out as an assistant coach for the high school soccer team. I met my future wife at school; we dated for a few months before we decided we should get married. She was still under eighteen, and we needed her parents' permission. I think what cinched the idea of matrimony for all concerned was the fact that I was going into the army.

But the army turned out to be more than she bargained for. I wasn't nearly through boot camp when she let me know she wanted me to leave. She didn't just hound me; she wrote letters to my commanders.

We were both awful young. Under other circumstances, it probably would have worked out fine. I'll take whatever blame God hands out, but the bottom line was we were not well suited for each other at that point in time, and the marriage failed almost right away.

I didn't accept that at first. The army tried to help by processing a compassionate transfer at my wife's request. They sent me to Fort Knox, which was closer to our families in Tennessee.

It didn't work. We tried a bit, but it soon became obvious even God couldn't make this union last. The worst part of it was that we had an infant daughter, and after we got divorced, I had very little contact with her, mostly by letter. I was lucky after my active-duty days to spend more time with her, and today she's graced me with a good, adult relationship. I'm proud of her and how she's turned out. I paid child support, spoke with her when I could, but otherwise I had little hand in raising her.

I have to admit, the divorce was tough on me emotionally. I'd grown up at a time when you didn't get divorced, you worked things out. Whatever my parents had gone through, I thought I was different.

But, no, I was human. I made mistakes, and I'd made a mighty one there. I struggled to admit it to myself. I had to learn that there are just some things that are out of our control, and I couldn't control a marriage.

Tough lesson, but one that would be valuable from then on.

KOREA

At Knox, I was part of a FIST team on a 113 and went from driver to RTO to FO to NCO.

Yes, the army loves acronyms.

In English: I was part of a fire support team (FIST), assigned to drive an Armored Personnel Carrier (M113). That's the vehicle that civilians sometimes think is a tank, even though it doesn't have a big gun or thick armor. Think of it as a big, boxy, metal truck that goes into battle on a set of treads rather than tires. It's not exactly sexy, but it did get us where we were going.

I was then promoted to a radio operator (RTO). That's a much more responsible position—the person who maintains contact with the commander, relaying things like target information back and forth. Communications (or "comms") technology then was not as advanced as it is now; the radios and other equipment we used were pretty heavy and at times complicated to use.

From RTO I went to FO—forward observer, the person who is actually spotting the target and directing fire at it. I eventually was promoted and became the noncommissioned officer or NCO in charge of the team. NCOs are enlisted personnel who command other, lower-ranking enlisted personnel.

I was still pretty young, but very gung ho. I was trying to be *that* guy.

I wanted to be all I could be. I wanted to achieve.

So I was psyched when I was assigned to Korea in 1987.

Officially speaking, I was going to a war zone. In June 1950, North Korea invaded South Korea, starting the war. While an armistice has been in place since July 1953, North Korea has resisted signing a permanent peace treaty. The US has kept substantial manpower on the peninsula, in hopes of preventing another invasion or helping South Korea defend itself should the need arise.

Relations between the two countries have ranged from pretty bad to extremely bad in the decades following the fighting. When I went over, they were extremely bad. Both sides had exchanged gunfire in 1984 when someone from the Soviet Union attempted to defect across the Demilitarized Zone (DMZ) separating the country. Two North Koreans and a South Korean had been reported killed in the skirmish, and an American had been wounded. Less than a

Serving as a forward observer, South Korea, 1987

decade earlier, the two countries had nearly gone to full-scale war over the trimming of a tree that blocked the view northward; two Americans were killed in the fracas.

Both incidents and a score of others, less publicized, were very much on everyone's mind when I arrived. So I was ready for whatever came up.

Except a fancy hotel in downtown Seoul.

A hotel?

In the army?

In a country at war?

Prior to being transported up to our actual duty stations, the army put us up in Seoul, South Korea's capital. I don't know if it was intended as a reward or just one of those things that happened to work out, but it was definitely culture shock on many levels.

Promotion to sergeant, South Korea, 1987

It wasn't the last. Soon after we arrived, some friends and I were told by those more experienced in the ways of Seoul that we had to visit the "turkey farms." So we set out to do just that.

Whatever it is you're thinking turkey farms are, you're wrong. This was an area of brothels, lined up on a narrow block. The buildings had these large windows—imagine Christmas displays in a city shopping area, except it wasn't Santa Claus or Christmas trees on display. I'd never seen anything like it. I don't think I even knew what a "sex worker" was until I took that stroll.

Our sojourn in Seoul ended the next day. I was picked up at the hotel and ferried to Camp Stanley, where I was assigned to work with an artillery unit. I wasn't there too long before I was transferred to Camp Casey, a base in Dongducheon, north of Seoul and near the DMZ.

When I got my room with the two other team leaders at the end of the Quonset hut, I thought to myself, *I have finally achieved something. I am a leader in the army.* As a soon-to-be-promoted E-4 (corporal),

South Korea, 1987

I shared the room with an E-5 (sergeant) and an E-6 (staff sergeant). Both of them treated me with respect I had never had before and didn't expect as an E-4.

I'll spare you the pay-grade information and promotion versus duty stuff, and only say that ordinarily the leadership position would have gone to an E-5 sergeant or above. Heck, lowly E-4s like myself practically bowed to an E-6. Here, I was being treated almost as an equal.

We did a lot of fun stuff: We trained all the time.

One thing Korea and Camp Casey did for me: it erased any sense of shyness I had. Body image issues? Not after serving there. There were no showers in the huts. To take a shower, you had to walk across the yard to an open bay building, where you cleaned up with a half-dozen or more other guys. I'd never done that before, not even playing ball in high school.

I did have my guitar with me. I piddled a bit, tried to write a little. I couldn't tell you one song I wrote, and it's not going out on a limb to say not one of them was any good. I did a lot of covers—Charlie Daniels comes to mind.

Forgive me, Charlie. I'm sure I played them terribly.

The real things I remember about my off time came from my mom. I think all or at least nearly all of my pay was all going to my ex-wife, and I can't remember getting any of it. My mother, though, would send me a modest check every once in a while, which at least put some coins in my pocket. And once a month, without fail, I would get an enormous care package, stuffed with homemade cookies, brownies, and all sorts of goodies.

I was extremely popular when those came in.

At the time, the army was holding a worldwide contest for something they called the US Soldier Show. A series of contests were held all over the world, at each base and command, looking for the most talented soldier musician. It was kind of like *American Idol* or the old TV series *Star Search*, except limited to GIs. The winners got to travel around the world and entertain the troops.

Easy duty.

I polished up my singing skills and entered the contest as a male vocalist. I sang "Bad to the Bone"—the classic rocker by George Thorogood. Maybe not something you associate with me these days, but . . .

I won!

I won!

I was named the Korea US Army male vocalist.

I'm thinking, *pack the bags. I am skating for a year. Shammin'. This is going to be the best thing ever.*

It was all set. The organizers came to me and said, you'll be on your way, son, as soon as higher command gives the OK.

Higher command said . . .

ABSOLUTELY NOT.

They used official army language, noting that my MOS (or job) was critical to the army, in short supply, of utmost importance, etc., etc., etc. However they phrased it, I was not to be released from duty in Korea for any purpose, including and especially to sing around the world. If I was so important, you'd think they would have given me a raise. Or at least a promotion.

I didn't get to go. But I did get to open up for a USO show featuring Sawyer Brown.

Sawyer Brown had just won a big Nashville talent contest, *Nashville Star*. The band members, Mark Miller, Gregg "Hobie" Hubbard, Bobby Randall, Joe "Curly" Smyth, and Jim Scholten, had all been with country singer Don King's band and gone on to form their own group when he retired.

So this was the big time.

I stood up there and played guitar. What I sang, I couldn't tell you if you offered me a million dollars and a clear shot at a twenty-point buck. But it was the high point of my year, I'll tell you.

Fast forward almost a decade. Sawyer Brown opened for *me*. I went over to Mark Miller before the show.

"I got a story for you, Mark," I told him. "Do you remember when you all won that *Nashville Star* talent contest and you went to Korea?"

"Do I remember?" he answered. "Yeah! That was our first USO Tour."

"You all went to Camp Casey."

"We did! I do remember that."

"Do you remember there was a guy who came on before you—"

"I do remember. That guy sang his ass off, but he couldn't play a guitar for crap!"

"That was me!"

"I guess some things never change!"

Gotta give him the last word on that story; it's too good to top.

The army wouldn't release me to sing . . . but they decided they could spare me for a two-and-a-half-month beatdown at Korean Ranger school.

The Republic of Korea Army—ROK to us—earned a ferocious reputation in Vietnam, where several units served as allies to America and South Vietnam. The standing army numbers are just over five hundred thousand, with reserves several times that. They're well-equipped and well-trained. Though they are organized differently, like the US Army's 75th Ranger Regiment, ROK Rangers are elite soldiers specially trained for a variety of missions, including patrolling the DMZ and scouting for other combat groups.

The Koreans decided to take Americans into the school to help build morale and camaraderie between the forces. Most recently, they have been hosting an event that brings American and Korean units together for some friendly competitions. The allies have also set up shorter exchanges and programs to help improve their ability to work together. When I was there, though, the program was very simple—we'd go through the same nine-plus-week course as the Koreans. No special treatment. And no translators. Everything would be in Korean.

Which I didn't speak. But I wanted to take the course for two reasons. One, my command let it be known that if I passed the course, I'd have my choice of assignments afterward. You can't always take promises like that to the bank, but I figured the odds would be relatively good they'd follow through.

And two—hell, it sounded like a lot of fun. Be all you can be, Korean style.

There were thirty of us Americans at the start. I don't know how many Koreans there were—a lot more than us, that's for sure. While the Americans were there primarily as a goodwill gesture between allied forces, the guys we were training with were trying to live out their dream of joining one of the top military units in the world, ROK's Black Horse Battalion. Korean Rangers on steroids.

The routine was nonstop. In the morning, I'd find the nearest Korean and stick to him, learning what I was supposed to do by watching him do it. Our days would typically kick off with PT, the same as in the US Army. Except it wasn't the same. Instructors would walk up to a candidate as he did a push-up and boot him in the stomach. The candidate would be expected to keep doing push-ups.

And they did. I saw a guy get lifted off the ground by a kick, lose his wind, but come right back prone and continue through the exercise. These guys were some of the physically toughest people I have ever met.

I said that we were treated exactly the same as the Koreans, but that's not precisely true. The instructors had apparently been told that we were not to be touched—and thank God for that, because I'm not sure what an American's reaction would have been if he was kicked in the stomach during PT.

Learning that we couldn't be physically attacked made things a bit easier, but only a bit. Run twelve miles with a full backpack? Sure. I was in pretty good shape, but as a lot of people who go through special operations training will tell you, these sorts of trials are as much about your mind frame and mentality as strength or physical endurance. You have to want it, and you have to be hard-core about wanting it.

The first ten days were probably designed specifically for us Americans. They were basically PT and more PT and a lot more PT, with some PT thrown in to round things out. Sixteen to eighteen hours of exercise, marching, running, whatever. Which wasn't so bad, maybe, except that the food they gave us was the worst sort you can imagine. There wasn't much of it—which, maybe was a blessing in disguise. One barely edible meal a day—call it the Korean Ranger weight loss plan.

At this point, the Americans were invited to opt out with a hearty "well done."

"End of the gentlemen's course," said one of the instructors. "Now who wants to go through the real thing?"

I stepped forward, along with five other volunteers.

Hey, I'm Airborne, right? You can't hurt me.

Heh.

For the next phase of training, we were taken to a camp with bamboo cages and locked inside. Our meals consisted of rice thrown through the bars, with the occasional green supplied by reaching down through the bars and grabbing a few blades of grass.

There weren't instructions for the exercise, but I figured out soon enough that I ought to try and escape. My first plan was relatively straightforward—I'll piss off the "jailers" until they haul me out of the cage. They can't beat me, let alone shoot me, so I'll figure out some way to run off.

As soon as one of my keepers approached, I launched into a tirade of the worst possible insults I could gather. "Bucket Head" was one of the few I remember without four-letter words attached.

Didn't work. Maybe it would have been more effective if I'd known Korean.

I tried spitting on them, but none noticed.

By the third or fourth night, I had hooked up with another American and two Koreans to plot an escape. I'm not sure how we got the cage open—it may have been opened as part of the exercise, or one of the others figured out some way of working the lock free. Anyway, as soon as we were out, we ran for the nearby fence, squeezed under it, and then set out for the safe house we'd been told about at the start of the exercise.

We ran most of the way once we got our bearings. At some point, one of us saw a chicken and grabbed it from its yard. Honest to God, he began plucking it as we ran, and I swear he took bites on the run, alive and all. We were *that* hungry.

But raw chicken wasn't on the menu that night for the rest of us— the safe house was filled with all sorts of food, chocolate and apples and incredibly good-tasting food. We ate like pigs, then spent much of the rest of the night throwing up.

The instructors came in the next morning. Instead of congratulating us for successfully completing the exercise—or better, giving us the next five or six days off while the others suffered—we were hauled back to the prison. In acknowledgment of our achievement, we became trustees, entitled to the full privileges of the camp: an actual meal consisting of rice and kimchi.

Just once a day, but better than nothing. And not bad tasting. It was almost as good as *real* Korean food.

It was in the mountaineering phase of the program later on that I established my reputation among the Koreans. I have all kinds of admiration for those guys, but let me just say: their equipment was some of the shabbiest, worn-out junk I have ever seen in my life. Which is something to keep in mind when picturing the pair of ropes spanning a vast gulch we were tasked to cross. The depth of the gulch was difficult to estimate—at least sixty feet, but maybe six hundred. The ropes, one over the other, appeared to have been strung around the time dinosaurs roamed the earth, and to have been nibbled by a good number of them.

In fairness, they did give us a safety harness to loop into the top rope, so if you slipped you had a fair chance of not hitting the rocks at the bottom of the gulch. Assuming the reason you fell wasn't because the fragile, ancient rope had snapped.

I started across. The instructor on the far side started yelling at me, in Korean of course. The instructor behind me joined in.

Maybe they were telling me to go faster. Maybe they were saying to be careful. Whatever they wanted me to do, it wasn't what I did:

I let go of the top rope, bouncing downward to hang by my harness.

I glanced left and right. Both instructors had turned their backs, apparently unwilling to witness my death.

I had other plans. I got back up and clambered across to the other side. The instructor still had his back turned; I had to tap his shoulder and tell him I was done. He reacted the way a man reacts when he's seen a ghost—and probably he thought he did.

The instructors were scared of me the rest of the phase. They thought I was possessed. Or nuts. Or both. Not so far wrong, I guess.

The rest of the training was easier. The hardest, or at least scariest, exercise was a parachute jump out of a hot-air balloon. It was a static line jump, and it felt like you were falling forever . . .

. . . and ever.

While relying on equipment which, as I mentioned, was not categorically the best.

Finally, the chute popped out and I landed, hard and fast. Intact.

I was one of three Americans who completed the course. We were awarded—and authorized to wear—the Korean Ranger badge on our uniforms.

I was proud of that badge. So proud, in fact, that I was wearing it later when I was at the 82nd Airborne and a sergeant major came up to me and began poking me in the chest.

"What are you doing wearing this," he demanded. No question mark, there—it sounded too much like a threat.

I happened to have the paper authorizing it with me and pulled it out for him. Maybe he couldn't read.

"I don't care what your paper says. Take it off."

He stomped away. I felt sorry for his unit the rest of that day.

I was gung ho and committed to the army. Being all I could be.

As time goes on, you think back and ask yourself, was I really that hard-core? Was I really that committed?

I was. And I shared that commitment with others.

I ran into a friend of mine, not long ago, who'd served around the time I did. We got to talking, and he reminded me that I had picked him up when he first arrived at reception.

He was downhearted, fed up with the army, ready to quit.

I talked him out of it and kept tabs on him in the unit. He stayed on and made a good career out of the army.

I don't take credit for doing anything other than recognizing another good soldier with potential.

As for myself, I didn't yet know I wanted anything else.

Fort Bragg, North Carolina, 1990

THREE:
TRUE LOVE

GLOW MUCH?

I made sergeant or E-5 shortly after ROK Ranger school. The extra pay wasn't much, but it did let me rent a small apartment in Seoul. We're not talking about a palace, but it was big enough to hang out in while off base on pass.

My divorce had come through while I was in Korea. I met a local girl and dated for a bit—she even introduced me to her family—but the relationship didn't go anywhere, and it ended when I got orders to return to the States.

About that, I got to rank my choices on where I wanted to go. Hawaii wasn't available, so I put Fort Campbell at the top. Campbell is on the Tennessee-Kentucky border, and I figured if I couldn't go to paradise, at least I could get close to home. Now understand, my assignment had a lot more to do with the needs of the army than my personal preferences. Fortunately, 13F was a job in high demand, which did give me a little more pull and probably some opportunity. Needs or luck, the army sent me to Campbell, assigned to the 101st Division Artillery—"Divarty," as we called it. I was tasked to Third Battalion, 320th Field Artillery Regiment, aka "Red Knights Rakkasans."

Awesome unit, great guys, but I wasn't there very long. I was sent to air assault school, and then stayed on for a few weeks as an instructor. From there, the army tasked me to a job that would have seemed straight out of *Star Trek* to someone raised in the 1970s or '80s. I became part of a COLT—a Combat Observation Lasing Team, assigned to work with the division's LRS or long-range observation team.

The "lurse" guys would work behind enemy lines, watching high-value targets: munitions dumps maybe, railyards, bases, something big and important. The teams were trained to enter an enemy's territory and remain undetected for a specific period of time—six or seven days would not be unusual.

The army took a few 13Fs such as myself, paired them with a driver/radio operator, and trained us to use what at the time were leading-edge laser designators to guide bombs to a target. This two-man section was a COLT. While in this case I was working with an LRS team, I'd be capable of going behind enemy lines with any unconventional force—think commandoes if you're a civilian.

This was perfect for me in just about every way: working with a small team, using my skills to survive and thrive off the land in a hostile environment, learning new tech.

As senior NCO, I ran the COLT teams assigned to the LRS teams. I and the teams working for me would be assigned wherever the division commander wanted us, "attaching" us to a unit that needed our expertise. The idea was maximum flexibility for the force—basically move the experts to where they are needed the most. Maybe one week it's a "routine" mission working directly with an artillery unit. Maybe another time it's hooking up with Green Berets advising a local guerrilla force as they attacked a command center miles from the front. We were expected to be ready to do both—and ten other things besides.

And always, there was something out of the ordinary.

At one point I was working with a guy I'll call Squared Away (because he was a very soft-spoken kid and good soldier). To give you an idea of how respectful he was, when he wanted to get married, he came to me and asked permission.

"If the army wanted you to have a wife, son," I told him in my best drill instructor voice, "they would have issued you one."

I was only joshing. The line is an oldie but a goldie. Thing is, he had a worried look on his face until I assured him it would be fine.

Squared Away and I were out doing a training mission one night, hauling butt through the woods in a Humvee. We had a Ground/ Vehicular Laser Locator Designator (G/VLLD)—the laser gizmo—in the truck with us. It was big and new, far heavier than what's generally used now, or even the man-portable units that were also being intro- duced into service at the time.

We were tooling right along, psyched to use the thing, when suddenly we went over a huge bump.

Huge bump. Hit-your-head-on-the-roof bump. The designator went flying, broke its lens and cracked open some critical parts.

Did I mention the G/VLLD was brand new? So new that we'd actually had to read the manual to figure out how to properly operate it? A manual which came with a number of warnings about the possi- ble emission of nuclear radiation in case it was broken.

Like it was now.

"Get out the manual," I told Squared Away. "I think we're supposed to quarantine ourselves."

Squared Away started reading through the long list of precau- tions, each one scarier than the other. I finally stopped him and called command.

Sure enough, it was a big deal. A freaking big deal. The people we talked to had to talk to higher headquarters to find out what to do. And higher headquarters had to talk to still higher headquarters.

Apparently, there was great concern that we were now radioactive. Squared Away and I shuffled around a bit, waiting in the cold. Finally, we got an answer:

"Put marking tape around the vehicle. Make sure no one comes within thirty yards. You may have to stay the night. You may be going to the hospital."

We looked at each other. At least we weren't glowing.

Yet.

We got further instructions, directing us to proceed to a nearby hospital. When we pulled up to the emergency room, a nurse met us at the door.

Not quite at the door. It was more like shouting distance. Apparently not fully briefed, she asked what the problem was.

"Possible radioactive contamination," I replied.

"I'm sorry. What did you say?"

"Possible radioactive contamination."

She backed up a few feet. "Can I get you to wait where you are, please?"

We sat out in the vehicle for a good thirty minutes before the hospital door opened again. Two guys in hazmat suits moonwalked in our direction, stopping a good distance away. They gave us new instructions:

"Drive over to the helipad. Remove all your clothing when you get there."

"Buck naked?"

"Everything."

More guys in hazmat suits were waiting when we got to the helipad. They laid out some gowns about thirty yards away, then directed us to "disrobe" in the Hummer.

It was maybe twenty degrees out, but we did as we were told, walking as quickly as possible to the gowns. From there we were directed to a decontamination facility.

You're expecting that was some sort of high-tech lab area where special rays are used to neutralize the harmful effects of the radiation. So was I. What we were led to was a storage closet, where we stood and waited for them to clear a shower area for us. At least we got to warm up under some heat lamps after washing off.

They kept us in isolation for a few hours. Finally, a doctor who specialized in nuclear contamination arrived, took some blood, and pronounced us good to go.

It was a bit disappointing, to be honest. I didn't want to get sick from radiation poisoning—apparently something that couldn't have happened, though neither we nor our commanders knew that at the time. But with all the fuss being stirred up, we kind of felt important.

That incident aside, I settled into a good routine at Divarty. I had a high-speed job, but that only made it more interesting. It built on skills I already had and took them further. And honestly, coming back to the States as an E-5 was great. Life was a lot different as a sergeant than a private. The army was *almost* like a "regular" job, at least at that point.

I'd go to work first thing for PT, come home for breakfast, go back in time for first formation, do my job, appear at the end-of-day formation, then go home to my folks. Not quite a nine-to-five but a heck of a lot better than a typical field deployment. I had weekends off. And thirty days' worth of vacation or leave to use as permitted.

In the middle of all that, I fell in love with the woman of my dreams.

Hell, she was so perfect for me I couldn't even have dreamed her. She was straight out of heaven.

KAREN

My mom and her mom played matchmakers.

It was 1988, early May. On one of my visits to my mom in Dickson, she began talking up this girl who was the daughter of a friend of hers from work. I didn't want to hear it. I'd just gotten out of one bad relationship, I was moving up in the army with a new job and responsibilities, and . . .

Who wants to be set up by their mom?!

One day I went to see my mother and got a message that she was at her friend's house. So I went over to see her and was welcomed inside, where this college kid was laid out on the couch, working real hard at ignoring me. Finally, she sat up and I forgot all about the fact that my mother had undoubtedly connived for us to meet.

This girl was PRETTY. Capital letters, PRETTY. Beautiful. Angelic. All those adjectives, and more. Tongue-tied, I introduced myself and sat down. Awkwardness filled the room.

Her name was Karen. It wasn't all that hard to guess that her mom had been in on the plan. I found out later that she'd been talking me up to her daughter for weeks. Karen had told her, again and again, that there was no way she wanted to meet me.

No way that she wanted a relationship, *no way whatsoever, whatever, no!*

I'm not sure how long we sat there before my mom called in from the kitchen. "Craig, why don't you go get your mother a pack of cigarettes?"

Being a dutiful son, I got up to comply.

Karen's mom chimed in. "Karen, why don't you keep Craig company?"

Karen's response was not the most enthusiastic "all right" I've heard in my life, but it was good enough.

One of us broke the ice on the way by saying how hard our mothers were working to set us up. We started laughing, and laughing led to talking, and a few days later we went to the Grasshopper arcade.

"No, it was that night. We went that night."

That's Karen, adding her two cents. But she's right, as usual. We did go that night to the Grasshopper, the little amusement store in the mall where Guy Eddie and I used to parade. There was a new Mario game, and I ponied up a few quarters to try it out.

We got Mario to the first pipe—which we thought was a chimney—and bumped into it. Trapped, Mario died.

Next time . . . same thing.

Next time again, ditto.

How many times we did that, I have no idea. We kept doing it, laughing, doing it again—neither of us was adept enough to realize Mario was supposed to jump over the pipe to escape. Heck, I'm not sure I could figure that out even today.

Who knows what might have happened if I was a better video game player? But by the end of the night, I'd gotten Karen's phone number and completely lost my heart.

"We were laughing so much that night," Karen adds. "And that was important to me. To me, it wasn't so much an instant fireworks explosion declaring I was in love. It took more time. I had to know who he was first. What he stood for. How dependable he was. What he valued.

"And he was cute, especially in that uniform. But then he left and didn't call! I thought I'd never see him again."

All true. The army almost cost me the love of my life. As soon as I got back to base, I received immediate orders for a training mission that sent me away for two weeks. I don't remember now what we did or where we went, except that it was somewhere either without phones or a place where I wasn't allowed to use one. There was no warning. It was one of those things where I was told, "Get your things and report to so-and-so."

Very common in that line of work.

What I do remember is spending those two weeks away from Karen as if in purgatory. I couldn't wait to see her again. I knew from just the few hours we'd spent together that she was the one.

Finally, we returned from the training mission. It was already pretty late when I reached the base, but I didn't stop to check my watch. I hopped in the car—no shower, no packing, didn't even change my clothes—and beelined to Dickson.

I got to her mom's house after dark. It had to be past ten. Late. But there was a light on. I went and knocked on the door.

Her mother answered. A little late, I realized I should have washed my face; it was still dirty and probably covered with the remains of the camouflage makeup I'd had to wear during the morning exercises.

Fortunately, her mom didn't slam the door in my face. But she did explain that Karen was sleeping.

"Don't wake her up," I said. "I just wanted her to know why I haven't called. I'll call tomorrow."

> *"That's my gentleman," adds Karen, "I thought when I got up that morning. It's not the uniform—he really is a gentleman."*

I got off duty the next day and this time managed to get there by five thirty. She wasn't sleeping or pretending to ignore me on the couch this time. We had a good ol' time together, talking easy like we'd known each other for years. Not too much later, days maybe, we were cutting up and laughing about something, and one of us—we're not even sure who it was, but I think it was me—said, "What if we got married?"

And the other said, "Yeah. OK."

Eight or nine weeks later, we drove down to her father's house in Texas to meet the rest of her family and make things legal. Karen's dad met us on the porch. Big fellow, six-four at least, maybe two-fifty. Bear of a man.

"Am I to understand that you want to marry my daughter?"

More of a threatening bark than a question. But I was full of cocky self-confidence, so I shot right back. "I've been sleeping with her, so I figure it's the right thing to do."

He laughed so hard he could hardly stand up. He grabbed my hand in one of his massive paws and pumped it. "Son, we're gonna get along just fine."

A little bit of my confidence melted away as we shook—he had a grip so hard my fingers felt like they were being squeezed to a pulp. From that moment on, though, he was like one of the greatest people in my life. He really was a good man; a great father-in-law.

On July 30, 1988, we were married.

Just under nine months later, our first daughter, Alexandra (Alex or Aly to the family and friends—and often "Alleycat" to me), was born.

Our wedding, 1988

"Hold on," Alexandra said years later, counting out the weeks. "You were married in July, and I was born in February?"

Mmmmmm . . .

"How far under nine months?"

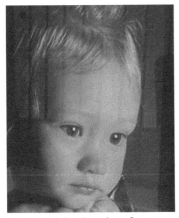

My darling baby Alexandra, reflecting amid reflections in the glass

Who's counting? Honestly, we didn't know at the time we said "I do" that we were pregnant, but it wouldn't have changed a thing if we did. And while I may not have believed in love at first sight before meeting Karen, I am a very firm believer now.

I knew when I saw her on the couch. That day, that moment, I knew I was going to marry her. I had never felt anything like that before—wasn't looking for it, didn't expect it.

Yeah. When it comes to true love, I'm a believer.

We celebrated our honeymoon halfway home, in Hope, Arkansas—Bill Clinton's hometown. We didn't meet him, and I haven't become a Democrat, but the location has caused a good amount of ribbing and sly jokes over the years.

Since I'm telling the whole story here, there's a bit more that I ought to reveal. Before we'd gone down to Texas, we went over to the justice of the peace in Dickson and got the paperwork for the license. The judge told us to have the official at the ceremony sign it, and we'd be good. So we did just that.

We were back about two weeks later, at Karen's mom's house, and for whatever little reason at the time, we started having a bit of a fight. Not a big fight at all, but when you've only been married less than a month, any sort of disagreement can seem major.

Her mother came into the room while we were in the middle of it. "The justice of the peace is here and he wants to see you," she said.

"I made a mistake," he told us. Apparently, the directions about just getting the paper signed out of state were wrong. "You're not legally married. For you to be legally married, I need to do it."

We looked at each other. In that moment, we each had a chance to back out.

We didn't. The disagreement evaporated and we were in love again. Sometimes you need a little shock to remind you what's important.

Karen dropped any plans to go into the army.

Actually, her memory of those days adds a little something:

> "His exact words to me were," she recalls, "no wife of mine is going to be in the military."

True. I insisted. Because with the deployments and everything, raising kids—it's very difficult when one spouse is in the military, but two? Close to impossible if you want a family. And I knew I wanted a family, even before we found out that Karen was pregnant.

It was arrogant, I admit. But I knew the reality. And the truth is, I didn't even understand yet exactly how much a service spouse does while the serviceperson is gone. I knew vaguely, but *really* understanding how hard it is to be married to a military person takes up-close and personal contact. Seeing how much Karen did as our lives went on gave me tremendous, unspeakable respect for military spouses.

Let me admit this: I was not easy to live with. I had an NCO's mentality about how the house should be run. I made Karen keep the hangers in the closet two inches apart, just as if we were standing inspection for a VIP visit. That's not an exaggeration. We GI'd the house the way my subordinates were supposed to GI their quarters. I felt I couldn't tell my guys what they had to do if I didn't do it myself. If they came over, I wanted them to see I lived like they did, or at least by the same rules.

It was a different army back then. Stricter on those sorts of things, I think. Lower enlisted were expected to keep their quarters—on base and off—in GI condition. The idea was, if you squared away the easy things, the big things would fall into place. If your life was orderly off the job, you were effective and efficient on the job. There's a saying: *Make your bed correctly first thing in the morning, and you'll accomplish a lot the rest of the day.* I believe there's truth in that.

I look back now, and I realize that Karen may not have signed up for the army, but she sure had joined it. She'd gone to school for psychology so she could help people. She did that as my wife, becoming an informal counselor not just to the wives and girlfriends of the younger enlisted who worked for me, but to the guys as well. She would do anything for them, anything for her kids, and anything for me.

I praise God that she had so much patience, especially with me. I pushed the envelope, I'm sure.

True story—there were nights I came in and checked for dust above the refrigerator or in the closet. And this was when she was home with one and then two kids.

How did she live with me?

"I had someone who literally went to work every day prepared to die," she says now. "There was nobody else I could meet who would ever do that for me. And I wanted to do all I could for him."

Like I say, thank God for Karen.

Karen and I at the grand opening of the Gallery at Morgan Farms, 2017

FOUR:
WAR

As part of the 101st, and especially while attached to a LRS team, you expect to spend some amount of time overseas. I'd been to Germany on a training assignment, but that was only a few days, maybe two weeks. I knew eventually I'd be tasked to go with a unit outside America for an extended period.

So I wasn't all that surprised when, eight months or so after Alex was born, I received orders to go to Panama. At first, the assignment seemed routine: it would be a two-year tour, with dependents. In other words, Karen and my daughter would come to Panama with me and live off base. We were both excited.

That changed a few weeks later when the army told me Karen couldn't go at all. And I had to get down there ASAP.

No, I wasn't happy. But the army's needs come before personal preferences. And the way the orders came down, I suspected my family wouldn't be safe with me in Panama.

There had been American military bases in the Central American country since the construction of the canal in the opening years of the twentieth century. The treaty that allowed the US to build the passage included a lease of the property flanking the canal, known as the Canal Zone. American ownership and operation of the canal was always controversial among some Panamanians, and as time went on, tensions increased, until a treaty was signed in 1977 to grant full control of the canal to Panama on New Year's Eve, 1999. With the pact signed, the US gradually reduced its presence, closing bases and sending troops home, anticipating the handover.

We still had a good-sized presence there in 1989; in fact, outside of the military, somewhere in the neighborhood of thirty-five thousand Americans lived in Panama. But our relationship with the country's government, headed by Manuel Noriega, was deteriorating rapidly. Noriega, a dictator who'd been in power since 1983, had been indicted in the US for his role in smuggling drugs into the US. While he occasionally cooperated with the US Drug Enforcement Agency, allowing or making seizures of illegal drugs, he more often allowed dealers to use the country as a staging area for sizable shipments, helped them launder money, and generally protected them. All for a fee, of course.

The US took various measures to stem the flow of drugs through Panama, including freezing government bank assets and trying to get Noriega to resign ahead of national elections, which had been promised to restore democracy to the country. In response, Noriega began courting aid from the Soviet Union and Cuba, seemingly changing sides at the tail end of the Cold War between the West and Communist Russia.

In May 1989, Panama held a presidential election. Counts at the polls showed that Guillermo Endara had handily defeated Noriega. Noriega then annulled the results, claiming the US had engineered massive fraud. Harassment against Americans accelerated. President George H. W. Bush (the senior Bush) began beefing up troops and security at US installations. I was part of that.

And a little more.

I landed in Panama that October without knowing much about what was going on. Someone picked me up at the airport and took me over to the base, dropping me off at reception. I went in and sat down in the dayroom, waiting for someone to get me situated when a sergeant first class barged into the room.

"There a Sergeant Greer, here?"

I rose.

Outside my barracks in Panama, 1989

"Come with me."

The sergeant did a quick about-face and set off double time.

OK, I thought. *Kind of gruff, but right to the point.* I followed down the hall, down a flight of stairs, and found myself in a supply room, where I was handed equipment. Not tourist gear, either. They gave me a ruck, a blanket, and a shelter-half—a kind of pup tent you share with another soldier who's destined to become your best friend in the field. I was also issued a Kevlar vest, a weapon, and ammo.

I was then introduced to a PFC and handed a map. "He's your RTO. There's a coup. We have a helicopter standing by. You are to board the helicopter, fly to this position, and issue sitreps for as long as they are needed." (Sitrep is military shorthand for situation report, basically a summary of what's going on.)

The position turned out to be a golf course on an American base in the Canal Zone. Officers in the Panamanian Defense Forces had decided to oust Noriega on their own, and a full-blown revolt was underway.

Or might be underway. The intel was still hazy. Our job was to watch the area in case there was an attack against the army installation.

My RTO and I were just setting up when a Panamanian kid who barely reached my chest came over with a tray of green mangos.

Was he a spy? An agent sent to poison us? Or just a kid trying to hustle a few bucks from gringos?

It looked like the last. There was no one else nearby and he was way too young to be attached to any sort of army, legitimate or otherwise. Still . . .

Damn, that fruit looked good.

"You eat it," I told him. "Go first."

It took a few gestures and a phrase or two in my stunted Spanish to put him to the test.

He smiled as the fruit went down.

I waited a moment. There were no ill effects, at least none I could see.

I handed over the equivalent of a few cents. Money tucked away, the kid sliced one of the mangos, dipped the slices in a little cup of vinegar, then applied a bunch of salt before handing them over.

They tasted pretty good. Very good.

We settled down to business after the snack. From our vantage point on a high point at the edge of a rough, we could see one of the main routes connecting Panama east and west out of Panama City. We could also make out the edge of a large urban area on the outskirts of Vista Alegre. Anyone in western Panama with an idea of either crushing or joining the coup in Panama City would likely take that route. More importantly for the US, it was the likely route a force would take to attack American bases near the ocean.

We soon spotted a group of Panamanians gathering near the road. A few had weapons. They formed themselves into a parade line and began marching, protesting against the American presence or maybe trying to create a diversion for an attack—we were too far away to get a good grasp on what they were saying, let alone their intentions, but it didn't look like they wanted to play golf.

We called the information in and continued to watch. The protesters looked angry but made no move to express that anger in our direction. My RTO and I stayed there that night, and I believe the next, before things in the country finally calmed down to the point where surveillance was no longer needed. We packed up our gear, folded our map, and went back to base.

I still have the map and my notes to this day.

A footnote: The coup was led by Moisés Giroldi Vera, who apparently tipped off the US beforehand but, according to US administration officials later, didn't want any help and didn't receive any. Giroldi and his force captured Noriega on the morning of October 3, but apparently couldn't decide what to do with him. While they debated whether to give him over to the US—he was under indictment for the drug charges by then, and probably would have been shipped back to the States for trial—Noriega phoned for help. Defense Forces loyal to Noriega arrived; Giroldi surrendered.

Ten members of the coup party, including Giroldi, were executed shortly afterward; an eleventh was tortured to death. Later reports pegged the coup as a key moment in what would happen later, as the US realized that Noriega's hold on power in the country was far stronger than they had realized.

Excitement over, I was driven over to Fort Amador, an army base on the Pacific end of the canal, on the tip of the ocean. I was assigned to Delta Battery of the 320th, which was attached to First Battalion of the 508th Airborne Infantry. As a forward observer, we were kind of living in two different worlds. One was the infantry's; the other was the artillery's. We bunked and did our morning PT and some activities with the artillery battery. Then we'd head over to the infantry unit and work with them.

We soon learned that the arrangement made for a bit of . . . flexibility. We could tell artillery that we were going to go over and work with infantry today, and tell infantry that we were working with the artillery. We were loose cannons. Excuse the pun.

I have to confess that our activities day to day depended on who was doing what. The more interesting the exercise, the more likely we were there. On the whole, we were with infantry far more than with artillery; I can only remember training with the artillery for things like our certification for the job.

Among the more rigorous training gigs we did were night jumps into the water. I'm not a big fan of these; you have to release your parachute the moment your boots are wet, and even then you can end up with the chute covering you while you're trying to stay upright and get situated in the water. I had floats on my arms and a vest to help keep me upright; still, it was disorienting, and could take a bit to get into the right position to do my job. But that's why you practice.

There was a bonus. The water was filled with an iridescent algae that glowed blue. It was like jumping into a pool filled with blue chem lights. Although the thought occurred to me that if I was able to see the pretty blue light in the dark, any nearby sharks surely could too.

While it seemed like things with the US had simmered down, there was a lot going on behind the scenes, and the Bush administration was getting more and more worried about the future of the canal and Central America in general if Noriega remained in control. We didn't know any of that. All we knew is that we couldn't go downtown. Which was a real shame for me especially, since I was the only guy in my unit with a private vehicle, thanks largely to luck and timing—I'd had it shipped immediately when my orders still called for me to bring my family, and it was already en route when things got hot and the army started tightening up.

It was a Jeep—a *civilian* Jeep, as the army had long ago replaced the ubiquitous utility vehicle that earned so much fame in WWII with the Humvee. There was no mistaking mine for a military vehicle—it was red. Stood out in the jungle, urban and otherwise. But all-around, a hoot to drive.

The infamous Jeep, Panama, 1990

Though downtown was off-limits, we were able to spend a good portion of time at the beach and going fishing during our off-duty hours. I made some good friends; among them was John Davis, another fire support guy who like me was heading a company. John was Bravo or B Company; I was Alpha or A Company. As senior

NCOs, we set the tone for the rest of the guys, both on and off duty. Work hard, play hard was our motto.

Meanwhile back home, Karen decided to move in with her dad temporarily. That made things a lot easier for her. Not that being, in effect, a single mom, was easy. Service wives make a lot of sacrifices, and Karen was no exception. Dad and other family members certainly helped ease the burden, but she still had a full day every day. Not only was she taking care of our daughter and herself, she also occasionally had to tend to things I would have done had I been home. Paying bills, keeping up with family—routine, maybe, but it lengthens the day, every day. She bought herself a little Yugo to get around. Those cars didn't have the best reputation, but hers soldiered on. I never once heard her complain, about it, me, or the situation she found herself in.

On December 15, Panama's general assembly passed a resolution declaring that the country was at war with the US. The same day, Noriega declared himself "Maximum Leader" and made comments strongly hinting that he planned on attacking Americans and taking over the Canal Zone by force.

The next night, Panama Defense Force (PDF) troops stopped a vehicle driven by a Marine captain, Richard Hadded, in downtown Panama City. When the PDF ordered Hadded and his three passengers, all servicemen, to get out of the car, they declined. The PDF soldier inserted a magazine into his AK-47.

Hadded hit the gas. The Panamanian began firing. So did others at a second PDF guard station. By the time the Americans reached safety, Hadded and two passengers had been hit by several bullets. One of the passengers, Marine First Lieutenant Robert Paz, died at Gorgas Military Hospital.

Two other Americans, a Navy SEAL and his civilian wife, were detained by Panamanians after witnessing the incident. The pair were beaten and the wife assaulted while being questioned.

Americans had been harassed in the weeks before—the so-called police would often stop civilians or soldiers dressed as civilians and rob them. But that incident was the last straw. In Washington, President Bush authorized a plan to overthrow Noriega and allow the elected government to take over.

A day or two after Lieutenant Paz died, we got orders telling us we were going into action. By December 18, we were set and ready. Roughly twenty-seven thousand American servicepeople were directly involved in the operations, which stretched across Panama but were mostly concentrated on the coasts.

The infantry unit we were working with was part of Task Force Bayonet. Their objectives included securing an American base, protecting an area where American dependents lived, and securing some roadblocks and police stations in the area of Ancon Hill and Balboa. The Panamanian Defense Force and the police had considerable men in that quadrant, which included the highest terrain in Panama City. It was a large and strategic area.

Bayonet had a subtask group organized as Wildcat, which included me. The units were directed to secure the grounds around the American command headquarters on Quarry Heights. Alpha Company, 508 (Airborne), the group I was attached to as fire support NCO, would land on a golf course near residential units, gather up the dependents nearby, and evac them to a safe place.

Different golf course, in case you're wondering.

We didn't know the whole plan for the country, of course, and we weren't privy even to the details of the different task forces working near us. We did hear a lot, though. We knew a good portion of the 82nd Airborne was coming in; we knew the Rangers would be there; we knew a SEAL team had something going on. They'd all be operating nearby. This was a big show, the real thing.

At zero dark thirty (12:30, or half past midnight) 19 December, we headed to the Black Hawk helicopters tasked to take us to the target area. One thing struck me right away as I boarded my aircraft: the seats had all been removed. That would allow for maximum flexibility—emergencies, more passengers, whatever. The crew could pack

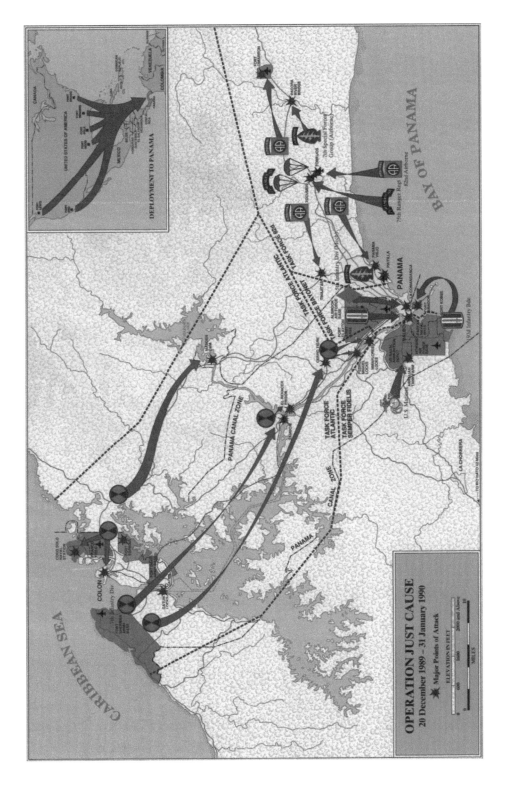

OPERATION JUST CAUSE
20 December 1989 – 31 January 1990

★ Major Points of Attack

ELEVATION IN FEET
0   600   1600   2000 and Above

MILES
0   10

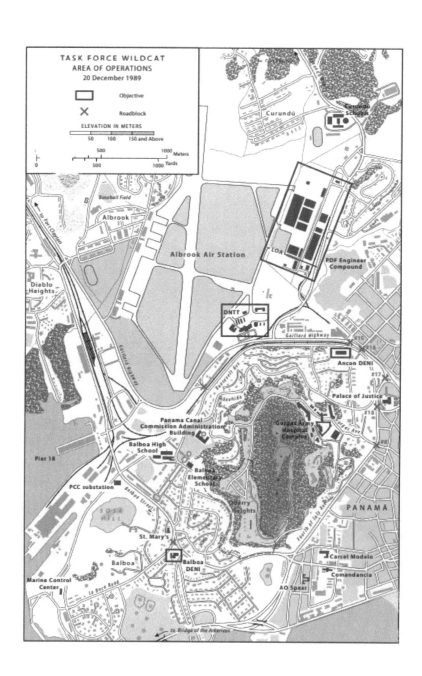

TASK FORCE WILDCAT
AREA OF OPERATIONS
20 December 1989

Objective

Roadblock

ELEVATION IN METERS

50   100   150 and Above

500   1000
0   Meters
500   1000   Yards

Curundú

Curundú
School

Baseball Field

Albrook

to Fort Clayton

Albrook Air Station

LOA

PDF Engineer
Compound

Diablo
Heights

DNTT

Gaillard Highway

#15

#16

Ancon DENI

#17

Palace of Justice

#18

Panama Canal
Commission Administration
Building

Gorgas Army
Hospital
Complex

#8

Balboa High
School

Pier 18

Balboa
Elementary
School

PCC substation

PANAMÁ

SOSA
HILL

Quarry
Heights

St. Mary's

Balboa

Balboa
DENI

Carcel Modelo

Comandancia

Marine Control
Center

La Boca Road

AO Spear

to Bridge of the Americas

in as many people as needed. It was something you only did if you're in combat and expecting the unexpected.

I was tasked to stand by the helicopter hatchway—the doors were off, replaced with a safety strap. When we landed, I'd remove the strap and leap out, leading the pack.

We started taking fire on the way in. One of the helicopters with us got hit bad. Damaged, they had to break off and find a place for an emergency landing. My commander, a lieutenant, was aboard that helicopter. Wounded by the gunfire, he would end up out of action not only for that night but for months. That injury made me acting commander that night, and for the rest of our time in Panama.

At that particular moment, though, I didn't know any of that. I was looking down at the ground, trying not to fall out of the aircraft.

"Sergeant Greer! Get ready!" yelled the crew chief.

I was more than ready. Adrenaline was flowing. I leaned forward, ready to get out and fight.

We were coming in very hot. Muzzle flashes, tracers. *Pop. Pop.*

Bullets snapped against and through the metal hull of the helicopter, but I couldn't register the sound; I had no idea what it was.

There was no time to figure it out. The ground was getting real big below me.

"Now!" yelled a voice in my head. "We're down."

I pulled the hook off the door strap, waited a second, and jumped out. But the ground wasn't quite there.

Damn.

I must have practiced the procedure I don't know how many times. And I'd never misjudged the distance to the ground before. But this time I had—badly. We were still twenty feet from the grass when I leapt out, expecting to be no more than two or three.

I hit the ground, rolled, and dislocated my right shoulder. The guys behind me, keying on me, came out right behind. They fell all over me.

Out of the corner of my eye, I saw the tail wheel of the Black Hawk coming right toward my head. All I could think about was the rear rotor, spinning somewhere above the wheel. A meat grinder.

I flattened. I don't know where that rotor went, or exactly where the helicopter set down; all I know is it didn't hit me.

I got up as the Black Hawk pulled off. My right arm hung limp off my body.

Hurt like hell too.

Realizing it was dislocated, I tried yanking my arm in place as I headed toward my position with the headquarters element, where I'd be available to call in fire support if needed. I still had my M16, but using it with any sort of authority was pretty much out of the question. I spotted a tree as I ran. Could that help?

I ran into the tree as hard as I could, thinking the impact might hammer my shoulder back. I don't have to tell you, all that did was make it hurt even worse.

There was gunfire everywhere. It was your usual combat situation—confusing as hell, dark night, everybody scrambling around trying to figure out exactly where they were and what was going on.

I made it to the headquarters element in time to hear the commander give an order—"Shoot out the streetlights."

Guys started popping off rounds. The area got even darker, but somehow less confused.

"Hey, there're American civilians here. Be careful where you're shooting!"

Our soldiers moved in from the perimeter, gathering up the civilians and securing them in a safe area where we could protect them. If there had been Panamanian forces there, they retreated pretty quick, and except for the target practice on the lights, things calmed down quickly.

My shoulder still hurt like hell. I found a light pole and went back to my homemade therapy, bashing against the pole as I tried to get the joint back in its socket.

"What are you doing?" shouted a soldier running up to me.

I explained.

Turned out he was a medic.

"Lay down on the ground," he commanded.

I dropped. He grabbed my arm, wrapped it in a poncho liner for leverage, then put his foot in my crotch—none of this was gentle. He did some other contortions, got a knee on my leg, and warned me that he was going to yank real hard and that it might hurt.

"Go ahead," I told him. What he was doing already hurt. How much worse could it really be?

Pop!

That much worse. *Damn!*

But it was like a miracle. My arm snapped back into place. The pain—a lot of it, anyway—was gone. I got up and resumed my post.

A year later, I found out that I had probably torn my rotator cuff when I dislocated the shoulder. But at that moment, all I felt was relief.

I'm not sure how much time passed, whether it was a few minutes or hours, but at some point a busload of Panamanian soldiers tried driving up the road in the direction of the houses. They were cut down quick, bullets splaying through the vehicle. The vehicle went off the road into a ravine. Worried that the bus might be booby-trapped or that Panamanians nearby were plotting an ambush, our commander on the scene decided no one would go down until morning light. So we held our position.

We could hear the groans and cries of some of the injured through the night. It would turn out most were dead by the time anyone got to the bus.

The area was secured to the point where the civilians could be bused out and then evacuated to an airstrip to be flown out of the country the next day. By then, I had moved with some of the unit down toward the water, where the navy had secured some twenty or thirty Panamanian Defense Force soldiers earlier. The PDF soldiers— they weren't sailors as far as we could tell—had been intercepted and brought to shore nearby, and the unit I was with was tasked to take them to some trucks and transport them to an area set up as a tempo- rary containment center.

A sergeant major came over. "Hey, anybody speak Spanish?"

I looked around. Surprisingly, no one did.

"Uh, I do, a little," I admitted.

"Come."

I went over to the Panamanians. They were standing around, stripped naked. I guess you can't blame the navy for not taking any chances.

"Sergeant Greer, tell them to put their clothes on," commanded the sergeant major.

I hesitated, desperately trying to think of the right words. Ready phrases like *cómo estás* seemed wildly inappropriate.

Pants. *Pantalón.*

Put on. No. Take off . . .

My store of Spanish was quickly depleted without noticeable effect. Finally, I resorted to a more universal language—I pointed to the pile where their clothes had been left, and mimed getting dressed. I got the idea across, but unfortunately with their hands tied, they had a hell of a time even picking up their clothes, let alone getting them on.

"Sergeant Greer, tell them to get their pants on!" demanded the sergeant major.

"I did!"

"Well, they're gonna need help. Get it done!"

"Yes, Sergeant Major."

I employed all of my training as an NCO to solve the problem—in other words, I looked around and found a private.

"Help these men, Private!"

I grabbed three or four privates to assist. They'd get the prisoners clothed, then walk them over to the truck. Unfortunately, the soldiers worked it out so that as the prisoners arrived, they "inadvertently" bumped their heads against the back of the truck. I didn't catch on until the second or third loud smack. At least one of the privates objected when I put an end to it.

"Sergeant, these may have been the guys shooting at us."

I understood the attitude, but that didn't make smacking them around "accidentally" right. I found out later on that a lot of the PDF members had been forced to take the job in the first place. These guys, I think, had probably tried running away when the attack started, going AWOL because they didn't want to fight and kill Americans.

At some point later that day—my personal timeline has blurred a bit over the years, but I believe I have the sequence correct—my company was assigned to guard the Presidential Palace, a few blocks away in Panama City. It had been secured by the time we got there, but hadn't been fully searched. We started going through methodically, working our way around. For some reason, a notion jumped into my head as we entered the room: *Maybe there are booby traps.*

"Whoa, hold on," I yelled as one of the guys went to open the first door. "Better check for booby traps."

Sure enough, a grenade was rigged to go off in one of the rooms. We proceeded carefully after that.

Noriega had a stash of gold and money in the palace; it had already been found and was being guarded. But no one had gone through his mountain of Christmas gifts. We found something like forty bottles of champagne apparently earmarked for foreign supporters around the world. Rumor has it that a bottle intended for Muammar Gaddafi made its way from that stash into someone's private possession. And according to said rumor, the bottle was later relocated to somewhere in the States, where it now rests in a secure storage area.

At some point in the future, I plan to pop it.

If I were the person who ended up with it, that is.

Sitting in Noriega's office, at his desk, was unreal. There were some cigars in a humidor box, and I believe one or more might have been smoked—someone had to make sure they weren't booby-trapped, you know?

I didn't have much of a chance to enjoy the good life of a dictator, as word soon came that members of the task force near Balboa DENI police station were fighting Panamanian forces there and needed fire support. I was the closest fire support guy, so I temporarily put the ranking NCO in charge of the rest of the teams and took off with my radioman.

Our first problem was getting there. Balboa DENI was at least a mile or two away. The solution presented itself when a car appeared on the nearby road. We pulled the driver over and saw that he had a bunch of guns in the car. Now, I don't know what all he was up to. I can't say that he was going to use those guns against Americans, or if he had some peaceful and logical reason for them. All I knew was that we had to get over to the police station as quickly as possible. And I couldn't just let him go.

We took the guy, bound him, and put him in the trunk of the car. I figured we'd get him over to the containment center when whatever we had to do at Balboa was done.

Honestly, I didn't think there would be much to it, given all that had happened so far. But the firefight at Balboa when we arrived was hotter than a five-alarm barn fire. Well-armed Panamanian forces had holed up in the police complex and were putting up such a fight that the assault teams tasked with taking the building couldn't make any headway.

My radioman and I reported in, then found an overwatch building about a football field or so away from the police station where I could get a good read on what was going on.

It wasn't long before we got the order to bring in "fire on the target." The sun had set, which meant we could count on fire from an overhead gunship which had just started circling above.

The AC-130 Spectre is a four-engined Hercules aircraft. While most Hercules C-130s are basic cargo planes used to ferry troops or supplies, AC-130s are armed with cannons. The exact configuration depends on the aircraft model, but whatever version, they pack a serious wallop. You do not want to be on the receiving end.

I started feeding the coordinates to the gunship. The first shell from the Spectre's 105 mm cannon hit the police station with a bang so loud my ears popped. I thought our building was going to collapse because the ground shook so bad.

They were good, those air force boys. Artillery you give a grid, and they hit anything in that grid. Generally. You close your eyes and hope for the best, at least in those days. But the Spectre shot with pinpoint accuracy. If they missed, it was by a millimeter or two. A good thing, since we were so close. The fire control officer in the plane knew my position thanks to a strobe we had, but even so—a few degrees off and I would have been 105 mm dust.

Funny. You don't think about that when you're in the middle of combat. You don't even pay attention to the bullets whizzing by while you're calling in fire, or at least I didn't. It was only later, when the sun came up and everything was calm that I realized the *fpppp* and the *klipppkit* I'd heard were bullets passing a few inches overhead.

Obviously not well-aimed, but tell that to the one that hits you.

Things calmed down some after the AC-130 strike. There were still Panamanians inside the police building, though most of the survivors had been severely wounded. The roof had been blown off; a lot of the concrete brick walls had been shattered and tossed every which way. No windows, no doors anywhere.

Mayhem.

By the time our troops began clearing the building at sunup, the bodies of some of the dead had stiffened with rigor mortis. War is exciting, but it's also a very ugly thing.

Remember that guy we left in the trunk of the car?

We'd forgotten all about him until the building was secured. We ran down to the vehicle and saw it had taken shrapnel or bullets at some point that night. I cringed as I opened the trunk.

Our prisoner was breathing and untouched. Petrified, probably out of his mind, but alive.

We drove him over to a school being used to process potential prisoners and got him checked in. On the way out, a news reporter came up to us and started asking questions. I can't remember exactly how it went, but it must've been something along these lines:

"Excuse me, Sergeant, can I have a word?"

"Uh, sure."

"What are you doing?"

"Escorting a prisoner."

"How do you think the war's going?"

Damn good from my point of view. I translated that sentiment into military speak: "I believe we have the situation under control."

"Did you get Noriega?"

I of course had no idea. I translated that into military speak: "I'm not at liberty to discuss that."

There were a bunch more questions. I popped out a couple more "I'm not at liberty to discuss that," supplemented by the occasional "I don't have that information," before managing to conclude the interview.

Honestly, I would have completely forgotten about that incident except for the fact that the interview ended up getting carried by some news stations and picked up by newspapers back in the States. Karen's father in Texas was among those who caught a broadcast—as did Karen.

That was how Karen and the rest of the family knew I was in the thick of things when, not all that long afterward, a US Army car pulled into Karen's father's driveway. A gentleman in uniform came to the door.

Karen looked out and saw him. There's only one reason an official army vehicle comes to a loved one's house, and it's not a very pleasant one.

"Daddy, I just can't answer," she told her father.

Her father opened the door with a heavy heart.

Karen couldn't hear what was said at first, but soon she felt as if she'd witnessed a miracle: The car pulled back out. They'd had the wrong address.

As badly as she felt for the family of the man who'd been killed, she was grateful that it wasn't me.

JUNGLE DUTY

People say that your training kicks in in combat. It's the truth. You get in the motion of doing what has to be done—what you've done before, what you know how to do.

What you can't do is let your thought process interfere, not at the crucial moment. Because if you do, you'll scare yourself into doing something that'll get you killed.

That's how I think about it now, looking back. At the time, it was all just happening.

This was my first test in combat, the real crucible of a soldier. You never know how you're going to react when the bullets fly until you face them. I think we did well because the men who had trained us had done a good job preparing us. My team passed a gut check, thanks to a lot of other guys who showed us the way.

Of the many honors, badges, and awards you can receive in the military, one of the most important is the Combat Infantryman's Badge, or CIB. You can get it only one way—by being in combat. Up where the bullets are flying, and you're fighting back. Ordinarily, the CIB is issued only to infantrymen; you *have* to be a "grunt" to get it. You're artillery—sorry, we have other badges for you. Good ones, just not CIBs.

But even though we weren't officially infantrymen, we got orders following Panama authorizing us to wear the badge on our uniforms. And we certainly did. (I'm guessing there's an obscure regulation relating to our serving with infantry during the combat, but no one ever bothered to show it to us.)

It may seem like a little thing, but I cherish that badge. I was

proud to wear it on my uniform, joining the ranks of men since World War II who risked bullets and death in the service of their country. You can never reduce yourself to a ribbon or piece of metal, but symbols are important, and I greatly appreciated the honor of wearing this one.

The fight was quick, but the US did take casualties, as the car that pulled into Karen's dad's driveway

Service patches honoring my duty in Panama attests. Twenty-three men were killed in action, and another 325 wounded. To the families of those brave men, it wasn't an easy war.

Panama also suffered casualties. Estimates go from 234 to 314, and those numbers aren't anywhere near as precise as they may look. Nearly two thousand members of the forces facing us—whether members of the Defense Force, police, or whatever—were captured and held, at least briefly. Task Force Bayonet was credited with twenty-four enemies killed, nine wounded. The force captured 463 Panamanians.

Organized resistance throughout the country wound down within days if not hours of the initial assaults. A SEAL team mission—one of the very few that has ever been publicly acknowledged by the US—blew up Noriega's yacht, the *Presidente Porras*, inside Balboa Harbor on the canal. Another team destroyed his Learjet and other aircraft at Paitilla field, but met heavy resistance there before completing the mission; four Americans died and eight were wounded. Noriega, cut off from escape, went into hiding at the Papal Nuncio, a building belonging to the Apostolic Nunciature, essentially an embassy complex owned by the Catholic Church and its Holy See.

The US command decided that we couldn't just charge onto the property and take him. So instead we would drum him out. Loudspeakers were set up, and for two days straight, the Nuncio and surrounding buildings shook to the loudest, most obnoxious rock music available. There was a lot of heavy metal in the rotation, AC/DC, Black Sabbath, Alice Cooper, with the occasional Doors and Bon Jovi song thrown in. Played at teeth-shattering levels, it was a PsyOp—a psychological operation, as opposed to a physical assault—without parallel in the history of warfare.

Noriega surrendered on January 3, coaxed out by priests in the Nuncio, whom I suspect had had enough of the music.

With Noriega corralled and the fighting over, American troops began returning to the States. In early January, the 82nd Airborne returned to Fort Bragg, staging a combat jump that caught a lot of media attention.

I saw none of it. I had been tasked on another mission, one involving the CIA and the Green Berets.

The details of that mission are still hazy to me, and not just because so many years have passed since then. As occasionally happens, information was handed out on a strict need-to-know basis. Even though I had to work closely with the ground commanders, I apparently didn't need to know much. I didn't even know the CIA was involved until many years later. Heck, I still don't *officially* know.

Not to say that we didn't *kind of know* at the time. But there's a vast gap between "kind of know" and "know for certain." What I do know for certain is this: the US wanted to find some men who were thought to be in the jungles on the border of Panama and Costa Rica. The people we were with were supposed to find them.

We jumped on the border of Costa Rica—or more likely a few miles inside that country—landing in an established landing zone. Established here meaning someone looked out of the aircraft and said, "That looks like a big enough clearing to land."

We made the jump with a minimum of hassle, organized on the ground, and then pushed into the jungle. I believe we had upward of a platoon of "regular" army in support. Obviously, they must have been airborne-qualified, but whether they were from the 82nd or some other unit at this point I can't recall. We all wore B-1s—battle dress uniforms and jungle hats, your very basic combat work clothes, with names and all insignia removed. I remember old-style flak vests, but I think they were ancient and lacked plates—easier to move without all that weight.

Moving through the jungle was . . . interesting. I've never seen so many bugs in my life. Or monkeys. The monkeys would steal your pants off you if you weren't careful. Anything not tied down at night became monkey property.

What spooked me, though, were the vampire bats. We heard they would fly down while you were sleeping, bite you, and lick the blood off. Something in their saliva acts as a numbing agent and they get quite a feast without you even waking up.

And then there were the snakes.

I'm not saying the stories were worse than the reality, but I didn't get bit by a bat or snake while I was there.

As the fire support guy, I stayed close to the Agency operatives and SF guys. It wasn't like in the movies; none of that *Rambo* bravado. The Group guys were low key, no name tags, easy-going. ("Group" is another name for Special Forces, SF, or Green Berets. The nickname comes from the way the teams are organized, which is unique to Special Forces.) They weren't a talkative bunch, but they were friendly enough, and pretty much accepted that we were all professionals. By contrast, the Agency people kept to themselves. You got the idea that they expected you to speak to them only when spoken to, and they weren't about to speak to you.

We pushed through the jungle that night, got some sleep, and continued the next day. It was a long, hot march, but without anything going on, until early that evening when the advance team came to a bamboo wall.

We'd walked without warning to the edge of a village. Apparently, this was our target, because orders were issued to set up a perimeter and prepare to go in. There was at least one aircraft flying somewhere above—"on station" as the air force would put it—and I got ready to call it in.

The SF and Agency guys moved to the village entrance. I joined them, mentally calculating targets, grids, everything I'd need to tell an aircraft if things got hot. One of the Agency guys turned to me and asked if I was ready. I'm pretty sure it was the first time he'd spoken to me since the operation started.

I ticked off some of the aircraft we could call in if needed; at least one was on station with us the entire mission. "Just tell me what you need."

"Thanks," was all he said, but there was a lot in that single word and the nod that accompanied it. It seemed pretty clear he'd done this before. It also seemed pretty clear that he liked the idea that we could nuke the place if necessary.

Figuratively speaking. As far as I know.

The team went in. I held back with one of the commanders, waiting for gunfire, careful to stay under cover in case I needed to call in support.

Nothing.

Really, nothing. The place was about as calm as a park on Sunday morning. There were plenty of people, but no gunfire, no fighting, no resistance. The locals quickly turned over two guys who were not part of the village—apparently the guys we'd come to find.

The Agency people made everyone but me and two of the Group guys leave while the men were questioned. What exactly they said, I have no idea. I'm guessing it was important information—*right?*—about the possibility of some guerrilla movement relating to Noriega, or maybe a rebel group that had been operating against him. Honestly, though, it could have been about anything—baseball, the weather, vampire bats. All I know is that when the conversation was over—and I don't believe it lasted five minutes—the Agency guy was satisfied. Happy, even.

"Pack up," he said.

And that was it. We didn't even take the two guys with us. We marched on back to the area where we'd landed and were picked up by helicopter the next day.

Mission accomplished, whatever it was.

LOOSE CANNONS IN CHARGE

Noriega surrendered January 3. Taken to the US to stand trial, he was convicted on eight counts of drug trafficking, racketeering, and money laundering. He was extradited to France due to charges there, convicted, and then later extradited to Panama, where he had been charged with murder. He was still facing those charges when he died in May 2017, following surgery to remove a brain tumor.

Those convictions were years in the future. The important things at that moment was that he was gone and the conflict officially over.

Panama was a fledgling democracy once again. We returned to Fort Clayton, relaxed a bit on base and off, and got ready to move on.

Now here's the thing. Like I said, our company lieutenant had been injured on the first night and was no longer around. That left myself and John Davis in charge. I was the commander, and John was first sergeant under me. As a practical matter, we worked as a team. We were still assigned to the artillery unit, 3/20, to work with the infantry. At this point there wasn't much chance that the infantry would need artillery, but that was our assignment.

Then one day the commander and the first sergeant of 3/20 walked over to John and me at the barracks and held out a set of keys.

"Sir?"

"Arms room. Building," said the commander, pointing to each one.

A brief explanation followed: 3/20 had been disbanded. All personnel, officers and enlisted, were to leave immediately for reassignment.

That happens from time to time in the army. They decide for whatever reason—sometimes a good one—that the way units were arranged no longer makes any sense. So they eliminate the unit and put its men elsewhere.

Come to find out, the army had issued orders for all of the artillery members. But not us. All of the attached forward observers, whom John and I were now in charge of, had no orders. It was as if we didn't exist.

We *did* exist, and the army knew we existed, because we were still getting paid. But we were in some sort of official limbo.

"What do we do now?" one of us asked the commander.

"I'm sorry," he said. "Y'all need to figure that out for yourselves. Good luck."

He and the sergeant beat a hasty retreat.

John and I looked at each other. I'm not sure which one of us spoke first. Probably John. He's quick like that.

"We're in charge. WE'RE IN CHARGE!"

Downtime after the conflict

Ordinarily in a military unit, you get orders from the command staff for training, schools, time off, and so on. But our command staff no longer existed. In effect, we were them. Which gave us a far greater authority than we'd had. Ever. We filled the void, at least where we could.

"Anyone want to sign up for any school?" we asked. We wrote authorizations for a number of different assignments, including in my case, Ranger school. I thought I would get through training and possibly join the regiment, the goal I'd been detoured off years before.

We also put everyone in for whatever leave they were entitled. John and I would grab a Humvee and drive all the way over to higher headquarters at Fort Kobbe to submit the paperwork.

Approved.

Approved.

Approved.

We didn't even talk to the infantry for a week or so. See, our function with the infantry *would* be to communicate with the artillery unit supporting them, but if there was no artillery unit supporting them, there was nothing for us to do. So there was no reason to be with the infantry; at best we'd get in their way. And you do not want to get in the way of infantry.

We went along like that for six months before someone caught on. I assume the infantry unit knew 3/20 was gone, but nothing they were doing even came close to involving artillery, so they really didn't miss them. What they thought about us, if anything, I have no idea. We trained with them on the few occasions that they had exercises, so maybe they just thought it was normal.

One of the buildings in Panama City after the defenders surrendered

Finally, someone in charge many pay grades above us decided that we should be attached permanently to the infantry unit, in effect giving their officers command over us. Little changed. The infantry unit had no place to put us, so we stayed where we were, and more or less went along as we had—training when called on, enjoying R&R when not.

What kind of R&R?

Some of our adventures remain so highly classified that even I cannot authorize myself to talk about them. But to give you a taste . . .

My team headed to Taboga Island, 1990

There's a resort island out in the ocean of Panama Bay called Taboga Island. It's a beautiful place today—and was even more beautiful back when we were there.

We're out there one day, partying, and for whatever reason someone started up a little fire. A soldier out there, who won't be named for reasons that will soon be clear, decided he was going to add some wood to it.

It turned out this soldier had recently had a vasectomy. And because of that, was wearing a special support in the critical area. Which was all he was wearing. What had happened to the rest of his clothes is a mystery, but I'd guess that the reasons for his state may have had to do with the prodigious amount of alcohol he had consumed just prior to turning his attention to the fire.

I'd further guess that alcohol had something to do with his falling *into* the fire, but that was secondary to him whacking himself with a stick he was trying to break to put in the fire. The stick—maybe it had been planted by a Noriega loyalist—somehow managed to whack him in the area that had been operated on. His support garment failed to provide much protection, and he thereupon fell unconscious into the flames.

I was elsewhere on the beach at the time, or I might've died laughing. The first I heard of it was several minutes later, when a member of our group ran and got me, screaming as they came: "[REDACTED] is on fire!"

I calmly gave the first order that came into my head. "Well, put him out!"

That had been accomplished by the time I arrived. We then had to find someone with a boat to get the guy back to the mainland. Said soldier seemed to have recovered to a semiconscious state when we landed, and so we didn't bother taking him to the doctor. Instead, we deposited him in his room, which he shared with another GI.

As I heard it, they were both all hugged up together the next morning, naked as the day they were born.

We didn't ask questions. Social media had not been invented at the time, so the incident passed without outside notice.

John, Gino Kerns, Rusty Shoemacker—the whole gang were great fun to be around. Everybody had their own specialty. Rusty loved to play golf. We'd do our formations, take care of army business, and adjourn to the golf course. After eighteen holes, we'd adjourn for shark steak and a beer; total tab, five bucks.

Somewhat more seriously, a bunch of us were part of the hundred-mile club—run a hundred miles and you earned a little patch. I think I got six. I also had a chance to do scuba diving and got dive certified while we were down there. Though I have to admit, "dive certified" in Panama at the time meant little more than you know what the equipment was and how to stay out of trouble. The instruction was basically, "Here, put this on and you're good to go." Years later, I went through an actual course and got a more official, and need I say rigorous, course.

Maybe the fact that we'd been in combat, that we'd been shot at, made us appreciate life a little more. Maybe the fact that we'd put our training to use—and that we had done a really good job using it— made us feel like we'd accomplished something important. I know that it made me feel more confident and proud.

For me, personally, Panama was also a time of music.

The big building we had to ourselves had a large room with pool tables and some comfortable chairs. Another member of our group, Tim Parris, had brought his guitar down, and we'd sit around in the evening and play some music in between shooting some pool. I didn't realize it then, but those off-the-cuff sessions were greatly improving my musicianship. I was learning without being all that conscious of it.

Army buddies John Davis, me, Gino Kerns, Tim Parris, and Ed Carlin got together to do some fishing and tell some tales in 2021.

STATESIDE AGAIN

As much fun as these weeks were, I missed Karen and the baby something awful. So I had no regrets at all when the army finally approved orders assigning me to Ranger school back in the States.

Truth be told, I walked right by Karen and the baby in the Texas airport when I came in to meet them. In the six or seven months that I'd been gone, Karen had lost the last of her pregnancy weight and changed her hair—she was always beautiful to me, but that day she looked hotter than a firecracker. I quickly realized my mistake and made it up to them with a great reunion. After a vacation that was far too short, we headed back north, me to Ranger school and Karen to our new place in army housing.

I was doing well there until I broke my back.

I believe I set myself up for the injury during a parachute jump into the training area. I landed hard and it hurt, but not so bad that I couldn't soldier on—or so I thought. A few days later when we were doing some hand-to-hand combat in a pit, I lost feeling in my legs.

Scary.

The docs at the hospital surprised me when they told me that, more than likely, I'd recover without surgery. But then they lowered the boom: "You have to stay off your feet and go easy indefinitely."

Not forever. But they made it sound like eternity, with no definite end date. I would be off jump status for a good three to six months, at least. Their pronouncement took me out of that Ranger training cycle. I was left to rehab on my own, struggling to get myself back into shape where I could complete the course without becoming a cripple for life. I had Karen and my family for support, but it was still a difficult time.

I slowly got to the point where I could start running. I gradually got my strength and mobility back. The hardest part wasn't the rehab, though I'm not going to pretend that was easy. No, I had to convince the medical people that I was in good enough shape to get through the Ranger course. Most guys who've been through any sort of special operations training say it's mostly a mental thing, and I agree—but your body has a lot to say about it, too, so I can't *really* fault the docs for holding me back. When I finally did convince them, they did so with a provision that under other circumstances would have truly killed me: I wasn't allowed to parachute.

Yeah. No jumping.

That alone would have most likely killed any shot at joining the Ranger Regiment after the school, but in any event, my personal time-line and that of most of the army was interrupted by the buildup for the first Gulf War.

In August of 1990, Saddam Hussein invaded and took over Kuwait. The US assembled an international coalition to kick him out, and as part of the preparations, I was called back to a unit at Fort Bragg. As always, the army was in need of 13Fs, and I imagined that with my training and experience, I'd be among the first to join the expected assault.

I imagined wrong. When I reported to the unit, it had already deployed. So instead of being sent to join what became known as Desert Storm, I was made senior noncommissioned officer for the rear detachment. To that point, it was easily the worst thing that had ever happened to me in my life.

My job was to deal with all the misery, heartache, complications, and just general BS that happens way behind the lines when a unit deploys. There were things that broke my heart—spouses cheating, people wanting to kill themselves for various reasons—and other things that made me shake my head and occasionally want to shake someone, like soldiers unfit for duty getting into serious trouble off base.

I was miserable. Maybe not as bad as some of the people I had to counsel or look after, but close at times. The only bright spot was the fact that my good friend John Davis had been assigned to Bragg as well.

One of us got orders to arrange for some gear to be shipped to the war zone. That gave us an idea.

We wrote orders for us to accompany the gear.

We made it pretty far—farther than you might think. Let's just say I'm still shaking the sand out of my boots.

We knew the end was near when an officer looked at us cross-eyed and asked us exactly what we thought we were doing.

"We're supposed to bring these weapons to the unit."

"No. You were supposed to make sure they got here, not come with them."

"Well, we're here now. We might as well go to work."

"No. The war's over. We're sending people home."

Desert Storm was so effective that the war lasted exactly one hundred hours, or less than five days. We probably wouldn't have gotten away with it even if the war had continued, but we had at least given it a try.

The army may not have seen it that way, exactly. But neither of us suffered any lasting consequences. We caught a flight back.

"You were gone for a long time," said my wife when I came back.

"You wouldn't believe where we've been."

And she didn't.

I was finally cleared to start jumping again. I set my sights on jump-master school and started educating myself on everything you need to know to run a jump and then some. It's a tough course. Even to get in—a panel of accomplished jumpmasters review you and your record before even deciding to let you take the course. I'd heard the attrition rate at the time was like 85 percent, and I worked like a dog to pass.

The good part was that I got to jump a lot. Before I left the army, I jumped out of every aircraft you could jump out of. My log has over nine hundred jumps, including the Korean balloon jumps. Not bad for a guy with a (healed) broken back.

At the time people associated combat jumps with BIG aircraft, namely the C5A, an aircraft just shy of a football field long. They make for very pretty photographs, stick after stick of paratroopers stream-ing through the sky. But here's the thing: the C5A has to be the worst plane to jump out of. Or at least it was for me. You step off that ramp, you are moving at maybe one hundred and eighty knots. The cord gets pulled, canopy fills—you're kicked in the pants.

A specific part of the pants where pain cannot hide.

The C-130, in its various guises, was a good plane to jump from, and probably the favorite of most paratroopers. But for me as a jump-master, the aircraft I loved parachuting from wasn't an airplane at all, but a Chinook C-47 helicopter.

Why was it my favorite?

On a fixed-wing aircraft, the jumpmaster ordinarily walks off last, making sure everyone else in the unit is out before he leaves.

On a Chinook, the jumpmaster leads. "Follow me!" you shout as you walk off.

Seems a lot cooler.

Still hate those night water jumps, though.

My son Kyle was born while I was stationed at Fort Bragg. I was right there—but I wasn't.

You see, I've passed out exactly three times in my life. That was one.

Another happened years later after I lost a bunch of blood working on a building we owned in Dickson. That was more due to lack of food and maybe sleep than loss of blood.

The other was a result of actual pain, and it happened while in the army.

We were doing a type of helicopter pickup that's used for a very fast extraction. The soldiers to be picked up are in harnesses; the helicopter comes in, soldier number one starts running in the direction the helicopter is flying, grabs the line dangling from the aircraft and hooks on. Next one does the same, etc., and away you all go.

The one thing you should know to complete that picture is that every soldier's harness is situated such that they can't fall out of it. This requires positioning a portion of the harness material in a crucial area of the body. The exact positioning of this harness is critical, but can and sometimes does slip in the process of the operation.

I forget exactly how we were arrayed during that exercise, but I do remember I was the last man to hook on. I had a solid connection, and the helicopter jerked me upward as I ran. As it did, it applied an ungodly amount of pressure to that sensitive area, and I lost consciousness.

This drill called for us to be ferried a short distance from the original pickup, whereupon we would be lowered to the ground and have to release—the flip side of the procedure we'd just performed. It was the sort of thing you might use, say, in a very hot insertion.

It does help to be conscious for it.

I woke up just as my feet hit the ground and we took off back running again and unhooked. I'm happy to report that I made a full recovery, with no lasting damage.

I can't blame helicopters or blood loss on my blackout when Kyle was born. I was right there, holding Karen's hand, talking to her as she started pushing and things got going.

Suddenly, the doctor pulled the baby out and one of the nurses said, "It's a boy."

"It's a boy," I said. And promptly fell—not to the floor, but right on my poor wife.

I recovered quickly. I blame my blackout on the fact that I hadn't slept much and had been training real hard and ... Aw, heck. Let's just say I was just so excited to be a father again and couldn't handle the excitement. Both mother and son were fine, and fortunately have not held my momentary lapse of consciousness against me ... much.

My combat experience in Panama, my stint with the Korean Rangers, my various schools—I was building a pretty good career base in the army. To get further along and earn promotion, I needed to punch a few more tickets.

I could have done that at Fort Bragg. I didn't *not* like Bragg, or the units I was working with. But I didn't really want to stay there for the next ten years. It seemed to me that once Bragg had you, they never let you go. So I looked around for another pathway to advance.

There were a few avenues I could have taken to move on up the ladder. I might have become a drill sergeant or a recruiter, jobs the army considers very important but which I had little interest in. So when I had the chance to go to Fort Polk and JRTC, I grabbed it.

JRTC stands for the Joint Readiness Training Center; it's army shorthand for a program that teaches combined arms training in a wide range of situations. In its simplest sense, the program teaches soldiers from different parts of the military—like infantry, artillery, and attack aircraft—to work together in combat. It's designed to be as realistically close to combat as possible, without actual blood flowing. Units engage in different exercises that mimic war conditions. It's common, for example, for soldiers on an operation to encounter actors taking on roles as civilians or guerrilla fighters who act the way they would in war.

My job as an E-6 staff sergeant was to evaluate the forward observers. Let's say the Rangers were doing an exercise. I would tag along with their forward observers and evaluate their job performance. They might set up a mock attack on a village occupied by the enemy. I would parachute in with them and live on their hips as they went through the mock battle. Every so often I would have to clarify some part of the situation for them, like a referee in a war game, but mostly I kept my mouth shut and took notes. At the end of the exercise, we'd review what they had done, praise them for what they excelled at, suggest improvements where they were subpar.

There was another reason I put my hand up for the job. I knew that at JRTC, guys regularly had four-day weekends. So if I took that job, I'd be able to spend a lot more time with Karen and the kids. We'd also be closer to her father and family in Texas, about a three-hour drive, though farther—ten hours or so—from the rest of our folks in Tennessee.

I was also thinking I'd have more time to write songs. At that point, it was still very much a hobby, if even that. But it was like the seed of something growing inside my soul, setting down roots, pushing through the soil. Playing the guitar in Panama on my off-hours had encouraged it, if only indirectly. I couldn't say I had a plan, just some thoughts. Maybe I'd spend some of those

Playing guitar at my in-laws', Texas, 1994

weekends going up to Nashville, seeing my family . . . and maybe trying my songs out at a small venue or with friends.

Fort Polk is in Vernon Parish, Louisiana. A lot of people refer to it as the armpit of the earth and down-talk it because it's so isolated. But as a training center, it has to be away from things. And there was a lot going on at the base. It would eventually become the prime facility for troops training up for Iraq and Afghanistan. So even though to the rest of the world there wasn't much going on, we were very busy and very important.

Still, my schedule was easy enough that I was able to be with the kids, especially on weekends. I coached rec soccer and was there for birthdays and even a 2:00 a.m. feeding or two. For us, it was a great place to be. Off base was an outdoor paradise. I had a buddy who was a fire support guy who lived outside the camp, and we spent a lot of time hunting and fishing. He showed me how to use a bow, which added a new dimension to my hunting.

On base was even more exciting. I never knew who I might meet in that job. The best example actually happened at Bragg. One night I was on the ground near an LZ, waiting for an exercise to begin. As the first aircraft approached, we saw it was a lot lower than we expected. I could tell it was going to drop equipment, not men—a deviation from the normal and briefed procedure. We scrambled to deal with it as two more aircraft flew in, disgorging their paratroopers in the sky. It was a very haphazard drop.

I finally spotted an officer hitting the ground and ran over to give him the brief on what his unit was supposed to do next.

"You Major So-and-so?" I asked.

"No. Who are you?"

"It doesn't matter who I am," I shot back. "I'm looking for So-and-so and you're not him."

The exercises were supposed to go according to a set of rules, and it seemed to me that this individual, probably a second lieutenant still wet behind the ears to judge from the way he landed, was trying to break those rules. Which, fine, good for him, but not with me.

"Who are you?" he asked again.

"You don't need to know who I am," I told him. "I need So-and-so. I'll brief him."

The light shifted—maybe a cloud had been covering the moon or something. Anyway, I suddenly realized this nugget lieutenant was as old as my father.

Hmmm.

When he asked a third time who I was, I asked him *his* name.

To be a little more specific, I said, "Who the f--- are you?"

With a lot of emphasis on the middle word in that sentence.

"Son, I am General Shelton. You can tell me who you are and you can brief me."

"Roger that, sir."

I can't recall if William Shelton was a two- or three-star general at that point. I believe he was still commanding general of the 82nd, though in short order he was bumped up to head XVIII Airborne Corps and eventually made a four-star in charge of the US Special Operations Command. He was promoted a lot in the '80s and '90s, and any of those posts would have brought him to that exercise. But which of those posts he held really didn't matter as far as my own future in the army was concerned.

The only way out of a situation like that is to find a way to fade from memory. Drop off the radar, go stealth, disappear. I would have gladly pursued that strategy and melted into the night, but for the fact that we had to debrief the exercise.

I found the most innocuous spot in the briefing room, as far back as I could go. I clamped my mouth and fixed my gaze as low as it would go, hoping to pass unnoticed.

The general, naturally, sat at the front of the room. I successfully avoided his glare until the brief was nearly over.

The general had a question.

"Where's 'Who the F--- Are You?'"

The room went silent. The colonel running the debrief looked like he'd been hit in the gut.

I straightened. Might as well make my demise as quick as possible.

"That would be me, sir." I mumbled an apology.

"I want you to tell these people what you told me."

No, not the curse words. Everything else relating to where people were supposed to be and how un-excellent the proceedings had been.

An order's an order, so I did. To my great surprise, General Shelton was actually pleased. Or at least, he didn't hold my candid discussion of the state of the exercise against me.

I will say this: I will definitely recognize William Shelton the next time he jumps into a field I'm monitoring.

My experience as part of a COLT team meant that I got a lot of the assignments with SpecOp units like SF or the Rangers. So I was working one night at Polk when the Rangers were executing a mission that involved a fast-rope infil, meaning they would descend by rope from helicopters and "infiltrate" the target area.

In this particular case, I stationed myself near the actual target, waiting for the team to arrive. They were late. Which, in my experience working with the Rangers and the 160th Nightstalkers ferrying them via helicopter, never happened.

One of the observers with me called over to the control unit to find out what was going on.

"Stand by," was the answer.

Moments later, we got the first inkling that there was a problem. We were given the grid location and told to get over there ASAP. We grabbed a Humvee and raced over there. The scene was horrific. Rangers were lying everywhere on the ground, between trees, seriously injured.

According to reports later on, the CH-47 they released from had been much further from the ground than thought when they went out. Apparently, someone had mistaken an equipment drop from the lead helicopter to mean that they had begun the insertion. The men piling out of the door had no way of knowing that their ropes ended well above the ground. The Rangers landed in trees, free-falling thirty and more feet. Twenty-one Rangers were injured. Another, Sergeant Alphonse J. Harness, died at the scene.

A lot of people don't understand how in the world that could ever possibly happen in training. But you train as you fight. You need to do things the way you would do them in combat, and that often exposes you to quite a bit of danger. Even if you're not being shot at.

One of the worst things I saw in the military. Haunts me to this day. Just a reminder that a soldier's job is dangerous, even in peacetime.

I loved the army. The army loved me. My next move was probably going to be back to a posting at Bragg where I would be in line to make E-7. My most likely career path would be to an artillery unit, where I would serve as a first sergeant, the noncommissioned officer in charge of other NCOs in that unit. From there, I would have worked toward becoming an E-8—a sergeant major. Somewhere along the way the army would probably ship me to Washington, D.C., and the Pentagon.

That all takes several years. And if you think that path would have taken me from the part of soldiering that I most loved—being in the thick of things, in the air and in the dirt, not to mention danger—you'd be right. But it would also involve more responsibilities. I'd have to learn a lot of new things. So I'd have new challenges—something I'd always welcomed, hell, lived for.

There were a few other possibilities. I could aim for what we called "the Unit" back then—Delta Force, the army's top secret anti-terror Special Forces group. The Unit didn't get much publicity at the time; civilians probably barely knew about it. But I'd met a couple of the members, and the little they told me was enticing.

There were lots of possibilities, but that's what they were: possibilities. It's not like there were guarantees that I'd make it that far, much less that I'd like doing any of those things. Delta, especially, puts heavy demands on your family life. You're away constantly, between training and deployments. That is one of the many reasons I admire those guys to this day.

Karen was extremely supportive, ready to back whatever I chose. She'd really taken to the army life, and I knew I could count on her for whatever direction I took.

Then, with all these possibilities and a really bright future, I made a decision to go in a direction that changed everything.

FIVE:
THE ROAD TAKEN

SONGWRITER

I don't pretend that things go on a straight line, and I sure am not saying that war feeds creativity, but something about my experiences in Panama kindled my creativity. From that deployment on, I found myself writing more and more songs.

I'm not sure what changed. I'd taken my guitar with me on every deployment, playing and singing in my free time for friends and my own amusement. But in Panama, things bumped up to a higher level. A tune and the words would start to form, and I'd work them together. Pretty soon, there'd be a song.

Then, another. And again. Gradually, I became a songwriter.

A part-time songwriter, whose real job was the army and whose nights and weekends were generally devoted to my family, but a writer who seemed always to have a song working through his head.

I met a few people at Fort Polk who encouraged me. One was an older fellow who was working on his own music like me. He told me about wanting to be a songwriter, and we kind of hit it off. I'd also grown up in and around music and songwriting, so it was natural that at some point it would take hold of my life.

Thinking back to Panama, it wasn't just the war that changed me. For the first time, I was not only away from home but truly missing it—my wife, my baby, my home. Powerful emotions can propel your creativity.

Longing.

My desire for all the things that I loved and missed and wanted to be around pulled out the creative side of me.

Emotion stirred the music. I didn't *have* to write. But I wanted to. And the more songs I wrote, the better I got at it. When we were in the Nashville area visiting family, I ran into some friends who were writing and playing songs. I started hanging out with them, sharing my own songs. One weekend I came up from Polk and they mentioned there was a writers' night at the Broken Spoke, a saloon/bar/restaurant that was pretty well-known as a place for budding songwriters to try out their stuff. My friends asked if I wanted to come along. I sure did.

Writers' nights let songwriters sit onstage (or wherever) and play some of what they're working on. The formats can vary, but in general you get some feedback, maybe suggestions, hopefully a little applause. I remember feeling awkward walking in—I was still in the military, still wearing my hair "high and tight," and everyone around me was a lot more casual. But they seemed to like me, and they definitely liked my singing.

I couldn't for the life of me tell you what I sang that first night—or the many nights I went back there, and to many other places, including the Bluebird Café, another locally famous place for songwriters. But the experience encouraged me to continue and helped make me a lot better. The Bluebird remains an important part of the Nashville scene, and it in particular has helped a lot of writers across a lot of different genres. You can hear a lot of different strains of greatness whenever you stop by.

I soon developed a routine. When we would finish work at Fort Polk on a Thursday, I'd hop in the truck and drive to Nashville. Thursday night and Friday I'd write. Friday night I would do a writers' night, meeting with other songwriters and performing informally. If I could, on Saturday I'd hook up with someone and do some more writing. Another writers' night Saturday night. Sunday morning I drove back home. Most of the time I was alone, but every so often Karen and the kids would join me, visiting our extended families while there.

Writers nights were very common then. You'd have them all over Nashville. Writers would get together in a semicircle on a stage and perform their songs. People would come to hear their friends or someone they'd heard of, or maybe just someone new. You never knew who was going to be in the audience. Or onstage with you. You'd talk a little, decide to spend a few hours trying out different things together. For me, writing music became a collaboration thing where I worked with other guys, inspiring them and them inspiring me. Pushing me. Prodding. And back the other way.

What do you think of this?

Try this.

I ended up writing with some of the best writers around. I learned a lot in the process. I worked myself through an informal apprenticeship, until finally I got to the point where people were seeking me out, coming to me and saying they'd love to write with me. And these were guys I'd admired.

Back in those days, nothing was digital. Computers were mostly in offices, and phones were attached to the wall. We'd write the lyrics and music out longhand. To keep track of my songs, I'd put entries in a ledger book. Working title, who I was writing with, maybe a note or two about the person if I'd just met him. Gradually, my collection of ledgers grew.

I was performing, but only so that other singers could hear my music. I wanted to sell songs. I didn't want to be on the radio; I wanted my *music* to be on the radio.

The music industry is different today than it was then, but some parts have not changed. The performance of a song generates two different revenue streams. One of those streams goes to the performer (and probably the record company or whoever is backing them). The other goes to the songwriter(s), to be split with the company that published the song.

Even in those days, the system was incredibly complicated, with different percentages depending on where the music was being played, how it was played, who was playing it . . . this isn't the place to detangle all that. The important thing for me was that I realized that I could make a decent though not huge amount of money writing songs part-time. It didn't interfere with being a soldier, my family didn't object, and it was something I liked to do.

Loved to do.

I was still learning the craft, but I was getting a lot of encouragement, especially from my dad. I played a song or two for him one weekend, and he got very adamant. "That's good stuff, man," he told me. "We need to go somewhere and put those on a tape. We gotta get them down."

He wasn't just speaking as my father; he was talking as someone who'd been in the music business a lot of his life. But of course it meant that much more to me that he was my dad.

He'd been out of the business for quite a while by then, but he was still in touch with a musician named Jack Green, who'd had a few hits back in the day. He called Jack, and Jack made a phone call to a manager who got me hooked up with an artist. I got to do an acoustic opening for him at a show. Three songs. I couldn't even tell you where the show was. A few hours from Nashville's all I remember. But it was a personal milestone, a solo at a real show, with genuine applause at the end.

Then one weekend a guy came up to me at writers' night and said his name was Buzz Stone. I knew that name—he had worked with Skip Ewing, a musician whose music I'd heard and loved in Panama. He gave me a card and said, "I'd love to talk to you about a publishing deal."

I told him I was interested—very interested.

Even more than very. Working for a publishing company would mean I had a serious shot at making a life in music. There'd be a whole team helping me promote my music, and paying me for the privilege.

Two hundred bucks a month, as it turned out. Not a lot, even back then. But the fact that someone would pay me, even a little, made a huge difference in my status. Buzz's company was a small publisher, but it was a publisher. I was considered a published songwriter. If someone asked me who I worked for, I had an answer—Buzz Stone.

To clarify for people who aren't in the industry: Being signed as a staff writer doesn't mean that you're going in and punching a clock. It's more like a commitment to write a number of songs for a specified period of time, which the company will then try to get artists to record. The terms can vary a great deal, and usually the monthly "pay" is actually a draw against royalty commissions for the songs you license. (Songs are licensed rather than sold; you can think of them as pieces of real estate being rented out for use, with the rent based on how much income the song earns. When a consumer buys a single, some portion of that money goes back to the songwriter and the producer.)

Basically, a writer is partnering with a publisher. The writer handles the creative side; the publisher takes care of the sales and business end. Publishers want to work with writers whose work they think they can sell; writers want to sign with publishers they think can market their work. There's a lot of feedback both ways; the relationship has been compared to a marriage by many.

The gig didn't conflict with the army because there were no set hours and the only thing I was expected to do was write, which I could do on my own time. But they gave me an *actual* office in the building on Music Row or thereabouts, with my name on the door and everything. I brought pictures in, found some furniture—hand-me-downs and throwaways—and set myself up.

I had made it!

At that point, the only singing I was doing was intended to get some attention for my songs. Songs aren't often sold on paper; an artist needs to hear a demo to get an idea of whether they like it or not. I cut a demo myself, playing and doing the vocals, saving a few bucks. Then I did a few more. Again, the point was to sell the songs, not the voice. But the voice was good enough that others started to notice. Songwriters began asking me to do their vocals. When I'd do a writers' night, I began getting attention for my voice as much as what I was singing.

I started to think that maybe I could make money singing as well as writing. With both of them together, I might be able to make a living. It wasn't a plan—not yet, anyway. But it was headed there.

One thing I always took for granted—I was country. My songs

were country. I performed country. I'd grown up with the music, and the lyrics and melodies that came into my head always seemed to track with that. I never really questioned it. Then or now.

Which isn't to say that there weren't a lot of different influences behind what I wrote. I'd listened to a range of music growing up, from rock to pop, R&B and gospel. Unconsciously, all of those things were forming what I was doing, even if the finished songs were country.

One influence that might surprise a lot of people: Elvis.

That's right. Elvis Presley. I've been infatuated with him since I was a little kid. I blame my parents. They went to an Elvis concert when I was young and became big fans. They talked about the concert and about him, played his music in the house. In my opinion, anybody that can do what that guy did is the bomb. He had such a voice. He was a real, real singer. And he had the ability to cross every genre.

You know, that was a hard era in our society. We had racism and civil unrest, and he was a white guy singing in a band with Black people, back when that was frowned on, or worse. Elvis didn't care. He did what he thought was right for the music, and for society, I think, in that regard.

He was also one of the first people to incorporate television into what we'd call his "brand" nowadays. And he was in all those movies— another first, at least at that level, for pop music. Now, you can tell me he was a horrible actor. That's what the critics said back then. But I've gone back and watched those movies, some a couple of times. He's no worse than most of the other actors in that period.

I think a lot of people just didn't want him to be a good actor. Kind of like a professional jealousy. He's such a great singer, we're not going to like him as an actor, or at least we're going to pretend not to like him.

We're all a little like that. But his movies packed people in. They wouldn't have kept making them if they didn't. The reviews maybe said one thing, but the fans said another.

I could watch an Elvis marathon any day of the week. I'm breaking into a little song just thinking about them:

Sweet tea . . .

You know, they didn't doctor voices back then. What you heard was the real singer.

One for the money . . .

If Elvis is an unexpected influence on my music, probably the most obvious are the values I was raised with. I don't mean musical values, though the connection to country music is pretty clear. The importance of family, duty, God—those are as present in my music as basic guitar chords. I haven't once sat down and told myself, *now it's time to write a song about the importance of patriotism.* Themes like that just percolate out of my experiences and into my songs. Having been a soldier, being a father—certain things are just so interwoven with my life that when I take my life as the seed for a song, they grow with it.

Anyway, I started being offered more chances to perform. In fact, there were more offers than I could comfortably take. Being based in Louisiana, I was a long drive from Nashville. Even when I was reassigned to Fort Campbell in Kentucky, it was a good haul. And as always, the army had first call on my time.

To make country music a career, I'd have to devote a lot more time to it. It would have to be the most important thing, after my family, that I did. On the other hand, I already had a good career in the army. I was on a track to join the ranks of the upper enlisted, the top NCOs who really run things.

Two different roads.

Being in the army is not like having a "regular" job. You commit yourself to active duty for different enlistment and reenlistment periods, which typically run two to five or six years. My current enlistment was coming up; I had to decide whether to renew my commitment for at least another two if not four years.

At the same time, I knew that opportunities in music can be very fickle. People who love you today may forget you tomorrow. If you don't grab an opportunity offered this evening, someone else will take it by morning. If the expression, "make hay while the sun is shining" wasn't thought up by a songwriter, it should have been.

I couldn't decide what to do. I'd been in the army roughly eleven years, and loved it. On the other hand, there was this opportunity that not only would fulfill a deep desire in me, but would also feed my family fairly well—maybe very, very well if I worked hard at it and had a little bit of luck.

Tough. There were no guarantees either way.

My father urged me to leave the army and concentrate on music. He sensed my talent. He'd faced a similar decision himself and gone the other way. Why was he suggesting the opposite? He thought I was better than he'd been. A lot better.

But he was Dad, and bound to be prejudiced. Trying to decide, I talked to my upper command, including General David Petraeus, who at the time was G3 for the 101st, in charge of the training among other things. They all encouraged me to give music a shot. But the biggest influence was my unit commander, Colonel Bill Greer. We had the same last name but weren't related. I've had the privilege of working with a number of excellent officers. Greer was one of them, and then some. I considered him then—and even today—a good friend, someone who not only knew me, but had a perspective on the world that made his advice especially valuable.

I sat down with him in his office and laid out my dilemma. He knew about the publishing company. I told him that I was being offered more gigs and that the people in the industry I was working with thought I had a good chance to succeed.

Greer gave me a hard look. "You know, Craig," said the colonel, "if you stay in the army, you'll be Sergeant Major of the Army someday."

Sergeant major—E-9—is the highest enlisted rank. But Colonel Greer wasn't just talking about the rank—he meant top dog of the entire army, "Sergeant Major of the Army," the highest position an enlisted soldier can attain. There is only one at a time in the army, and while it might seem an exaggeration to compare Sergeant Major of the Army to a four-star general, in a lot of ways the job is even more special. The courtesies and privileges are considerable; the responsibility awesome.

To have an officer you respect even hint that you might be able to achieve that is more than a bit flattering. But Colonel Greer didn't stop there.

"I also think you're a great songwriter," he continued. "I think you're a good singer. And I'll tell you something else: I think if you don't try this, you will regret it for the rest of your life."

The colonel then offered a suggestion—why not switch over to the army's active reserve? In that way, I could stay in the army while I tried music as a career. If things didn't work out, I could change back to the "regular" army.

I hadn't thought about that.

The reserves are an important part of the military. During times of conflict—such as the war on terror which would begin a few years later—reserve units are activated and are tasked just like regular units. In less stressful times, though, reservists generally train one weekend a month and two weeks each year. They are essentially part-timers, though as fully trained in their army jobs as soldiers in the active army.

It may be that the other officers thought I'd get music out of my system after a year or so. It's relatively easy to get back to active duty from the reserves. I may even have thought I'd be back myself. But Bill Greer really believed in me as a singer and a songwriter. He may even have believed in me more than I did. To this day, I am grateful for his faith and support at that moment.

The reserves offered the best compromise possible. I'd leave the army without actually leaving the army. If music didn't pan out, I'd switch back and pick up where I'd left off.

I joined a reserve unit based at Fort Campbell. Eventually, I was able to get with a unit in Nashville, which was a lot more convenient for my budding career.

I don't have any regrets about leaving the army. I miss it, still. But that's different than having regrets. I took the right road—and even if my career hadn't taken off, it was still the right decision.

But I do miss the army. I miss the camaraderie. The esprit de corps. The feeling like you're doing something good, and part of something bigger than yourself. The army gives you that feeling, even on a bad day. Even on a day when you're doing nothing special: you're part of a bigger organization that is serving your country. I knew I was going to miss that feeling once I was out. Big time. But I was also going deeper and deeper in this other world that excited me. Music.

STRUGGLES

There's no such thing as an overnight success. A big career may look like one from a distance, but up close there are odd jobs at crazy hours, old cars that break down at the worst possible time, kids who have to be fed—all of the complications of a normal life.

Before I left the army, I'd gotten a deal on a prefab house and five acres up in Tennessee not that far from my folks. It was a small starter home, affordable even after I left the army, but it felt like a palace. To that point, Karen and I and the kids had always lived in army housing—small, old, much-used structures. Nice, but not *too* nice, if you know what I mean. This really was a palace compared to them. The neighbor across the street was golden. And heck, there was great turkey hunting just down the road.

I had some money saved up, and with side jobs and such supplementing my songwriting, the first year, 1995, wasn't that bad financially. The second wasn't terrible either. But as time went on, money got tighter and tighter. That made things tough not just on me but on Karen, who was still caring for two kids largely on her own. She drove a 1972 Chevy, and about the best you could say about the vehicle was that it had air conditioning and more seats than my latest Jeep. (I am partial to the vehicle.) Our parents helped out with small gifts every month and on holidays. I worked a long list of jobs while writing and playing wherever I could. I did some construction, hung siding, worked as a security guard and part-time sheriff's deputy, and even did a stint at Walmart. Whatever paid and still let me pursue music.

Karen picked up some income by working at a daycare. That meant long days for her, and rushing from work to pick up our daughter from school. My mom played babysitter when she could, picking up the kids and minding them when we needed her. It was a true family effort.

Karen supported me all the way, but the truth is, she had loved the military almost as much as I did, and our new life had to be rough on her. She says now that she cried for two years when I left the army. That's an exaggeration, I'm sure, but the point is, I did make our lives difficult.

We never had a lot of debt, maybe because we only had one credit card. That was maxed out plenty. There were plenty of times when we paid the absolute minimum, just to have enough credit so we could go get milk and bread.

Money's not the only thing valuable in life. We'd always wanted a big family. Karen got pregnant with our third child, Wyatt, in 1997.

In the meantime, we got Jerry.

Jerry was supposed to be a foster child, but he never had that status in our hearts or in our heads. Our interest in becoming foster parents had started years earlier, back when I was at Bragg. Karen was the driver in that.

I'll back up a bit and let her tell the story of how we got to be foster parents:

> I was watching the Oprah Winfrey show one afternoon. She did a show in front of an audience with all foster children. She spoke about the need for foster parents, and how important they are. Then this little boy stood up and I think he was eight or ten. He had blond hair and blue eyes and he looked just like Craig when he was young, with long curly hair and the cutest smile. Beautiful, big blue eyes, seriously.
>
> He stood up.
>
> Oprah asked him what he wanted in a family.
>
> "I just want a dad to take me fishing," he said.
>
> Craig came home at four thirty and found me crying on the couch.

She told me why. You don't have to take too many guesses to figure out what happened next.

We signed up for foster parenting classes at Bragg and went through the screening and education process. They don't just throw a kid on you; there's a lot of checking, formal and informal, trying to make sure you're ready and a good fit. We ended up not fostering anyone at that point, because of my military commitments—I was only at Bragg a short time, remember. But we renewed our interest after I left the army.

Fostering children was a way to care for kids and have a large family without having the lifelong financial and other responsibilities. It was also a different way of serving the community.

There's a big need for foster parents, who typically care for a child for a short period of times while the natural parent or parents deal with a range of issues. The average length of care in the US is between one and two years—it's a lot different than adoption, which is meant to be permanent. Fostering a child can be a trial as well as a blessing. Many of these children have left abusive family situations and don't really know what it means to be loved.

I'm not going to make this into an advertisement for foster care, but I will say that the need is great. I can tell you that what you feel in your heart caring for these children is incredible. And the impact that you have on their lives can't be measured in words.

We had fostered one or two children already when I came home one day from working at the mall as a security guard. Karen met me at the door. There was a little boy with her. She told me his name was Jerry.

"We're keeping him," Karen announced. "I don't care if we don't have two dimes to rub together. He is our son."

She was right. There was something about him, an immediate connection, not just between her and Jerry, but with me as well.

How do you describe such a thing?

Karen:

> Scott, the social worker, brought him to the house. Scott got out of the car and went to the back to get him.

"No, I want to get him," I told him.
The minute I saw him, I knew he was mine.

I've tried many times, but it can't be described in any more detail than that. It just *was*.

Something we felt. Something you feel as a parent. Period. Whatever the backstory or events leading up to that moment. It's just—that's my kid. You just know it. We knew it.

We would end up fostering eight or ten kids over the years, but with Jerry—no, we just knew right away. Other folks in the same situation describe it the same way: it just is.

But another kid meant more adjustments. A little more side work for me. I sold my Jeep and bought a 1980-something Plymouth minivan, burgundy with wood grain panels down the side. But the kids more than made up for the little sacrifices we were making.

My army reserve job in Nashville was with a rigger unit that was part of Airborne. Parachute riggers are the folks who "rig" parachutes—an absolutely critical job for a force jumping out of aircraft. Riggers are experts on parachutes, not just for people but for cargo. They maintain a variety of equipment, are usually detail oriented and very good at fixing things and coming up with solutions on the fly—excuse the pun.

I chose the unit because of convenience; being located in Nashville, it made it a lot easier on the family, since I could get there and back quickly. The unit was great and helped me maintain my airborne status, but to be entirely honest, after everything I'd done to that point in my career, the job felt less than exciting. I know every role in the military is important; I truly believe that. But on a personal level, I craved the excitement I'd felt, whether in combat or training. I ended up transferring back over to Fort Campbell, when the unit there made it clear I could have a flexible work schedule.

There were weeks where our money got even tighter than usual. I remember my mom giving us twenty bucks to spend at Shoney's, and feeling like that was a huge treat. Other times, the floor seemed ready to cave in—like when the truck I'd gotten as a hand-me-down from Karen's dad to help with my side jobs was stolen with all my tools.

Our church took up a collection to help me replace what insurance didn't cover. God bless them.

Another time the parishioners put four new tires on our minivan. Even random strangers helped out. Karen was shopping one day and the kids wanted strawberries and some other fruit she couldn't afford. Right as she was telling them this, an older gentleman walked over and stuffed forty dollars into her purse. God bless him. She sometimes tells people it was an angel, but I know there are people doing God's work without a thought for reward, and I'm happy to say I'm grateful.

Looking back, I knew we were struggling moneywise. But so much was going on, both for me musically and with my family that it didn't feel stark or hopeless. It was the opposite.

But money problems could be solved by working harder, and I did when I needed to. It was losing people close to us that was difficult to take.

I was driving home one day when Karen's sister called me on the cell. That was a little unusual, but what happened next was way out of the ordinary. I answered, and she just started screaming and yelling. I couldn't make out any words—if there were words.

What came through crystal clear was the pain. God-awful pain. The only thing I could do, finally, was hang up and call Karen's brother. He explained their dad had just passed away.

I had to tell Karen. That wasn't going to happen on the phone. I drove home; she wasn't there.

Where was she? Shopping?

I debated waiting, but it just seemed to me I had to tell her right away. Like the rest of her family, she was very close to her dad. If things had been flipped, if she had that kind of news for me, I'd want to know immediately, even if I was in the middle of a firefight. So I had to find her. I called her phone.

"Where are you?" I asked.

"I'm at the parlor, getting my legs waxed."

"You need to come home."

"I—"

"You want to come home right now."

That tone in my voice got her attention. She left immediately—with one leg done. Tears were shooting out of my eyes by the time she walked through the door. I was filled with all sorts of sadness, for her dad, and for her.

"Oh, Craig, I'm so sorry," said Karen, running and hugging me. "I know how close you are to your parents."

"No, it's your daddy."

She started to fall and I caught her. We sank to the couch, consoling each other.

Moments like that—those are the hard times. You can get past them, because you have to, but they're the ones that you never really forget. Even if you find the strength years later to make a joke or two about them, or remember the one funny bit—Karen's one smooth leg—you never erase that mark in your soul.

Among the part-time jobs I had, sheriff's deputy was the most important. The sheriff liked that I was in the reserves; he felt my service was important for the country, and that the connection might have a side benefit for the department if a need ever came up in an emergency. But the biggest benefit he saw was the experience the army had given me, not so much with police skills as with judgment and leadership.

For me, it was steady work. It even opened up some other very temporary security gigs, which could pay pretty well on an hourly basis. Music forced me to take less and less hours as my career progressed, but the department kept me on with their auxiliary, a reserve unit that gets called on only when truly needed. Dickson County has grown with the rest of the state—when we first moved there, I believe there were twenty-five thousand people all told. Now we're closer to fifty-five thousand. The department has gone up as well. I'd guess there must be one hundred and fifty deputies by now. It's a big area to patrol.

Still has small-town values, though. And if you go downtown in the morning, you can catch up on the local business and politics over coffee. For me, it's close enough to Nashville without being *too* close. But I'm getting off the track, sounding like I'm working for the Chamber of Commerce.

Being a deputy was a civilian version of some of what I'd been doing in the military. Except for the traffic tickets. Truth is, I hardly ever gave out any of those. A lot less than the department would have liked, that's for sure. Most of my stops resulted in warnings. Unless he saw some other sort of infraction, DWI say, Deputy Greer was generally inclined to issue a warning and set you on your way.

I worked a lot of second and third shifts—late afternoon into early morning—and a lot of times I was on with a deputy I'll call Cary. Those were shifts when the bad stuff would tend to happen, domestic violence especially. People got home from work, they'd get to arguing, and ... bad stuff.

And then there were the drunk and disorderly cases. One time we had a call that there was an intoxicated male banging on someone's door in the middle of the night. The guy who'd called it in had been woken from his sleep, and was not too happy. We were directed to get there ASAP.

"If he comes in the door, I'm going to shoot him" were more or less his exact words to the 911 dispatcher.

We got there just before the lock would have given out. A few shouts from the man at the door made it clear the perpetrator (a) thought he was at his own home and (b) was drunk out of his mind.

You can envision a happy ending: Deputy Greer goes around to the side of the house and alerts the homeowner that it's all a terrible misunderstanding, and the drunk will no doubt come by tomorrow with a hangover to apologize. The caller puts his firearm away, shakes my hand, and goes back to bed. We deliver the drunk to his own house, tuck him peacefully under the covers, and go off to write up a brief report over coffee and donuts.

Didn't happen that way.

My partner and the drunk left the front peacefully, talking very friendly-like at almost reasonable decibel levels. Passage clear, I went in the front door to talk to the homeowner. Soon enough, there was a commotion at the side door. I went through the house to the side, where the drunk was trying to turn my partner into a punching bag.

It took us quite a while to get him subdued and then cuffed.

Pounding on a neighbor's door by mistake in the middle of night might be passed off, but not this. I don't remember what bail the judge might have set, but he was less than happy about being woken up in the middle of the night, so it couldn't have been too cheap.

Years later, I ran into the drunk—now sober—in town.

"You're Craig Morgan," he said.

"Uh-huh."

"They said you used to be a police officer in Dickson."

"Yeah?" I answered, with a little of an edge.

"Man, you arrested me one time."

"Yeah?" Even more edge this time, thinking, *Oh God, we're going to have this out.*

"I just want to tell you I deserved it, man. And uh, I, really enjoy your music."

LEARNING TO PERFORM

The music publisher I was working for was sold to Maypop Music. I went with it. It was a natural, easy move for me. I had written with some of their writers. They introduced me to management, and I was offered a *real* publishing deal, better than the one I'd had. I think it paid probably a thousand bucks a month—not immense, but it let me cut back on some outside jobs. Maypop was owned by the country rock band Alabama at the time; a year or two later in 1999, Maypop and its catalog were bought by Sony Music, which also kept me on. I stayed with Sony for about four years, then started my own publishing company.

We'll get to all that down the road.

Besides writing my own songs, I cut demos of other songs the publishing company had the rights to, which brought in a little more money. In fact, I eventually got to the point where I could make a thousand dollars a day recording demos.

Not every day, not even every week. But this was real money. And it brought more connections to writers and performers.

In the process of that, I met a guy named Brian Kennedy. He was a songwriter and was working with Garth Brooks at the time. I went along with Brian to a writer thing one night, where he introduced me to some mutual friends—actually reintroduced me, since I'd known a couple of them years and years earlier, growing up; they'd all lived near my Uncle Willie. Among them was Marla Cannon-Goodman, whose father Buddy was a producer and hit songwriter. Marla was already a well-respected songwriter in her own right; Lee Ann Womack took Marla's song "The Fool" to number one on the country charts back in 1997 when Marla was still working as a nurse. This is an extremely talented family; her sister, Melonie Cannon, is a well-respected singer herself.

By and by, I played some stuff for Buddy. "You have some promise, kid," he told me. "But you gotta work on your singing."

Now, remember, I hadn't planned on being a singer, and I still wasn't sure I wanted to be a performer, but advice and encouragement from someone like Buddy—Academy of Country Music Producer of the Year in 2006, among a whole slew of other awards, accolades, and notices—is not something to ignore. Especially when he puts you in for an audition somewhere like Country Tonite.

Which he very generously did.

Country Tonite, then and now, is a theater up in Pigeon Forge, Tennessee, about two hundred miles east of Nashville near the Smoky Mountains. It's a country music mecca, a place whose shows people plan vacations around. Country Tonite started out in 1992 in Las Vegas, moved to Branson, Missouri, in 1994, and then went over to Tennessee in 1997. They generally do two country music shows a day, six or seven days a week, featuring a variety of acts.

Buddy called Craig Morris, who was the music director at the show, and Craig set up a time to hear me. I guess he liked what he heard because he offered me a full-time gig.

Every musician the theater had hired in the past, the male performers at least, had been hired as musicians. Meaning they would play as part of a band, then do solo songs at some point in the show. But I was strictly a solo act. There's a chance that was by necessity: I wasn't a great guitar player; I'm still not. You do get better playing twice a day, six times a week. But there are limits.

I will say one thing. I look back on the songs I was writing and singing then, and I wonder how anyone saw anything in me. That's a real talent to have, to know that a person has something you believe will turn into something bigger. Because honestly, I don't know if I saw it myself. I thought my writing would get better. It felt like it was. But I never thought I could turn into the kind of singer you need to be in this business. I wasn't a performer; I was a songwriter hoping to get his work noticed.

Country Tonite turned me into a performer. I learned a lot about playing guitar, singing, and most of all entertaining a crowd. Those are different things, even if they are pretty closely related. You can be phenomenal at guitar and a virtuoso singer, but to do a show at two o'clock and then a show at six o'clock over and over, you have to be a performer. You have to learn stage presence. Fill the space when you're not singing. Show people the words are coming from your heart even though you haven't slept all night or your kids are sick.

I learned to entertain. That's what Buddy was after. To be successful, I'd have to perform before all sorts of audiences. This was like army basic training, boot camp for a would-be country singer. And it was *paid* boot camp. Just like the army. Better, in terms of dollars and cents. And a lot less push-ups.

It was good money at the time—I think it may have been as much as fifty thousand a year—which meant I could stop doing construction, drop all of the other part-time jobs and concentrate on music. There were some complications—we had to get special permission to take Jerry there, since the adoption hadn't been finalized yet. But overall, it was a huge step up. Karen and I found a house near the theater, rented out our home in Dickson to pay for it, and concentrated on our family and music.

I was still in the reserves. So the one weekend I wasn't playing at Country Tonite, I was at Fort Campbell doing maneuvers. It was a scramble, but a good scramble.

I mentioned earlier that Garth Brooks once gave me some advice.

Garth reached the big time with his very first album in 1989, and he's been a huge success ever since. By the mid- to late-1990s, he was known all over the world, having played before audiences from Nashville to New York—where just about a million people crammed into Central Park to hear him, the park's all-time record. Outside of the US, he'd played Brazil, Canada, Ireland, England, and Lord knows where else. What I'm saying is, the man was BIG.

You'd never have known it the way he acted that night at the writers' meet where I sat next to him. Of course, everybody knew who he was—he was GARTH BROOKS! But you know what I mean. He was friendly, matter of fact, and down-to-earth genuine.

I'm not claiming that we became best friends and started hunting together all the time, or anything like that. But just having his encouragement, and occasional advice, was truly important to me, especially at that point in my career.

And the one piece that really stuck with me was to not use my "real" name. Until that point, I'd been Craig Greer on the playbill.

"You're going to want some separation," he told me. "A little privacy."

It was good advice, but I wanted to keep things in the family. So rather than picking an entirely new name, I used the one I already had—my middle name, Morgan.

And so a singer was born.

It was 1999, the year before the end of the century and the beginning of the new millennium. Some people thought the world would end December 31. Others thought ATMs and banks would fail because of a worldwide bug in the dating system financial institutions used.

I don't suppose what happened for me was anywhere near as dramatic. But it was certainly life changing.

Here's the scene:

My music starts doing well. I'm writing songs that stars like Joe Diffie are recording. Alabama and the like are starting to do my music. I'm hanging with some of the best writers in the business. I've got artists like Blake Shelton and Tracy Lawrence talking to me about my songs. I'm performing at Country Tonite and drawing good crowds. I'm writing and doing demos, sitting in on writing nights, making as many connections as I can.

Meanwhile, a buddy of mine named Jeff Averett has a barn and some nice acres in Kingston Springs where he does a good business renting out space and caring for local horses. I'd go see him when I could, once or twice taking a turn on his champion quarter horse, Joe Go Quick. Joe definitely lived up to his name.

I'd give Jeff copies of some of my demos, partly as a thank-you and largely because I valued his opinion and friendship. He'd tell me that he'd stick me on a slow horse if I gave him a bad song; that must not have happened, because the horses were all fast as the wind.

One day an owner walks in to check on his animal. Jeff has some music playing. By coincidence, it's one of my recordings. The conversation goes something like this:

"Who's that singing?" the man asks.

"Friend of mine," answers Jeff. "Known my wife since they were kids, and me almost as long."

"Can you put me in touch?"

Jeff does. And that's my catching-lightning-in-a-bottle story, because the man with the horse was the vice president/general manager of Atlantic Records Nashville, Bryan Switzer.

CRAIG MORGAN, THE ALBUM

I went in and sang the song for Bryan and Al Cooley. I sang a few others as well. I walked out with an offer for a record deal.

While I'd been around the business a while, I didn't know that much about recording contracts or how to deal with a big corporation. It was time to get a manager. But I didn't even know how to do that. So I called up one of my writing partners and told him that I'd just been offered a deal and needed a manager to negotiate it for me.

"I know a woman named Christie Fortner," he said. "Call her."

I did, and we hit it off. We signed the deal in December, and I went to work.

Given how important that one song was for my career, you would think I would be singing it in my sleep. You'd at least think I would remember the title. No on both counts.

I combed through the ledgers. I called up Bryan. I called up Christie.

Christie: "It had 'blue' in it. It was about bullying."

Bryan: "It had an address. Like a number. It was a woman with an address . . ."

Nothing rang a bell. I sat down and went through my notebooks. I enlisted various helpers. We could not figure it out. I remember singing it a cappella. I remember it was a big vocal song. I remember . . . that I can't remember which song it was.

The search goes on. The problem is I wrote so much. Song after song after song. Too many to keep track of.

Anyway, that song never got cut. That may have been because it was a "piano song"—I think. Hazy as my memory of it is, I think I wrote it with a guy who played the piano, and it was very suited to that instrument. But because it was done with a piano, I don't have quite the same memory of it that I would have had if I were strumming the guitar to it.

Maybe.

There were two things about Al Cooley that made him unique in my opinion:

One, he would listen to anybody. Just anybody.

And two, he would tell them absolutely frankly what he thought.

I was in his office soon after we closed the album deal when a man came in, wanting his songs to be heard. Al invited me to listen to the kid, maybe thinking I might hear a song that could be included on my record, or maybe just being Al—he was very open, very inclusive.

And very to the point.

The fella mentioned that he'd just sold his house and moved to Nashville to follow his dream of becoming a singer-songwriter. Al asked him to play one of his demos. It hadn't gotten very far when Al rose up. "What else you got?"

The guy played another song.

Al looked disappointed. He stopped the music a few verses in. "What is your best song? Play that."

The man played another. I think it got to the chorus before Al tapped the button on the player.

"You sold your house already?" Al asked.

"Yes, sir," said the young man.

"Call the real-estate broker and see if you can cancel the deal."

That was Al saying, he didn't think the man was going to make it. He was that harsh, or to the point, depending on your point of view. The musician stayed in Nashville, playing around. No, he never made it big. Al may have been harsh, but he was seldom wrong.

My deal was finalized in December 1999. We had our first single out in February 2000.

That quick. Yes.

I asked Buddy Cannon and Norro Wilson to produce my first album. They were absolute blessings. I got to work with two of the guys who'd been in it and done it for a heck of a long time. And with that experience, they still had an ear for what was coming in the industry.

That's not an easy thing. Sometimes you get so used to success that you can't figure out what happens next—will it be a smooth transition or a jump into something completely different? They seemed to have that sixth sense, Buddy especially. He'd produced Merle Haggard and a lot of other big acts. Still does. But he was always tuned to tomorrow, and the tomorrow after that.

A good producer can add a lot to the sound of a song, and both of those guys really helped. I learned from the best on that first album.

The first single was "Something to Write Home About." I wrote it with Tony Ramey, and I have a strong memory of writing that one. We'd spent all day working on another song, working in Tom Collins's office. Tony was with Tom Collins—Tom had a string of publishing businesses and was well-known for shepherding the careers of Barbara Mandrell and Sylvia (Sylvia Jane Hutton), among others.

We pretty much finished up on that first song, and thought it was pretty good. Not necessarily great, though.

"What do you think?" Tony asked when we were done.

"I don't know," I said. "I don't know if, I mean, I don't know if it's anything to write home about."

"Well, we need to write something to write home about."

The phrase ignited my mind.

"That's what we need. We need to write that. I've never heard that before. She's something to write home about . . ."

Forty-five minutes later, we finished that song.

I remember going to Norro right after that to tell him I had just written a song that had never been written.

His eyes burned through my head with a world-weary look. "Son, there ain't never been a song that's never been written."

"I promise you, this hook has not been written."

"Go to bmi.com and type in the title. Tell me how many titles you find."

I went over to a computer. This is back in the days of dial-up.

Wzzz-whrr-kadang . . .

It turned out there were seventeen titles with the exact same words: *Something to write home about.*

"You're never going to write a song at this point in your life that hasn't been written," he told me. "You just gotta write it better."

I'll never forget that piece of good advice.

My father still calls "Something to Write Home About" the best song I've ever written. Whether he's right or not, it's always had a lot of meaning for me, commercially as well as artistically. The single reached number thirty-eight on the Billboard Hot Country Singles and Tracks.

Good, right?

Out of this world for a new artist who was hanging vinyl siding and handing out traffic tickets not all that long before.

I really didn't understand how big it was until I reported for weekend reserve duty at Campbell not too long after it came out. There were people at the gate, waiting for me. They were carrying signs with my name on it and wanted autographs.

Me? Really?

Very . . . different.

I went out on a national tour to support the singles and the album, with a dozen or so shows lined up from California to Florida. I was double-billed with Anita Cochran. Anita was great, a real pleasure to work with. She has had a bunch of number-one songs during her career, so forgive me for not remembering which one was getting big airtime while we were out. Whichever one it was, the single started sliding down the charts in the natural progression of things—to be replaced, not literally but figuratively, by "Something to Write Home About."

Somebody seems not to have liked that. A lot of my posters suddenly went missing in the places we were set to play. I'm not sure who did it—a jealous fan of hers, maybe. Or heck, maybe it was some-one who wanted to get in early on my memorabilia, even if it might cut down on attendance. I do know it wasn't Anita, and it certainly wasn't me.

Didn't hurt the turnouts, at least. Or my song's climb on the charts.

I was out on that tour when I shot a music video for the single. I was nervous doing it. Not just because I'd never done a video, but because the script called for me to walk down the street in LA holding hands with Morgan Schultz, a beautiful blond—and I'm a married man.

Probably seems naive now, but truly, I was a little worried. *Is she going to come on to me? Am I supposed to come on to her? Should I tell her I'm a married man?*

They took me over to her trailer to introduce me, and my fears melted away—she had her Bible out and was in the middle of a study group. I had nothing to worry about. We got to be good friends. She eventually gave up full-time acting, got married, and moved to a farm. Her life turned out a bit like the song, I guess.

There were other surprises. The hotel we used for some of the interiors had been a crack house, and not very long before. While we were out there, we also did a photo shoot at a ranch . . . where they also made adult films.

They didn't tell me that until after we'd left. Probably a good thing.

But the music video I really loved making for that album was "Paradise," which was the second single. It starts in downtown Clarksville, Tennessee, where I walk to an old movie theater. And the movie that plays is a reminder, for me, of my military service. We shot those scenes at Fort Campbell, the installation I'd been stationed at during my career. The army very kindly tapped some of the units there to support the filming. It was very cool, very nostalgic, and very much fitting with the words and mood of the song.

Being on the base made me want to really do a great job, not just for fans, but for the men and women who were helping us, and all the soldiers I'd served with. I felt—I still feel—like I owe people in the military my very best.

The album itself came out in May 2000, peaking at number thirty-nine on the country charts. All three singles we released off that album—"Something to Write Home About," "Paradise," and "I Want Us Back"—were all hits and got a lot of airplay from country radio stations.

Craig Morgan, 2000

By any measure, I was a success. *Overnight* success?

Sure, if you don't count those years singing in the barracks, working all those jobs, pounding the pavement in Nashville, learning my craft at Country Tonite . . .

And the truth is, I didn't think of myself as a successful performer, let alone a star. I wasn't, not by my lights. Now, I had a huge sense of accomplishment knowing that I had an album out and singles being played on the radio. But I wasn't making any money, or at least not the amount of money most people would associate with those things. I wasn't seeing any revenue from the sales, not yet anyway. A lot of the times I was playing for radio stations, which meant I wasn't being paid, or if I was, it was only for expenses.

We were still living in a comfortable but small house. I was still—what's the saying? I still took out the garbage every night.

Actually, I think Karen did that a lot because I was on the road, but you get the idea. My feet were planted firmly on the ground. I guess you don't notice the accomplishments when you're wrapped up in the race. Sometimes it's hard to see the milestones because you're just running across them so fast. I have no regrets, but if I had a chance to do it over, I think I might be a little more attentive to some of the great things that were happening to me. Little moments that I rushed through at the time, but that held huge emotions—which sometimes I only realized looking back.

WARNER OR . . .

Money aside, things were going very, very well. Atlantic was excited, I was excited, everyone I met seemed to be excited. Everyone wanted to know about my next album.

For good reason. The first had done really well, with three separate hits. Country radio knew who I was. The sky seemed the limit.

I started working on songs for the next album. Buddy was producing again, along with myself and band member Phil O'Donnell, who'd started playing and writing with me just around the time my first album came out.

I should point out that, while Phil's name is Phil O'Donnell, his *name*, what we call him, is Phil Billy. Or Philbilly. Because . . . because he's country. When you meet him, you'll know exactly what I'm saying. You won't find anyone more country than Philbilly.

Funny thing is, he's from Canada. He came down here, went to Florida, got into the music business, and moved to Nashville, where he started working as a guitar player. He worked for a friend of mine, Jeff Carson. When Jeff put his music career on hold, Phil was looking for a job. He auditioned and I grabbed him.

I have a lot of Philbilly stories, but this is one of the oldest and one of my favorites. It was very, very early in my career. The record company had arranged for me to perform somewhere, setting up a flight and the rest of the arrangements. Phil and I hopped in my Jeep (by now I'd managed to get another) and headed for the airport.

We were a little short of gas. Worse, we were short of cash—a search of pockets and every corner of the vehicle turned up a grand total of $2.65 between us.

"Think we can make it?" asked Phil, glancing at the fuel gauge as we rounded down toward the airport. We still had a good fifteen miles to go. We debated, maybe prayed. We knew if we made it to the airport, the record rep who was supposed to meet us there would give us our per diem, and we could use that to fill the tank up and get home.

But first we had to make it. And besides gas, time was growing short to make the flight.

We rounded a hill, and came up to an exit just as the Jeep began chugging. The engine choked as the fuel ran out, but thanks to luck and geography, we managed to coast into a gas station, where our $2.65 bought us just enough fuel to complete the trip.

That's how long Phil and I have been friends.

I was in a writing session for my second album one day when I got a call from my manager:

"Atlantic Nashville is being closed."

"Huh?"

"They're transferring some of the artists to Warner Brothers."

Atlantic Records at the time was part of Warner Music Group, which had bought the label back in 1967. Originally known for jazz, R&B, and soul, Atlantic branched into rock and pop and opened a country music division in the 1980s. Warner and Time Inc. later merged, creating the biggest media group in the world.

In 2001, the corporation decided to reorganize its music divisions, including Atlantic. The fallout affected a large number of people. Employees were laid off or reassigned. Artists were told their contracts would not be renewed, or would be transferred to a different entity.

My general impression was that most of the performers who had been signed to Atlantic's country division were, in effect, going to be dropped. A small number, however, would be transferred to the Warner Brothers label.

The company wanted me to be among them. Sorta.

I mean, they said they did, but they weren't exactly gushing about it.

"You're under consideration for transferring to Warner Brothers," one of the company execs told me over the phone. "What are your thoughts?"

"Do I have a choice?" I asked.

"Of course."

I thought about it for a moment. "Do I have to make a decision right now?"

"No."

That's good, I thought. *Gives me time to think.*

Then he added, "You have twenty-four hours."

It wasn't so much a deadline as a gun to my head.

I did give it thought—a lot. My feelings ran like this:

Warner Brothers was a big label with a ton of artists. If I was thrown in with them, I'd be low man on the totem pole. I don't mind a fair fight—or even a lopsided one. But I knew I'd have trouble getting attention at Warner, not only as a new artist but one who hadn't originally been signed by them. All the attention—and resources—would go to more established singers.

I talked to Philbilly and some of the other musicians, as well as my manager and friends who were in or knew the business. "A leaky roof is better than no roof," Phil pointed out. Most everyone else had a similar opinion—at least going with Warner would mean that I had a label and could get a second record out, which, after all, I'd already started working on.

After a long night of thinking about it, I called over the next day and told the exec who'd called that I was sorry, but I didn't want to be on Warner Brothers.

"You got no choice now," he answered.

"Huh? You told me I had twenty-four hours to decide. I'm calling you back in less than twelve."

"It's too late."

Apparently, Warner had put together a press release talking about the closing and some of what it meant. Somewhere in that press release was a list of artists who were moving over to Warner Brothers, and I was on the list.

I hung up and got in the Jeep.

I don't know how long it took me to get to Nashville and the label's offices, but it couldn't have been too long. Security met me; I never did reach the exec's office. What I would have said there, what I might have done . . .

I'm sure it would have made for interesting reading, either here, or possibly, the daily newspaper.

Didn't happen, though. The security people escorted me out peacefully. I was done with Atlantic Records.

SIX:
HOME

9/11

It's over twenty years now, but those numbers, that date—9/11—still mean a great deal to the Americans who were alive at the time. Most of us, I'm sure, can remember exactly where we were and what we were doing when we first saw or heard of Osama bin Laden's terror attacks on New York and the Pentagon.

Karen was at home with the kids. She'd started homeschooling them, giving them the personal attention and rigorous instruction the public schools in the area seemed to all lack. It must have been a little before eight in the morning our time—9:00 a.m. Eastern—when she saw the news on the TV that a plane had struck one of the World Trade Center towers.

She called her sister, who by then was at work. "Have you seen the news?"

Her sister had them turn on the TV at work. They were both watching when the second aircraft hit.

"Oh my goodness," said Karen. At that moment, our daughter, Alex, happened to come into the room. Karen shooed her away gently, telling her to go play with her brothers. She waited for her to go inside, then got off the phone as quickly as she could.

The kids knew something was very wrong.

"A plane crashed," said Alex, ten years old at the time. "Is Daddy OK?"

"Daddy wasn't on the plane," Karen said. "Daddy's OK."

Karen sat down with the children and explained as much as she knew, as gently as possible. It was a history lesson, after all—live, important history that they were all part of.

I was away, camping on an isolated ranch in New Mexico. A few of us had flown out a few days before, trekking into the wilderness to hunt bison.

It was the first time I'd hunted bison. I had a 45-70 Sharps, not unlike the legendary hunters of the nineteenth century would have used. We were staying in a teepee-like tent, ranging out from camp on horseback during the day with a guide. When we got back that night, there was a note: EMERGENCY. COME TO RANCH HOUSE.

We did. The folks there were still up when we arrived, watching what had happened.

I knew my reserve unit would be called up, and that it was my responsibility to get to the base as quickly as possible. My four companions were in the same boat, all with military obligations. We called around and quickly discovered that all flights had been grounded. So we crammed into the rental car we'd used to get from the airport and drove the whole way east to North Carolina and Tennessee, shoulder to shoulder, gear piled or squished into any crevice we could find.

My unit wasn't activated immediately; in fact, by the time we *were* called up, days or weeks later, I was back on the road, playing in California. I left the tour and deployed to . . . Mississippi.

I wanted to go to Afghanistan or Iraq even—this was before the second Gulf War, but I could see that coming. Whatever wherever, I wanted to do *something*, not sit around in the States. I talked to my commanders. It turned out that only a small part of the unit was needed at the moment, or for the foreseeable future. That part didn't include me. Since I wasn't needed, they released me to go back to work. It would turn out that the unit never left the US, though some reserve troops from Campbell and Tennessee were sent to the war zones later.

It's funny. When you get that first call, when you think you're going back to war, you're like, *Damn, this is awesome!*

That's what you think. Your heart skips a little faster. Your muscles get tighter. You want to fight. That's not to say war is anything but ugly and nasty. But it is exciting, and when you've trained to do it, you can't help but want to get into the middle of it.

My active reserve status ran out in 2004. By that time, I was ready to walk away. My music career was solid by then—more than solid. We were super busy with tour dates and recording; I'd started dipping my toe into TV as well. I was still a soldier mentally and emotionally, but the reality was, I was more a country singer and songwriter.

Band leader.

Dad. Husband.

Other guys had the skills and education I'd been privileged to earn in the army. I'm not saying they wouldn't have put me to work if I stayed in and was needed, but there certainly would have been some very good men and women ahead of me. I was no longer essential to the army. Music now was my life.

I LOVE IT

When I made my decision not to go over to Warner Brothers, some of the guys I played with were worried—"leaky roof better than no roof" and all that. But I didn't look at it that way. I knew I was taking a chance, but staying with Warner would have been a bigger chance. And the only guarantee they would have given me was that I was on the bottom of the pile.

My military experience doesn't seem directly relevant—I wasn't literally parachuting anywhere or using laser designators to pick a new record label. But the army did prepare me. When you're trained for a job like COLT, going over enemy lines, working with a small group under potentially the worst possible circumstances, you learn to assess risk and reward almost intuitively. You're taught to make the best choice for the mission. A lot of times that's not the safest choice. It was like that then. I knew I wouldn't be top dog at Warner Brothers, but I had the potential to *be* a top dog. I had to believe in myself.

I'd already had great success. That wasn't going to earn me a free ride to stardom, but it did tell me I had what it took. I just had to build on what I'd already done.

The question was: *Where was the best place to do that?*

I had plenty of time to figure that out; it took the better part of a year to formally leave Atlantic/Warner. Out of all the options, the ones that appealed to me most were with independent labels. Part of this was practical. As an up-and-coming artist, I wanted to be with a company that was going to be sure to push me, not wedge me under a stack of older artists they already had commitments to. I wanted a label that was as hungry as I was.

I also wanted a place where I felt comfortable musically.

I found those things, at least initially, at Broken Bow.

Benny Brown had started the label in 1999. Benny had been, and continued to be, very successful in the car business in California, where he had a string of dealerships. He wasn't what you might call a music industry guy himself, but he did have an ear for country music. He sure liked it—he'd play our music on his dealerships' sound systems all the time. More important, he brought some good people in to work the label.

This was also a time when some of the big corporations dominating the music industry—looking at you, Atlantic—were treating country music like a sad-sack second-class citizen, leaving room for upstarts to try and muscle their way in. In a lot of ways, Benny was the right guy at the right time to start a label and have some success.

Finally clear of the Atlantic business, Phil and I went to work on songs for what became my second album, *I Love It*, soon enough bringing in Mike as we got rolling. The album debuted in March 2003 and immediately climbed the Billboard charts to the top twenty.

Let me stop here and get to two questions a lot of people always ask:

How do you pick the songs that go on an album?

How do you come up with the name of the album?

The answer to both questions starts with the songs. After all, when it comes to putting together an album, a songwriter/performer like myself needs to write or at least find the songs before picking which ones will go on the album.

Writing is a mysterious process that you can't really explain or analyze too closely. Some songwriters will start with a melody they plunk out. It'll take hold of them and grow. It'll stretch itself out and become a song, or the skeleton of a song. Then they or a collaborator will add words. Things will get fleshed out, tinkered with, bothered around a bit, until eventually the song will be recorded into a form for an audience wider than the musicians they're working with.

Other songwriters will start with words—a poem, really. Notions leading to bits and then lines to stanzas, a refrain maybe, until finally the whole piece is there, more or less, just waiting to be set to music. The writer, or maybe a collaborator, will take inspiration from the words, weaving bits around them.

The point being, a lot of songwriters look at their craft as having two separate halves: music and words. For me, though, there is no separation. Things are always together, or pretty much always. The words and music spring up intertwined, two strands of the same vine twirled tight around each other.

Songs can take quite a long stretch to write. I might have a bit of something and it just doesn't jell for weeks or months. It's like an incubation period. It's not uncommon for me to be writing two or three songs at the same time.

My songwriting is usually very collaborative. I like working with other writers. There's energy there, and inspiration. You get another look at something from someone else's point of view, and lightning can strike.

Or not. All part of the process.

I've used different strategies as my career has gone on. I've organized my own writers' events. I'll take four writers and we'll go somewhere— New York maybe, or my place in Florida. We'll get up, have breakfast, hang out a bit, and then get started. I'll put one or two to a room and I'll go back and forth. I write better that way. Motion. I can't sit still too long.

The start is usually an idea about a melody. We gotta have a good hook. There are guys that are very melodically driven. Mike, my band leader and one of my dear friends, is like that. He and I have written a ton of songs together. I love working with him 'cause I can have an idea and he'll say, "Man, I got this melody," and he'll start playing it. I can tell him, "No, don't go there, go to this note." He's real quick. It's fun to write with someone like that. He's a decent lyricist but his real money's made in his melodies.

I think of a guy like Elton John, who takes Bernie Taupin's lyrics and puts them to melody—that blows my mind. Bernie's not knowing how it's going to sound. But there's a partnership, right? They found the right person to work with.

I can't do one without the other. I've never written a lyric without having some form of a melody in my head. That doesn't mean I can't change one part without the other. The melody or the lyrics can change. They *will* change. I'll modify the melody based on the lyrics, or the other way around. But usually, one is not going to drift a big way from the other as I work on it. The meat and potatoes—the chords—usually stay where they began.

As for the lyrics—maybe the second verse is stronger than the first, and that leads to something new or a switch, but again, usually the basic idea remains. I've done that on songs that guys have brought to me and said, "Man, we liked this, but there's something missing. Do you want to work on it?"

I'll listen. Sometimes the problem is relatively simple. They're singing a verse that doesn't have anything to do with the song. So I'll rewrite a verse and we'll have a song.

I go through dry periods. We all do. Those can be nuts. Sometimes they'll last for months. You can't force the issue. Oh, you can force it—to some degree, you know there's a format, you know you have to have an intro, and so on. But there's a difference between "just" writing a song and creating a great song story.

Most people, 99 percent of the people who record, don't use the same guys in the studio that they use on the road. That's because it's a different skill set. In the studio you need to comprehend what the writer wants you to portray. You have to take what he wants and add your own artistic touch to it as a musician, without ever taking anything away from what he expects the lyrics to deliver.

It's a little different for the guys on the road who have to play what you've already developed. You've already figured it out, developed it, played these notes, gotten a signature lick that sticks out on the recording. That's what the audience wants to hear. So the road musicians have to be able to play the song the same way, night after night. That's not nearly as easy it might sound.

I do use songs from other writers on my albums. It's not padding, or for meeting a mathematical formula for an album. If there's something I like and I think it will work, I'll pick it over my own work. When I heard "Redneck Yacht Club" by Thom Shepherd and Steve Williams, I knew it met all the criteria: something country radio would play, something people would enjoy, and something I could sing.

My number-one requirement of *every* song that has gone on every album was simple:

Will it be a hit on country radio?

Does this have the sound and everything else that will get it played all the time? Will it rise to the top? However else you want to phrase that requirement, it comes down to a simple question, again and again: *Is the song a potential hit?*

I have never included a song I didn't think had that potential. Well, there was one exception. We'll get to that down the road.

Now, judging what the public is going to buy is tough. Look at a song like "Red Solo Cup"—I'm not sure how anyone could have predicted that song even being written, let alone having the kind of success it's had. (Over sixty-one million views on YouTube alone, as of the other day.) But I think one of the keys is striking an emotion in people. That can be happiness or fun like in "Solo Cup." It could be sadness. Anything someone can relate to and attach themselves to musically, they're going to buy and support.

I do realize that not every song I put on an album is going to be a single. The business just doesn't work that way—or didn't when I was starting out. But I wanted that potential to be there in every song. I loved it, and still do, when someone says, "Man, such and such on this album was my favorite song and it should have been a single." I have to agree with them.

Beyond that requirement, the decision on what to put on an album is pretty democratic. I get a lot of input. I ask the people around me—but I'm sure I'd get advice even if I didn't. I do have the final say, but I can't remember going against the collective wisdom or votes of my producers, the label execs, and my management.

Let's say I have a bunch of songs that, when I started getting ready to record the album, I put down to include. It'll be a long list, way more than would fit on an album. Everybody hears the songs. If there's one song that gets more than one dislike, it's off the list. We whittle a bit more from the ones that are left, then cut the album.

The album title?

Everyone tries to be artistic and all when coming up with that. But really, we're just trying to sell records. So the end result has to have that in mind: *What is going to push people to buy this album?* Or at least get their attention long enough to think they should sample the music.

So "catchy." The title of the album has to have a bit of a hook, something to draw a listener in. But of course there's more. Again, it's a process.

I don't, or at least haven't, done concept albums or think about a certain theme that's going to organize everything before I record. There are certain themes that come out a lot in my music, but those come naturally from who I am, what I value, and the people around me. I don't choose a song because it's, say, about the military. I choose it because it sounds really good and—most important—should be a hit.

Once the ten or twelve songs for an album are collected, I'll listen to them and see if there's some sort of theme there, or if one of the titles for the songs seems to sum up the others. The title of my first album with Broken Bow was *I Love It*. The title came from the very first track on the album. The song is about an "unordinary" woman, an unconventional lady who is unique, goes her own way, and is the love of the

CRAIG MORGAN

I LOVE IT

I Love It, 2003

singer's life. Philip Douglas, Ron Harbin, and Jimmy Yeary wrote it, and I think it sums up what a lot of men think of their wonderful but occasionally baffling wives.

Probably goes the other way too.

The idea also describes the range and sets the tone for the rest of the album. The upbeat music, the notion that not every part of life has to be conventional, the importance of love—not just romantic love, but love of family, country, and God—this song opens the way for all that follow.

So there's the title.

And no, that song was not released as a single. There were four others that came out, starting with "God, Family, and Country" a few months before the album itself launched March 11, 2003.

The song that I included that no one on the team liked—not even me: That red ladybug song.

That's what I call it. And I'm not smiling when I say that.

Officially: "Look At 'Em Fly."

It was included as the last song on *Little Bit of Life*, released in 2006—appropriately, the last song on the last album I did with Broken Bow before our later reunion. Benny Brown begged me to cut it. He really wanted me to include it on the album. I mean, *really* wanted it on the album.

I don't know that he wore me down. I do know that he was the owner of the label, and I did feel that I owed him something. So I did.

But you know what?

My uncle David loved it. He loved it to death.

"That needs to be on the radio," he'd tell me all the time.

I'd shoot back, "Hell no. I don't want anyone to hear that song."

And I meant it. I've mellowed a bit since then, but that one's not making any of my favorite lists. With due respect to its writers.

Picking the singles is similar to picking the songs to record and include on the album. While I start with the idea that everything should be hit-worthy, some will naturally sound more like a hit than others when they're recorded. Catchy. Has a hook. Something people can easily relate to.

There are other considerations. One's timing. If it's going into summer, you don't want to release a ballad or a sad song, because it's summer, and everyone wants something up-tempo on the radio then. Radio being the most important thing. If it's not on the radio, it's not going to be a hit.

At least that's the common wisdom, or was when country radio ruled back in the '90s and early 2000s. Today . . . well, look at one of my recent songs, "The Father, My Son, and the Holy Ghost." That got very little airplay because the stations thought it was too heavy, too sad a song. (I don't agree at all but I'm irrelevant in this discussion.)

I'll talk more about that song a bit later. For now, let me just say that the song made it to number forty-eight or something most-played song on country radio. Good, but nowhere near number one. Plenty of stations said flatly they would not play it at all because in their minds it was too much of a downer. The opposite is true, but the point is that song became the number-one most-downloaded song of all genres. It was a *huge* seller, very, very popular with people, and not just country music fans.

Back before the dawn of the iPod and iPad and iTunes, no country song could become anywhere near popular without country radio playing it a lot. I imagine if you're under thirty or so, you may have a hard time understanding how important country radio was, let alone envisioning a world that did not have iTunes—or Spotify, Amazon Music, Napster, et al. Maybe the best way to think about radio's importance when I was starting out is to imagine what you might do *without* those services.

Nowadays, you can buy individual songs off of any album—if there even is an album. Back then, producing, distributing, and promoting a single was a fairly intensive and often expensive process, which is why you could only do a few. There was also a limit as to how many songs by a single performer a station would put into "rotation"—songs that were regularly played during a given time, which was how they became hits.

In those days, singles were physical vinyl discs played on turntables. Singles were important not only for their sales numbers, but for their ability to draw attention to the album. Albums mostly being on CDs at the time. Album owning isn't entirely obsolete, but it's nothing like it was during my time at Broken Bow. That's why we spent so much time in those days concentrating on singles and getting them played on country radio. The deejays were social media influencers before social media. Now it's different. Singles do help other sales, quite a lot. But they also bring revenue on their own.

If you're a songwriter, having your song chosen as a single by an artist is big. Having it unchosen—which will happen for all sorts of reasons—is big too. I have had to disappoint some writers. We've had songs picked out as singles, only to have thing change at the last minute because the label wants to emphasize something else. I know it's tough on the receiving end. I had a writer bring it up about a song that he had high hopes for, an old-style country tune that he'd been shopping for quite some time. It was real, real country. I liked it. I still like it. But the label wanted to go with a different song, and I had to tell him, "Hey, I'm sorry. Yeah, it was our intention. And it just didn't work out."

There are bad breaks in every business. I've had a few myself.

I've had my share of hits, but it wasn't all victories and roses; never is in life or the music business. The label promotions people would give me feedback. A lot of it was positive: "WKTF frickin' loves the new single." But there were plenty of times they'd say something like, "We can't get station X to play anything—maybe if you give them a call . . ."

I'd do that, of course. Which was why I told the promotions people to be totally honest with me. It would look pretty weird if I called up a studio to thank them for playing my music when they didn't even know my name, let alone play my single.

So I'd call the station that's not playing my music. Let's say I get the program director, who tells me he's not playing it because he doesn't like it. Not directly. Most station managers are way too polite to be that blunt. They'd tell me things like, "Great song, but we don't think anyone in our audience will like it."

That was easy to turn around. "Try it," I'd answer. "If you get ten phone calls, and five of them say I don't like this song, don't play it."

"If I get five people saying I like a song, I'm playing it," he'd say.

"Then you might as well chart it then. Because you're gonna get that."

And more often than not, they did.

We did a ton of shows for radio stations, formal and informal. I'd go in, sing on the air, do listener parties and that kind of stuff. I did their shows. I did 'em in malls. I did 'em in parking lots. I did 'em everywhere. Those were mostly free shows. Which meant I didn't make any money. The label would pay my musicians, but that was it, aside from the occasional per diem.

I was grateful just to get the shot. I figured eventually it would pay off. And, generally, usually, it was fun. I met a lot of nice people. A few not so nice, but mostly nice.

I talked to just about every radio person there was. I'd do ten radio interviews a day, in person or by phone. When we'd be touring, I'd have my motorcycle with me on the truck. I'd pull it off and head over to a station to visit, just to say thank you in person.

I owe my early career success to country radio. I tried to remember that as I moved up. Sometimes a programmer would call me up personally and say that there had been a last-minute cancellation for a show or whatever, and ask if I could step in. I'd say sure. And when I did a show, they'd hammer it for me.

ALMOST HOME

Traditionally, country radio had tended to emphasize the big labels. That was breaking down by the time I went with Broken Bow, enough so that I mentioned it at the time to news people covering me. I got a little credit for helping blaze the way with that first Broken Bow album, and specifically the second single off it, "Almost Home."

"God, Family, Country," the first single off the album, had done OK. It was a song close to me. I'd written it with Lance McDaniel and Craig Morris, and I can't think of a song that sums up what I believe in any better. It's all right there in the title. The words are a tribute to a member of the Greatest Generation, and if it reminds you of your grandfather or great-grandfather, that's not an accident. But it's also a reminder of timeless values that are still important, and of a time that at least in our minds was simpler.

"Almost Home" takes its own look back, but that comes from the voice of a homeless man who's remembering his childhood. There are at least two different ways to interpret what happens in that song when the singer stops to help an older homeless man—maybe he keeps him from dying, or maybe he was just dreaming. That's the beauty of a song sometimes: you get to decide yourself what it's about.

Kerry Kurt Phillips and I wrote that. It shot up the charts, peaking at number six in Billboard. BMI awarded it "Song of the Year," and the Nashville Songwriters' Association International gave us a Songwriter's Achievement Award for it.

That combination—both commercial and critical success—was big stuff for a guy who was only on his second album, especially after the Warner mess. And it was big for the label, which had just made a push to get bigger with a new outside publicity team. I'd had top-forty songs before; being in the top ten was like that on steroids.

Everything was great before. Now it was phenomenal. And fast.

But the song. I got the idea for "Almost Home" on the road, appropriately enough. We played a hell of a lot of dates those years after the first album came out—I think one hundred and sixty in 2000, which comes out to more than half of every week once you add in travel time. Karen and the kids weren't all that happy—can't blame them—and I remember talking to her one day when she was frustrated with me being gone so much.

"This is temporary," I told her. "Just relax. It won't be long. I'm almost home."

I got off the phone and I started thinking.

You know? That is not a bad idea, that line. Almost home.

Almost home.

Almost home.

I had the words and a kind of music hook there, the story starting to jell. I wrote it down. Not too long after that, I saw Kerry Kurt Phillips for a writing session and he asked, "What do you got?"

I told him the story, played the hook. He brought me out a bit, asking questions. I answered, and we went back and forth like that for a while. We wrote probably three or four times on the song in different directions, without really getting it. The song was there but not there. *Almost home . . . almost.*

Then one day I was driving into Nashville and I saw a guy with a sign.

WILL WORK FOR FOOD

He was an older guy, in very bad shape, at least from what I saw. I met up with Kerry a short time later and mentioned it.

"That guy's almost home," said Kerry.

We looked at each other. That was the key to the song. Until then, we didn't know it was about a homeless guy.

Bells went off, fireworks. We finished that song right up that session. I knew it was going to be a hit when I shared it with Philbilly, who offered to give me forty acres of land he had for half the rights.

I thought he was joking. He wasn't, not really. He believed in that song, and I think if we'd've shook on it that day, he would have gone through with it. Might have been a good deal for him, even though I wouldn't have thought so at the time—that land he had was sweet.

Joking aside, the popularity of "Almost Home" changed things for me, or maybe just accelerated them. I started getting a lot more mail at home—and this was at a time when it wasn't easy to figure out home addresses of celebrities through the internet, especially when they didn't use their legal names. I became better known on and off the radio.

I guess that was another part of the decision not to stay in the active reserves. My enlistment was up, and while I'd planned on putting in twenty years, the attention I'd get when reporting was, to be honest, embarrassing. And it had to be a little distracting for the other guys and especially for command. I tried not to act like I was any different than I had been before the hit. Hopefully, I was successful.

Sometimes, though, I wish I had stayed with the army for three more years, which would have brought me to twenty. Somehow being able to say I retired after a full career just feels like it would have been more of an achievement. Impractical, and not the best thing for my music or my family. But some feelings are hard to shake.

"Almost Home" near cost me a friendship with Trace Adkins. Unknown to me, Kerry's publisher took the song out and played it for Trace; he put a hold on it, or at least he thought he did.

A "hold" is just that—a performer who plans to record the song will put a "hold" on it with the publishing company, which in turn will tell other performers about the intended recording. Generally, there's no money changing hands, no guarantee that the song will actually be recorded, and usually nothing in writing. It's more a handshake kind of thing. But it has the power of tradition and honor, a commitment on both sides not to be taken lightly.

In this case, I had no idea that Trace wanted to do it. And he had no idea I'd written it—which explained why he asked me how I'd heard about the song when he found out I'd recorded it.

"Are you joking?" I asked.

"Do I look like I'm joking?"

He didn't. He calmed down when realized I'd written it and hadn't known anything about a hold. Probably still wished he'd recorded it first, though. Can't blame him at all for that.

SADDAM'S HOUSE

I was out of the army, but in many ways still very much a soldier. Then and now, I still think like a soldier. And some of the people who knew me as a soldier think of me that way too. Especially during the war on terror.

At the end of 2003, I joined a Stars for Stripes tour to Kuwait and Iraq. Jolie Edwards and I were the celebrity performers. Mike Rogers and Brian Tapley came along—Mike to play guitar, and Brian, my tour manager, to handle sound. Faith Quesenberry, who had replaced Christie as my manager, also came.

We spent Christmas in Kuwait, then flew up to Iraq. Poor Brian lost his lunch, either because the choppers we took were flying so fast and low, or the crews' practice gunfire roiled his stomach—he'll have to tell you which.

It was a cold ride, wind whipping through the open cabin of the Black Hawk. The US had invaded Iraq and kicked Saddam out of power just a few months before. Remnants of Saddam's army and foreign fighters recruited by al-Qaeda and others were building an army of terrorists aiming to kick us out and overthrow what would eventually become the democratic government. But most of the people we flew over heading out of Kuwait waved at us, and at least pretended to be friendly.

We transitioned to ground vehicles for the ride into town. A high-ranking general met us—we'll conveniently forget his name in light of what he was about to say—and after a word or two with some of the team, pointed at me and said, completely serious, "Anything goes down, this guy here is in charge."

That got everybody's attention, including mine. It was real life as opposed to real military—a recognition of my résumé, I suppose. And truth was, if I was still active I would have outranked everyone on the detail. But as far as they were concerned, I wasn't just a civilian, I was a *singer*. Nobody in the army takes orders from a singer.

I sat back and took in the sights. A short while later, we're driving over to the city from the airport. Suddenly, there was a commotion, people hollering on the radio. A guy had run out in front of the convoy, and somebody shot him. Apparently he had a bomb or had planned to detonate one.

The convoy started to stop. I started yelling. "Don't stop the convoy, move, move, move, move, move!" Which is what you do in that situation.

I can't say why they would have stopped. Maybe for some reason they felt like they were safe.

I grabbed an M-16 that belonged to the driver, and scanned the road, ready to use the gun if I needed to.

Troops nearby had rallied to the spot. The terrorist was lying in the road as we passed. Blood was streaming out. We whipped on by without stopping to investigate further.

Poor Mike. He'd never been outside of South Carolina until he moved to Nashville, and he hadn't seen anything like this.

You know what baffles him the most?

The fact that I'd had a bag of M&M's in my hand when the commotion began, and kept eating, even as I grabbed the gun and scanned for more trouble. But that's why M&M's were invented, or so I'm told. Very popular candy in World War II among infantrymen. They came in tubes and were sold exclusively to the military.

Those sorts of attacks would become very common and more sophisticated as time went on in Iraq. We were well protected, though, and there were no more incidents like that on the tour—or at least none that came that close.

From Baghdad, we went to a few other places around the country even less secure than the capital. Among the soldiers we visited and performed for were members of the 82nd Airborne. Had things gone differently for me, I might have been in the audience rather than on the stage.

But the SF guys were the most fun. I'll leave out some identifying details to protect the guilty ...

We met up with a contingent of Green Berets who invited us to a personal VIP session at their base, a fancy private home that had belonged to one of Saddam's officials. Unfortunately, the invitation was issued in the presence of the Stars for Stripes trip liaison, who adamantly insisted that neither I nor my guys were allowed to leave the safe confines of our present abode.

"No problem, guys," I told them. "I appreciate the invite."

The soldier who had offered the invite nodded solemnly, then waited while our liaison was called to attend some other problem.

"Under the west wall," he whispered, "there'll be a Conex. Climb up on that and throw your bag over. There'll be two Humvees there to meet you."

He added a time and slipped away.

In case you're wondering, a "Conex" is a large steel shipping container used by the army to store and ship things all over the world. The boxes have a multitude of uses besides moving gear and supplies, and a few hundred thousand have been used by the army since the Korean War.

Mike, Brian, Faith, and I showed up at the appointed time, found the Conex, and over the wall we went.

The Humvees were waiting. We were whisked away to a pretty nice house—so nice, in fact, that it had an indoor swimming pool. We stripped to our underwear, and dove in.

Those Green Berets know how to party.

If there had been alcohol in Iraq, of course it would have been there. But everyone *knows* there was no alcohol in Iraq. It was against regulations.

I played a few songs and joined in some toasts to fallen comrades. We all had a great time.

The soldiers got us back to the wall and the Conex a few hours later. We made our way up to our rooms . . . only to be intercepted by our Stars for Stripes nanny.

I mean, liaison.

"What have you been doing?" she asked.

"Laundry," I said. I had the wet underwear to prove it.

That was the same trip where I introduced Brian and Faith to the wonders of dumpster diving.

The civilian version of dumpster diving is really a hit or miss venture—you go into a garbage dumpster and generally pull out junk. Every so often there's something worth taking, depending on your level of desperation.

The rewards in military dumpster diving are far greater, and almost guaranteed. When troops are coming home from an overseas assignment, they usually have plenty of stuff they don't want to carry back with them to the States. These items could range from belts and half-tents to tables and chairs. The best we found on that trip were some brand-new combat boots that Brian, I believe, ended up wearing.

You can't dumpster dive for all your treasures and souvenirs. For those we went downtown to the bazaar, something that probably put our escorts on edge, and not just on that trip. The best pieces came out of Saddam's palace—the locals had looted the place for anything that wasn't tied down, and some pieces that were. Bits of marble were for sale, their authenticity sworn for by the vendor. Somewhere along the way, I picked up a few knives possibly used by the dictator himself.

That was the first of many trips I took to the war zone, both in Iraq and Afghanistan, for the USO as well as Stars for Stripes. I think at last count I've done a total of sixteen trips for those groups, and always aching to do more. The high point, every time, was performing with the troops. A lot of times the military would arrange small group meetings, where the guys and gals would talk about different things. They'd be shy at first, but you get one person asking a few questions and everyone will jump in. I'd sign a few hundred autographs every show.

Me, Betty Cantrell (Miss America 2016), and Peanut Tillman on a USO tour

The military always took very good care of us. Still, you could never forget you were potentially a target. We were in Kandahar, Afghanistan, at the airport one time, soon after an attack there—the townspeople were still sweeping up the debris. We were doing a show in a large tent when some loud and nasty booms sounded nearby.

My guitarist hit the ground. I just kept playing. I guess danger sounds a little different after you've heard it in a war.

It was on one of the Stars for Stripes tours, I believe, that we performed at the embassy in Iraq. It was an interesting show, not for the songs I did or even the audience, but for the people who weren't in the audience.

Iraq, 2011

There were plenty of VIPs doing the introductions, as there always are. But I noticed a bunch more in the back halls who didn't seem to have a real hankering for country music or mingling with the guests. And unlike most of my other performances, cameras had been forbidden inside.

We pieced out later that my show had been used as a cover for a meeting of different country factions, a face-to-face sit-down of some sort. The only reason I figured that out was because of some other guests who weren't there for the music, either. They were American. And the most prominent, at least as far as I was concerned, was a lady who came up to me while the boys and I were mingling after the show.

"How are you, Sergeant Greer?" she asked.

I had been introduced as Craig Morgan, civilian, singer, no army rank or connection whatsoever. Morgan, not Greer. But she seemed to know me and my background.

I couldn't quite place her. She introduced herself as Carol. That still didn't quite register.

"Panama," she said.

Carol . . .

Oh.

That had been the name of one of the Agency people responsible for the jungle mission I'd been on years before. I couldn't even remember interacting with her. She'd seemed to be some sort of civilian in the headquarters building. Her interactions with the others hinted that she had *some sort of* authority, but it hadn't been on display when I was present. No need to know, I guess.

"So Carol?"

"1989. Panama. You went into the jungle."

"Yeah," I told her. "I remember now."

We talked a bit, about nothing very specific. Then she thanked me for coming to the embassy.

"It was on the tour," I said.

She smiled. "We may ask you again."

"Any time."

It was only a lot later that I became friends with a Special Forces guy who knew "Carol" as well. She had apparently had a long list of escapades, we'll call them, in Panama and South America.

Carol wasn't her real name. Surprise.

At a different show, a fellow came up to me and said something along the lines of, "I was told you worked with us in Panama."

"No," I said.

"Yeah. In Panama."

I kind of shrugged. The guy described a little of what we had done and finally I admitted I'd been there.

"OK, cool," said the fellow, who apparently knew Carol. "That's cool. So now when we do the USO shows, we may ask you to do something.

We may ask you to do a show here that might seem unusual, but do your show."

Sounded like good advice.

Have I done other work for the Agency?

Maybe. They seem in the business of not making those things public, even if you're the one doing the work.

The audiences at the military shows are always the best. A lot of the servicepeople who'd come out would admit they knew nothing about me or even country music. I always felt like in doing those shows, I was making new fans, but also bridging a culture gap. You'd get people who thought country music was all super hokey because all they remember are some super old songs. They'd listen and walk away thinking, *Hey, this may not be as bad as I thought.*

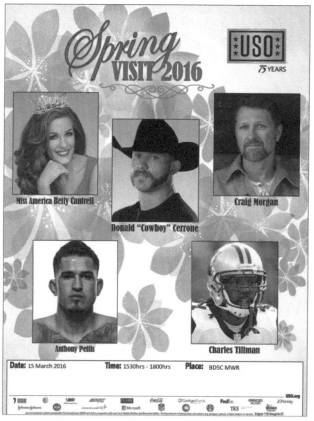

USO tour, 2016

You don't have to like country to like music. You may not like rock music, but that doesn't mean you won't like a particular rock song. Plenty of people I met told me they'd never listened to a country song in their lives, but would download everything I'd ever done.

A lot of the new fans were Black, and from communities where country music hasn't been very popular. That's one thing I like about the military—it's the one place in our society where people mix freely, where racism is less active. Now, I don't mean that racists don't exist in the military. But the military culture tamps a lot of that crap down, and shows people that you should be valued for your character, not your skin. My shows had audiences with as many Black guys as white guys, as Asians and Hispanics; it didn't matter.

I met a lot of interesting people at those shows, including a few celebrities and politicians. Al Franken before he became a senator, for instance. It's surprising—we were two guys from

VIPs often stop by before we go on. Here, Senators Lindsey Graham and John McCain say hi in 2011.

the opposite ends of the political spectrum, more or less, and we got along pretty well. We had something in common—wanting to do something for the troops.

Plus, he is one funny guy. Which you'd expect from someone who was a comedian, I guess.

We pulled a few pranks, including one or two that were not PC, or anywhere near PC. I'll let Al talk about that in *his* memoir.

Al had me on his radio show after we got back—not to talk about the trip or even an album, but as a hunting expert after Vice President Dick Cheney accidentally shot a hunting companion.

"Does that happen?" I think he asked. "Should it happen?"

"Should? No. Does? Well . . ."

I knew Dick Cheney as well. So I know Cheney didn't do it on purpose. But I expect Al knew that too. I think he just wanted to talk off-air about some of those pranks we pulled.

NEW HOME

The popularity of *I Love It* and its singles made a difference in my career that I can't measure. Huge. But in many ways the real impact of that album was on me personally. Making that album taught me a lot about making and recording records. Philbilly and I produced it. I hadn't done that before. I think I learned how to communicate my vision for the songs to my bandmates better as we worked on it. I also got a lot more confidence.

The funny thing about that: the more confident I was in my own abilities, the easier it was to let my bandmates have their own vision of a song. When I was sure of myself, I didn't feel threatened by their trying to add something to the music or push it out in a way I hadn't imagined. I didn't let them take over—I'm not that kind of guy—but I was like a platoon sergeant understanding that his squad leaders have a lot to contribute, a general letting his battalion commanders react to the situation, and so on.

You hear stories all the time about guys who have a hit race up the charts, and it changes their whole lives—for the worse. Those stories take all sorts of angles: blew the money, started acting like a jerk, drugs, booze, etc.

I'd heard them, too, and took them to heart. I didn't want to get overly excited. I didn't pay too much attention to the milestones—this song on the chart, this invitation to perform at a large venue, this chance to play with someone or other I'd always admired—but I did know I was having milestones. And I felt blessed. That was a powerful feeling and a spur to push on even harder.

That's a soldier thing too. You see it in combat. A new unit in the field picks up confidence in that first battle. Taste victory, push to another, bigger one.

Though my first album had done well, I hadn't made a huge amount of money off it. We had to save where we could. Rather than taking out the tour bus, I let the label cover airplane tickets where I could, charging the cost to my account. Right there was a fallacy—I had to pay that money back from the sales of the album. But in my head, it was their debt, not mine. There was some logic, I guess: if the album didn't sell, I wouldn't have to cover that cost. But that's not exactly high-level financial planning. At least they were paying per diem while we were on tour. I stretched what was supposed to be food money every which way imaginable.

Song rich, pocket poor. At some point I realized that if I was really going to make it in music, I had to look at it as a business. I had to learn where income could be generated. And more. I looked at other musicians, examining how they made—and spent—money. How do these guys generate income? How do they pay people?

I became "Mr. Why" and I learned to think long-term, like a businessman.

Why does this guy use a payroll company? Why doesn't that guy control the masters?

I was like a twelve-year-old, constantly asking people questions. But I learned a lot.

For instance: A "master" is the original recording of a song. It's base copy for any digital download or album pressing. Owning it means you can license or lease it out to others. Anyone who wants to use that track, whether for an advertising campaign or maybe a song reissue, has to approach the master's owner and arrange for its use.

Long-term, that can be a significant amount of money. Beyond the cash, owning the masters gives you a lot of control over where a song might be used. Like in a commercial, say. I ended up stipulating in all my deals that the masters would come back to me after a reasonable period of time.

The success of "Almost Home" in 2003 didn't eliminate the need for me to continue my business education. The album did not erase any question I had about my viability in the industry. But my success did convince me I could buy a little piece of land and build a comfortable place to live.

And just in case you think I had too much confidence, what I was really thinking was this: *If I never have another hit, or even an album, at least we'll have this property. We'll be OK.*

I told a few friends I wanted to find something a little bigger, and with a little more property—maybe enough to hunt on, though that was more a dream or wish than a plan.

One day the youth minister at First Baptist Church in Dickson tapped me on the shoulder at a church event.

"I heard you all are looking for some land," he said. "I have twenty acres I'm thinking of selling."

Karen and I drove out—it was a ways from town—to have a look. As we drove up the steep hill, two big ol' turkeys walked out of the neighbor's drive.

There was a sign if ever there was one.

The land was pretty, but it was steep. The only access was an old logging road. Good thing I'm so partial to Jeeps.

We made the deal, then started hunting for blueprints we liked. We found them, made a few modifications, and then put the money down for the foundation. I might have done a few things a little differently if I knew I was going to be as successful as I am. I might have—I guess I *would* have—built the house bigger. I like having my family and friends with me, and though we've added on, a couple more rooms would mean more family and friends, and there's not going to be a complaint from me about that. Let's be honest: the house we built won't ever be featured on *Lifestyles of the Rich and Famous*.

But to me it was, and still is, *gee whiz*. It felt like a mansion at the time. Heck, I thought I'd get lost in it the first year or so. We'd been living in a house the size of a double-wide, and before that, military housing. So this was a huge, and a very big deal.

We didn't have a gate on the property when we first bought our house. I told my wife, I won't be one of those gate people. I had songs on the radio, but I didn't feel like a celebrity.

The third time someone drove up to the house uninvited and unannounced, we called the gate company. I'd become a little too well-known to pretend otherwise. And I didn't want my family being bothered, or worse, when I wasn't around.

But if I was famous at that point, it didn't feel like it, and we certainly didn't act like it. As Karen pointed out the other day, we were still going to Shoney's for our big nights—we hadn't moved up to Cracker Barrel yet.

And I still like Shoney's, thank you very much.

Eating out did present a few moments of awe for the kids. Some people would come up and just kind of stand there, staring.

Things like that could be tough on Karen and the kids. As Karen says, "It's hard enough to raise kids without their daddy being famous." They did get a certain amount of attention, good and bad, because of what I do, but mostly any fuss was low-key. I appreciated teachers and coaches not treating my kids special because of my profession. On the other hand, that works both ways—don't give them any special privileges, but don't be extra hard on them either. I know for a fact Karen had some words on that subject with the school at least a few times. And anyone mistreating her kids quickly learned they had picked the wrong person to go up against.

There could be some funny situations. Way after the fact, Wyatt told me he'd bartered with a teacher who gave him a "B" on a paper. According to him, the teacher asked if it was possible to get one of my CDs. Wyatt told him it wouldn't be a problem—if the "B" became an "A." Apparently the grade got changed, whether for merit or initiative, who's to say?

We got friendly with the father of one our son's friends, sharing turns taking the kids to baseball practice and games. We'd been good friends for quite a while when one day he came over and I saw his jaw was just about on the floor.

"You're Craig Morgan."

"Um, yeah?"

"You're the singer."

I guess I figured he'd known who I was, but he didn't. He knew the songs, but hadn't quite made the connection, possibly because the kids used my real last name and it didn't really come up in conversation. If anything, he'd thought I was a famous dirt bike rider—we'd started a little family team and had our names on the motorcycle trailer parked in the driveway.

He might have been a little disappointed. Racing motorcycles is way cooler than singing in some circles.

He's a good guy. We're still good family friends and we love him. And nothing on him, because even I can be slow to figure stuff like that out. Awhile back, I stopped in a convenience store and the lady behind the counter was all excited and asked me to take a picture for her—of her and another customer.

Of course I agreed.

The customer and I got to talking a bit. He introduced himself as Luke Perry, and said he owned a farm nearby. He suggested maybe I might look him up some time.

That's nice, I thought. *Maybe there'll be good turkey hunting there.*

I got to where I was going and mentioned that I'd just met a real nice fella whose name was Luke Perry.

"The movie star?!?"

It turned out he was *that* Luke Perry, and he did have a great place for turkey hunting. He gave me the OK to use it even when he wasn't there.

He passed away in California after having a pair of strokes unfortunately. Died too young.

I mentioned motorcycles.

My son Kyle got into what are called "hare scrambles" when he was young. They're cross-country events where you race across a field, through woods and occasional hill stretches that can be as sharp as mountain patches. Being able to ride fast and true through a zigzagging patch of wilderness is only one of the skills you need to win. Endurance is often more important, because you have to ride the course for quite a while—two hours is common. There are different area circuits and championships; the events are popular up and down the East Coast, the Midwest, Texas, California, and Nevada—you can pretty much find a race in any state you care to look at.

I would ride around the property with Kyle when he was young. It was an expensive sport, and as he started entering races—Jerry joined a little later—I realized that if I were racing with the boys as a team, they would get some support from sponsors and the like. And

they did. Kawasaki—great bikes—ended up providing motorcycles. Fly Racing supplied all our gear. Fred Andrews, a legendary race-bike veteran who was the manager of the Kawasaki off-road team, went to bat for us and got us permission to pit in the pro area at races, even though we were amateurs.

Karen and me helping Kyle at a GNCC race

At first, I was the pit crew. Then I started racing with the boys as a senior. In the process of doing that, I got pretty good—but Kyle was *really* good. He was always top in his class.

Dad confession: I raced because my son was racing. I figured that if he got hurt, I'd be there to take care of him.

We got a little competitive, which made us both better. Kyle was small and light, and had a great feel for the woods. He could ride through mud better than most. His pain tolerance was through the roof. He might be sore or a little beat-up, but he could just drive through it. He might not have been the fastest on a straight, but he was the smoothest overall, and that counts for a lot.

We practiced on my property with trails we marked out. Twenty, thirty miles an hour on a bike—we wrecked a lot. Today, we mostly use the trails for walking, or, if you're feeling ambitious, running. But the bikes are in the shed, at the ready.

I will admit I've had a few spills on bikes. *Off* bikes, I should say.

Kyle and me getting ready for a GNCC race

Back in the army, I'd broken my neck jumping out of airplanes for Uncle Sam, and apparently broke it again in a different place racing. I've had surgery on both shoulders and had half a dozen concussions and had a really impressive fracture of my tibia. I guess I've had enough hurt to make me consider what I'm doing before I do it . . . then do it anyway, if the risk-reward ratio is right.

We raced until Kyle was just about through with college. The schedule was tough for him—and near impossible some weeks for me. I'd do a concert on Saturday, then get the bus to drop me off the next morning at the race. A lot of times I would get there just in time to hop on the bike at the starting line.

Karen would load up the trailer with him, then drive up to the race site and pit, standing there with his goggles and gas.

> *"I'll never forget the first time I gassed him up," says Karen. "I put the can up and didn't get it in right, and I just dumped a whole lot of gas all over him."*

Kid ran that whole race with a gas rash, and never complained.

They'd get home late Sunday night and Kyle would head on back to school so he could be up first thing for Monday morning classes.

About those races I couldn't make, here's Karen:

> *"Race day is amazing when Craig's not with us. We get up, we get ready, we leave, we get there. Everything is smooth. When Craig is with us—chaos."*

Not my fault! Problems with the RV, including a fire. Bad alternators, late schedule changes, inexplicable mishaps—they seemed to come only on my watch. I'm bad luck, I guess.

Pro motocross racers Kevin Wyndham and Fred Andrews encouraged Jerry early in his career.

We would do charity events every year, and have four or five hundred racers involved. The sport is a real family-type affair, filled with people with good hearts and acceleration in their veins.

I still ride a bit. A month ago I geared up and rode for a couple of hours over the trails.

Couldn't walk right for a day.

TOPPING THE CHARTS

The new house and my growing career made quite a difference for us. But you are aware that you're leaving things behind. Physical things, but more.

We had a lot of memories in our first house. And some good neighbors.

One day coming home I stopped to get the mail. The man across the street flagged me over. He happened to be a very distant relative, which neither of us had known until well after we moved in. His name was Earl Gray—like the tea. I imagine he might have been teased quite a bit for that when he was younger, if kids knew anything about tea. Even if he had gotten ribbed, though, he was a very friendly, neighborly sort.

"You have quite a boy there, Craig," said Earl. He was referring to Kyle, who would have been about seven.

"I do, thank you."

"When your dog was hit the other day," Earl said, "I told him I'd see to it."

"Really? Thank you." Our poor dog had gone exploring in the road one time too many. Kyle and I had buried him a few days before.

"Kyle wouldn't hear of it," Earl told me. "He was cryin', but he stood up and said, 'No, sir. It was my daddy's dog. He'd want me to do it.' There's a lot of man in that little boy."

There certainly was.

The story got me thinking. I told Phil O'Donnell about it and he said we need to write that. And so we did, with help from Tim Owens.

Sorry about the dog, but thank you, Kyle, thank you, Earl. "Lotta Man (In That Little Boy)" came right out of that encounter.

"Lotta Man" was on my second album for Broken Bow, *My Kind of Livin'*—not one of the singles, though it could have been. The album outsold my earlier ones and produced Broken Bow's first number-one country song, "That's What I Love About Sunday."

My Kind of Livin', 2005

It was my first number-one hit too. Not only that, but the Billboard Year-End chart marked it the number-one country single of the year. You can't go any higher than that.

Braggin' on it a bit.

I didn't write it, though, so I want to share a lot of the credit with Adam Dorsey and Mark Narmore, who caught what a lot of people like about Sunday—time off, a little church, a little shopping, a lot of relaxing. To an up-tempo beat. Almost sounds like they were hanging around our house on one of those rare occasions when we were all home.

The second single off that album was "Redneck Yacht Club," which also did very well, losing out to my friend Keith Urban for the number-one single the week it came out in May 2005. I knew as soon as I heard that song it was going to be a hit, no matter who recorded it. It was written by Thom Shepherd and Steve Williams, two of my buddies. I would have done a deal to share the publishing if they would've ever been crazy enough to let me.

What's great about that song is that it doesn't really matter what your financial status is, you're in. You might have a forty-two-foot yacht, or you might have an aluminum johnboat—you're a member of the Redneck Yacht Club.

I really knew it was going to do well when I played a demo for my wife, and she hated it.

Just kidding. She did hate it, though.

The song's fun, and so is the music video, which was released at the

same time. The best part of making it was inviting a bunch of friends and family to help out. Blake Shelton's in the video; Aaron Tippin, Michael Waddell from Outdoor Channel, Alex Rutledge, all my kids, and a whole bunch of friends are in there too.

It was a long shoot. We started like 6:00 a.m. and didn't finish till after dark. And it was nonstop the whole time. Having fun is hard work. And expensive. Believe it or not, that video cost in excess of a hundred thousand dollars—that was back when labels spent a lot of money on music videos and promotion.

While I didn't write "Sunday" or "Redneck," I wrote most of the rest of the album, including the third single off the album, "I Got You."

Phil O'Donnell, Tim Owens, and I started writing that while we were touring with Keith Urban, and at first, I was thinking I'd give it to Keith to sing. But you know what? We cut a demo and I realized I liked it too much to give it over—it fit my voice and style so well, and I had that sense about it that it would be a hit.

It was.

The song still gets good airtime. It's a big song with some nice hooks, but it's the words I love. They're about a simple guy with a not-too-easy life, who's thankful for everything that's come his way—but especially "you," the love of his life—in my case my wife, but I would imagine anyone tappin' their foot to it is thinking about their own special match, like the earth's got the sun.

Getting back to my friend Keith. We'd done a bunch of shows together the year before my album released. It wasn't really a tour exactly, more like a collection of dates where we played on the same bill. In that time, I got to know him and really liked him. He was ahead of me career-wise, but still in his early stages, like he was a sophomore and I was a freshman. I remember some fun times from Vegas, the Iowa State Fair, the Minnesota State Fair.

The Minnesota State Fair—we did that three or four days, switching back and forth on the bill. One night I would open; the next night he would.

The first night, I was onstage singing a song . . .

Lately I've been lonely . . .

Suddenly, in my ear monitor, I hear some woman whispering "Craig."

In a bedroom voice: "Craig. Craig."

While I'm trying to sing.

I pulled one of my earphones out and glanced to the side of the stage. There is this woman I don't know, whispering into the microphone—and who do you think is laughing his butt off behind her?

OK, I thought. *Payback's a bitch.*

The next night, Keith was onstage.

Now here's the thing to know about that. Keith was playing to tracks that night. He had his band and he was singing, but he filled that out with tracks. Which meant he couldn't stop in the middle of the song or it would be really messed up.

In the middle of his set, on one of the songs he had tracks on, I had a forty-piece band march on down through the middle of the crowd, banging and howlin'.

Keith is a good sport. He thought that was a hoot. And he kept singing. Didn't miss a beat.

As pranks though, that wasn't nothin' compared to the time we released a thousand crickets loose on Brad Paisley's bus.

Oh, Brad was mad about that for quite a bit. Can't much blame him.

He didn't hold a grudge, though. He played with me on "Blame Me." A song that has nothing to do with the crickets, I swear.

John Conlee sang on "Blame Me" as well. Phil and I wrote it along with Tim Owens. I love that song. It's us as entertainers accepting the responsibility for the people who love country music. So, you know, we're saying, blame me for the steel guitar, blame me for the cowboy boots and that stuff. Oh, hell, blame me, blame us, for it all.

You know, we'll take the blame where we're honored and proud that there are people out there that enjoy country music and our lifestyle. And we celebrate that same lifestyle.

So blame me. All that foot tappin', back slappin', and wide-grinnin' smiles are on me.

Putting a show together, you try to mix things up. You can't do all ballads, for example. People need to feel some energy, some love and fun. The serious songs need to be balanced. For a long time I left "Tough" out of my shows because I had too many other ballads, even though it was a top single and a song I love to sing. Now it's back—at the expense of some other hits.

Those fair shows had huge crowds and favored a lot of up-tempo, "fun" songs. That's how it is with fairs and festivals. Everyone's out there drinking beer and having a fun time even before they get to the show, and you want to keep that mood going. If you're in a theater and everyone's sitting down and a bit quiet, you can play more ballads.

Clubs can go either way. I'll open with a pair of up-tempo pieces, then take it down a little and read the reactions from there. "This Ol' Boy," "That's What I Love About Sunday," "I Hate the Taste of Whiskey"—I bring it down gradually. You can't go from "Redneck Yacht Club" to "Tough"—I'd be halfway through the ballad before the crowd even knew what I was singing.

I vary what I play depending on the crowd and the crowd's mood. My band knows all my songs and never makes a mistake—but I've messed up. I've given an introduction to one song, and actually wanted to sing another song, but of course they have no way of knowing that.

I've had to turn around and tell them, "No, no, not that one, not that one."

Crowd usually gets a bit of laugh at least. And the boys'll give it to me later.

SEVEN:
BREAKING TIES

LITTLE BIT OF LIFE

The first two Broken Bow albums Phil and I produced were very successful commercially. We had seven hit singles off them, including one of which was the most-played song of the year on country radio.

That's insane.

Just as importantly, the albums won the awards and praise from critics and industry groups. Artistic and commercial success don't always go together, but somehow we managed it. So Phil and I were feeling pretty good when we went in to talk to the label and get things in order for our next album, which would eventually become *Little Bit of Life*.

"We want to bring another producer in," said the execs. "To raise the bar."

"I don't know where the f'in' bar can go any higher," I told them.

That's the calm version. And, yeah, I think I could have found a place for the bar. Sideways, at that.

But we were polite. I remained calm.

The label insisted. And Keith Stegall joined us as producer for Broken Bow record three.

Now let me say this—I love Keith Stegall. I love what he does. He is a talented individual. He would have been on my short list at the time . . . if I'd been looking for a producer.

I hate being forced to do something. I'd say most people do, especially musicians.

We ended up with a very uncomfortable situation, for all of us. In my opinion—and that's all it is—the reason the label wanted Keith on the album was for his name. Phil and myself were no-names as producers—at least in the label's eyes.

What's that saying about not being a hero in your hometown?

Broken Bow was still a pretty new label, and I suppose you could argue that they were trying to establish themselves as well as their artists. Maybe getting Keith hooked into them was important in their minds.

Benny, the owner of the label, had a good ear, I'll give him that. But he also had concepts and visions that were a bit different than the industry's. That cut both ways. He was willing to take chances on new performers, and let established ones chart their own course—generally. But he often came at things like he was running a car dealership. The salesmen, a lot of times, seemed more important to him than the musicians, or the music.

This came out in subtle and not so subtle ways. He'd hold back on giving acts money to tour when they had a new album coming out, a real silly move since the few thousand bucks he might have kicked in per show would have yielded many times that in album sales.

An act that might be opening at, say, a state or county fair might get only a thousand or two for a show that would cost them eight to put on. That's going to be a nonstarter for most bands; you can't afford to be doing shows where you're losing money. The guys in the band can't play for free, and usually can't rely on music sales they may not be getting a part of. The label has to think of those shows as an investment, not an expense.

Benny learned that was a mistake, eventually. Still, musicians were cars to him in a lot of ways. Wax 'em up nice and shiny and push 'em out the door.

But back to my album.

Keith and I worked together, and we got along well, but I think we were both uncomfortable—each one of us wishing getting together had been our idea, not the label's. Early on, Keith came in, sat down, listened to the session for a bit, me and Phil running things, and then got up.

"Man, I'm sorry," he told us. "You guys know what you're doing. You don't need me here."

He made sure he was there for the track sessions and he'd always have some good comments. But in my opinion, he was as embarrassed by the whole deal as I was.

Album came out fine though, and I do appreciate his contributions, even if I hadn't asked.

Like I've said, I never worry about a theme on an album. I just want to cut ten or twelve songs that I think country radio will play. Once we have the songs, then we sit down and figure out the order, and what the name of the album should be.

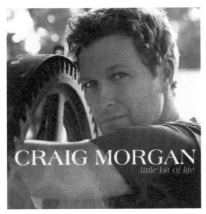

Little Bit of Life, 2006

Little Bit of Life jumped out because all the songs had different takes on everyday life. The song itself sums up a lot of the little bits of my life and probably yours. Take a little bit of country, a little bit of pickup trucks, a little bit of this and that, and it all comes together.

No surprise, "Little Bit of Life," written by Danny Wells and Tony Mullins, was the first single off the album. The video we launched it with has to be one of my favorites, because it was another family-and-friends production. I don't believe there's a single actor in that video, at least not inside the warehouse shots.

That is an actual warehouse in Nashville that we rented for the day. I got everyone to come on over and, well, do everything you see them doing in that video. Basically, it's a crazy little party.

Elvis even stopped by.

Elvis?

Yeah, that's me in an Elvis getup.

The motorcycles? My son Kyle and I, bouncing for the camera.

And on and on.

Funny thing: the video starts with a report about how hot it is outside, and shows a businessman walking through the heat. As it happened, while we were in the middle of the shoot, someone ran into a telephone pole a few blocks away. The electricity went out for hours. Hours. In a very warm warehouse with no air conditioning. There was backup power for lighting and the cameras, but nothing else.

Hours.

So there's a little bit of life in that video. Hot, sweaty life.

"Little Bit of Life" was a hit single. So was the next song off the album— "Tough."

Very different kind of song, and a very powerful one. It's about how strong women are, how much they have to do in just everyday life. And then comes something impossible to deal with—cancer, a disease, maybe some other tragedy—and you learn how *really* strong they are.

I have learned that from personal experience. I've been blessed with powerful women in my life—my mother, my wife, my daughter. I didn't write the song—Joe Leathers and Monty Criswell did—but it sums up what I think of them and a lot of other women too.

Some people have asked whether I picked the song because my wife or someone else I loved had cancer. God had spared us of that affliction to that point. It was only afterward, when my mom suffered and then passed away, that I experienced firsthand how devastating the disease is. But as I say, I have benefited from the strength of good women since the day I was born.

Another song on the album came from Shane Minor. He and I toured together when my career was just taking off. He opened a bunch of shows for me, and we became good friends. He's a former cowboy, LA police officer, and a great or great-great-nephew of Wyatt Earp.

By the time I was getting ready to cut my album, Shane had backed off on touring to focus on his writing. We got together to write a little together, and at some point he played "International Harvester," which he'd written with Jeffrey Steele and Danny Myrick.

As soon as he finished running through it for me, I told him I was recording it. It's one of those fun songs that brings people to their feet at a show as soon as they hear the opening. It's become something of an anthem in the Midwest, and maybe a reminder of how important farming is. Smile and wave at the man up on the tractor next time you're stuck behind him.

I know somebody's going to ask this, because it comes up online a bit: that's a Case IH 1460 combine in the video. We shot it in Wichita, Kansas.

For the record, I'm not a farmer myself. The closest I came was helping my grandfather and joining the Future Farmers of America (FAA) in high school, where I became the state reporter. (The reporter serves as a volunteer for the organization, traveling around the state to represent FAA at different events and fairs.)

Here's another thing about that song—my wife, Karen, hated it. She practically begged me not to put it on the album.

Sense a pattern? If I play a song for Karen and she doesn't like it, it'll go straight to number one.

CHRISTMAS

One of the cool things about the music business is that you get to celebrate Christmas in July.

Broken Bow decided that I ought to do a Christmas song. Not a bad idea, except that it had to be recorded at the beginning of summer, and I was in California.

Phil and I went into a hotel room and jacked the air conditioner way up. We circled around for a while until Phil said, "What would Christmas be like in Dickson?"

Rudolph the Red-nosed John Deeres, light-draped houses, carolers going door-to-door . . .

The idea sparked us. We got to work and within a few hours, we had the song written.

Might've had a little frostbite too.

The song is called "Merry Country Christmas," and it's included as a bonus track on some of the *Little Bit of Life* albums.

I've done a few other Christmas songs and been on a holiday special or two. I also had a nice part in the Lifetime movie *A Welcome Home Christmas* (2020), which was close to my heart because the story concerned veterans coming home for the holidays and the difficult transition they often have to make. The character I played wasn't that much of a stretch for me—I was playing an officer supervising the counseling staff helping soldiers. As a senior NCO, counseling was often part of the job officially and unofficially.

The most fun I had in a *police* uniform had to do with Christmas too. It was during December of 2014, when I went out on patrol with the Dickson County Sheriff's Department. Instead of handing out tickets, we gave out gift certificates to families, including a few we stopped on the road. I'm not a real emotional guy, especially when in uniform, but tears welled in my eyes at the gratitude people showed.

It is *fun* to play Santa Claus. You can't help everyone in this world, but you can make a few people's lives a little brighter, especially on that holiday.

There was a bonus to the gift campaign. It reminded people—and the deputies, I'd say—that the role of a rural police force is to protect and serve. They—we—are not the enemy.

Small-town values? The country is made up of small towns.

Police agencies have gotten a lot of bad press over the years, but the majority of officers care about the people in their communities, and do their best to be good neighbors, directly and indirectly. Even when it may not look like it: it stinks to get a speeding ticket, true, but maybe that saved a life.

Soldiers know what it's like to face the uncertainty of combat; knowing that you can die at any moment changes your body chemistry. Police officers and other first responders know that, too, or at least something close to it. That's why I have a special feeling for them.

I gave up my part-time job in law enforcement when I got too busy and a little too famous with the music career—can't be pulling over someone for speeding and have them ask for your autograph; it just doesn't set right with the judge. But I'm still part of the department's auxiliary, ready to be called out if necessary.

Who knows? If this music thing doesn't work out, maybe I'll become a homicide detective. Or at least play one on TV.

BNA & SONY

Three hit singles, solid album sales, more dates than I could handle ... but I wasn't happy.

The situation with Broken Bow had become unbearable. Them bringing in a producer on me—whether I liked the guy or not, whether the guy was a great producer and musician or not—all facts, besides the point—did not sit well with me.

And guess what? We had fulfilled our contract.

We started negotiating a new one, but I had a bad taste in my mouth. I wanted out, a new start. Faith, my manager, came over one day. She'd talked to them and they weren't interested in agreeing to our terms. That was it; I was done.

My wife was happy; she knew they'd been giving me all sorts of trouble.

"That's it; we're out," I told Karen.

"Thank God," she answered.

I think at that moment she would have been happy to see me just up and rejoin the army. That's how upset I was with them.

But I didn't. I found a new deal pretty quick—with BNA, part of Sony Records

Let me say, though, before I go on—even though the label and I parted ways, I have to recognize that without Benny Brown and especially Broken Bow's promotion team, I would not have a career in country music. I owe them my sincere gratitude.

Sony is a big place, but switching from an independent to a label under the umbrella of a large conglomerate wasn't all that big a deal. The labels themselves are all the same when you get down to it. The people you work with make the difference.

In this case, that person was Joe Galante, the head of Sony BMG Nashville, which included BNA. Joe had pulled their whole country operation together following a merger. He was one of the masterminds of the industry, and one of the best at what he did. He wanted me, and the label backed him up with what's said to be the largest signing bonus a country artist had received at the time. That's saying a lot, given all the stars they had.

It was another one of those moments where you take a breath and say, *OK, we're going to be OK. We can make it from here.*

Joe's idea was to establish "Craig Morgan"—the performer or "brand"—with country radio. He actually told me he didn't care how many records we sold on our first album; he was more about the second album, which he was aiming to be the big splash. He was talking Grammy's and the whole works.

We had a two-record deal, and the first disc did great out of the gate, with a bunch of top-ten hits. The album was *That's Why,* which came out October 21, 2008. And by the way, it peaked higher on the album charts than *Little Bit of Life* had.

Not that I wanted a little "told-you-so."

Much.

"Love Remembers" was the first single off the album, hitting the top-ten list. I wrote the song with Philbilly, who also coproduced the album with me—no third wheel assigned from the label this time.

I remember Phil and I coming up with those two words, "love remembers." Once we had that, I just fell into the rest of the song. *Love remembers.* Those two words felt kind of sexy. The whole song is passionate, and very specific. I could see the images we put into that song. Feel them, taste them even.

Cotton candy on your girl's lips.

And then the idea tying it together, the way hurt comes back after a breakup. You have the taste of something sweet on your lips, and it all goes bitter.

Love remembers.

"God Must Really Love Me" is a song that spoke to me then and really speaks to me now. I imagine it's that way for a lot of people. God does love me, in spite of all my deficiencies. He must, because I have been so blessed. A lot of times, despite my faith, I've not been the man I should have been, done the wrong thing or gotten in trouble—but God's still there.

Jim Collins was one of the writers on that song, along with Troy Verges. I'd written with Jim but I believe I heard that one during a pitch session without him being there. It struck me right away and I called him up and told him I was putting it on the record.

There's another song from that album that has a similar effect—"Ordinary Angels," by Angelo Petraglia, Steven Lee Olsen, and Richard Supa. Again, it's about God and faith, and how when you're at that point when you just have no way to get out, when you just can't go on, God is there, sending down an angel to help you through it. You may not recognize it at the time, you may not know who's pushing you through, but there's an angel at your side.

Strangers, kids, somebody on the street—God's there in every one of us, ordinary or not.

It felt more like a pop song than a country song. Maybe here's the reason—Richie Supa is a guitarist who's pretty tight with Aerosmith. He subbed in for Joe Perry in 1979 and cowrote a number of their hits. He's also worked with Richie Sambora and a mess of others. Talented guy. I believe I may have heard the song first from him.

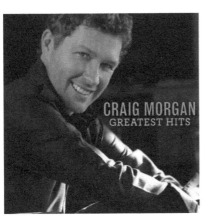

Greatest Hits, 2008

Broken Bow released a greatest hits album right when my new album came out.

Now maybe they were just cashing in or being "opportunistic," as "suits" like to say. But by putting out an album with old songs, radio would be less likely to play my new songs. It's easier to play a hit, and there are only so many times a day a station is going to play an artist. It's as if the new songs are competing with the old songs, and it's harder to get traction.

I've heard since that Benny Brown made the decision to do it and has since said he regretted the decision. But done is done, and I did make a lot of money off it.

GRAND OLE OPRY

A month before the album came out, I played a concert at Fort Bragg, North Carolina. It was a show I'll never forget.

Fort Bragg covers a little over two hundred and fifty square miles in North Carolina. It houses from forty thousand to fifty-seven thousand troops, depending on who is doing the counting and when. It's the head-quarters for the XVIII Airborne Corps, which includes not only my old units the 82nd and 101st—but the 10th Mountain Division, the 24th Mechanized, intelligence, and a slew of others. (Most of those other units are located elsewhere—Campbell for the 101st, for example—but their personnel come in and out of Bragg all the time.) No matter their job, the soldiers connected to Bragg are the tip of the spear, the most likely to be sent into harm's way when trouble starts anywhere in the world.

Doing a concert there was a literal homecoming. A lot of guys I had served with were stationed or had assignments there, and of course they made sure to hook up for the show. I visited around, reliving military and nonmilitary landmarks of my life. My son had been born at Womack Hospital, on base. I also had fun showing some of those young kids that you can't smoke this musician when you take him out for the morning run and PT.

Part of the fun was the fact that we were doing it all for TV—we were filming a special called "Back to Bragg." And while I was in the middle of the show, who pops out as a surprise to sing along? An old friend and performer I especially like: John Conlee.

I've always been a huge, huge fan of John's. He began singing and play-ing guitar on a tobacco farm at the tender age of ten, but he had a few professional detours—working as a mortician and a disc jockey—before going full-time into performing. He signed with ABC Records in 1976; "Rose Colored Glasses," his first big hit, charted in 1978. He's had at least seven number-one singles and a whole bunch of other songs in the top ten.

I have a history with "Rose Colored Glasses." My dad and his brothers used to play in an annual softball game in our hometown, and at some time during the proceedings, people would come up and sing songs. My father would always get me to sing "Rose Colored Glasses." He claims now that I hated doing that, but if I did, it wasn't because of the song. It remains one of my favorites, often included in the set list.

It was in my show at Bragg. We get ready to do it, and John walks out from backstage, singin'. "*I don't know why . . .*"

Total surprise. He got me good. You can find that moment on YouTube somewhere, with me acting like a little kid at Christmas when he comes out.

We finished the song, and John looked at me, still holding the mike, and asked, "What are you going to be doing October twenty-fifth? Do you have any idea?"

October 25? What the hell? Was he planning a barbecue or something?

"No, sir," I told him. "I don't know."

"You don't?" John was a great straight man. "Well, I believe you're scheduled to be on the Grand Ole Opry. How would you like to become the next member of the . . ."

He said something else but by then I couldn't hear anything; my senses were in orbit. I stomped around the stage looking for my mind, crying like a little schoolgirl with pencils poked in her eyes.

Couldn't help it. It was such an honor to be asked.

Karen was off in the wings, crying herself. I just soaked in the moment.

Any description of the Grand Ole Opry will leave some important part of it out. No single parallel to a hall of fame, to an entertainment mecca, to a flagship broadcast network, can rightfully capture its status in our industry.

The short story is that it started with a radio broadcast in 1925 on Nashville station WSM. Uncle Jimmy Thompson took his fiddle out and burned the airwaves down for a show called The WSM Barn Dance broadcast from the National Life and Accident Insurance Company headquarters in downtown Nashville. Two years later, WSM Program Director George "The Solemn Old Judge" Hay called the show the "Grand Ole Opry," putting a name that would not only last but tickle listeners' interest for almost a hundred years now. The Opry moved permanently to the Ryman Auditorium in the city in 1943, giving it a location worthy of the country royalty it had attracted. The show moved to its current location outside of city center in 1974 (Ryman continues to be used for shows after extensive renovations). Weekly cable broadcasts began in 1978. The Opry has survived changing musical tastes and floods, becoming not just a local attraction but an institution known worldwide.

Unlike your typical musical venue, the Opry's roster of regular artists are members, chosen by the board and management. They're all-stars of varying ages and musical temperament, hall-of-famers still in their prime. There are more people in the Country Music Hall of Fame than there have ever been members of the Grand Ole Opry—the last count showed a nudge over two hundred musicians and groups had ever been Opry members.

Needless to say, the Opry is very selective about whom it takes on as a member. It's not just your career. They take it for granted that you've had a number of hits, commercial and critical success. They want more than that.

The members size you up. Among other things, they have annual hunts where the members go out with *possible* candidates and get to know you. If they don't like you, you're not getting in. Period. No matter what other qualifications you may have.

I'd been on a couple of hunts, but there wasn't a whisper of an offer of membership. And I wasn't expecting it that night. I pride myself on being able to suss things out in advance, but John caught me completely off-guard.

I looked over at the side of the stage, tears running down my face.

A few friends from the special operations community were there—they looked teary-eyed as well. That made me feel a little better about my waterworks. If they can cry for me, I could certainly do it on my own. They were as excited and proud of me as I was.

My induction into the Opry came a few months later. Mom and Dad were there—I can still see Momma in the front row, big ol' tears rolling down her cheeks. She'd always been proud of me, but this was one of those moments that goes beyond even the pride you feel for your children.

And I was proud of her. Proud of everything she'd taught me and what she'd done for me growing up, coaxing me through the bad times, and having faith in me to do my best no matter what it was I was doing.

Dad—well, I thought a couple of buttons would burst off his shirt. As a country musician himself, he knew firsthand what the Opry stood for. I remember him taking us to a few shows when we were little and talking about the place in glowing terms. And now here we were, his own son onstage. I can't blame him for beaming like a lightbulb.

It was fun to see him be so happy. He never argued against the military, but I know he was nervous a lot, worried, and I'm sure he found it more relaxing when I got out. If anything, he wanted me to get out earlier so I could work at music full-time.

I suspect he had a joke in there somewhere. Like if I'd listened to his advice, I'd've gotten in sooner.

All in good fun.

Now that I've been a member since 2008, I've become part of the Opry's backbone, I guess. I'm not one of the old guys, but I'm not a new guy either. I'm one of the people the new guys in our industry who are making an impact ask, "How do I get on this hunt?"

I'm happy to offer advice and a helping hand if I can, but I tell them straight that it's not just an honorary thing. The Opry expects you to perform. I believe members play there ten times a year. You're not doing it for money, and while you're getting exposure to some of the biggest country fans in the world, there are plenty of other ways to build yourself up commercially once you've been recognized. Being a member makes you responsible for carrying on and spreading a tradition.

It's a good, fun, entertaining tradition, country music. But it is something you have to keep working at. And the Opry has a certain sense of values and moral standards they expect you to follow.

For a while there, the Opry had the reputation of being a little out of date, catering to older audiences strictly. Fair or not, Pete Fisher had a lot to do with changing that perception. There's been some controversy along the way, but now I think the audience is diverse, age- and taste-wise, from six to sixty and beyond. We have the influence of a younger generation as well as the longevity of the older members.

Thinking on the Opry, I have to admit that I've outlived the typical span of a country artist. I'm ten years past at least . . . and with God's help, still going.

I don't take the credit. I've been really fortunate to have great songs, and great people to work with. A lot of what's happened to move my career along has been due to God.

I do work hard. I do try to do the right things. During the spells when the music wasn't being played a lot, I started doing other things to keep awareness up: movies, TV. I've been talking to country radio for twenty years, so unless I'm doing something new, they have nothing left to talk about. Even if you have a new album, people need to hear some new twist, some new thing you're doing, besides the music.

When your career hits a plateau, you need to find a way to spike it higher. I've been fortunate that the spikes have kept coming, and those plateaus keep getting higher and higher—kind of like climbing mountains, going higher and higher.

OUTDOORSMAN

If someone were dividing my life up into different parts—which is more or less what I'm doing for this book—then the major parts would be my family, my military service, and my music. Those are all truly important pieces.

But there's another, and while it may not rank as high in the grand scheme of things, it's a true part of me and has brought me a great deal of fun over the years.

Along with a little frustration at times.

Hunting.

If you're a hunter, I don't have to explain the attraction. If you're not a hunter, nothing I say will explain it. It's a challenge, it's an immediate purpose, it's an escape; it's a test and it's an education. All of those things, always.

And in my case, it happened to work itself perfectly into my career.

I always loved hunting, but I don't suppose I ever dreamed of doing it on TV when I first learned how to aim a rifle or dress a deer back as a kid. Unlike my musical career, I didn't start out with a plan. There was just a cascade of events, a tumbleweed rolling downhill and picking up steam.

Back in 1999 when I was in the army and just starting to pursue music, I was invited to a celebrity turkey hunt out in Missouri to help provide a little entertainment for some big shots. I did a couple of songs and then, as I was stepping off the stage, a fella came up to me and introduced himself.

"Hey, I'm the president of Quaker Boy and Kirby Game Calls. I'd like to talk to you."

If you've ever hunted turkeys, you probably have heard of Kirby. Turkeys are very elusive prey, a lot smarter than most people give them credit for. The males especially avoid humans, and they can sense them from quite a distance. A tom'll change course as soon as they realize you're anywhere near them. Long-range army scouts have nothing on them when it comes to operating in the bush. They change up movement patterns and make use of natural camouflage as well as an Army Ranger.

But Nature drives them to mate. And they will do a lot to find the right hen.

They have to eat as well, defend their territory, maybe just meet up with old friends—all of this is accomplished vocally, which is where turkey calls come in. There are various ways of making the sounds turkeys use; Kirby then and now makes some of the best devices.

"Sure," I told the guy. "Let's talk."

It turned out the man wasn't just the *president* of the company— he was the founder and owner, Dick Kirby himself. A barber by trade, he'd started making hunting calls back in the 1970s. By that point, his work was legendary, used by some of the best hunters around the country.

He asked me to tell him a little bit about myself and I did—in the army, working on a record deal.

"I'd really like to offer you a pro staff deal with the company," he said.

I had no idea what that all entailed, but I was for it. He ended up outfitting me with a whole bunch of gear I needed for hunting, including his famous calls. All I had to do for them was take photos of me using his equipment.

I think they were hoping that I'd be successful as a singer, and when that happened, I'd already be on board. Which is how it turned out.

Skip ahead a bit, during which time Mr. Kirby introduced me to some other folks in the sporting business. One day I got a call from Michael Waddell, who was shooting a TV show called *Realtree Road Trips*. He asked if I wanted to go on a hunt, which would be filmed for the show.

Why not?

One thing led to another—another show asked if I'd be on, then another, and another. Michael then started a show called *Bone Collector*, and I went on that as well. Doing those appearances, I met the show's producer, Marc Womack. Eventually he decided to split off from Michael's company, and asked if I'd be interested in hosting my own show.

Heck, yeah.

It'd be fun, I thought. We'd film while I was on tour, mixing two of my favorite things, music and hunting.

Red stag, New Zealand, 2010

I got a piece of the production company in exchange. A very small piece, which to be honest didn't really turn into much money, ever. But heck, I was hunting, all over the world. And the exposure was great for the rest of my career.

It took us quite a while to get things off the ground. The records show that the first episode *Craig Morgan: All Access Outdoors* didn't air until 2010; I seem to remember it debuting a lot earlier than that. But whatever—we were on for eight seasons on the Outdoor Channel. Besides showing me hunting and touring, we had a bunch of racing and even family life on the shows. We won four Golden Moose awards for top shows and bagged some beauties.

Warthog, Namibia, 2014

Maybe the best—no, definitely the best—was one that got away. Kind of.

We were hunting Black Hill Deer in Alaska. They're actually considered a "melanistic deer." You've heard of albinos? Well, the Black Hill is the exact opposite. I made a 480-yard shot on the deer. But before I could get to him, a big ol' Kodiak bear and her cubs came over and started feasting on the corpse.

We watched Mama Grizzly and her cubs eat for six hours, filming it the whole time. Finally, we packed up and retreated, walking out three miles through brown-bear country to get back to our boat. According to Alaska Fish and Game, it's probable that was the biggest black tail ever shot on Kodiak Island. Or would have been, if Mama and her cubs hadn't gotten to it before we did.

It wasn't a total loss, though. That episode won a Big Game Hunt award from the Outdoor Network that year. A shocker, since we weren't a big-game show. And I had to share my kill with the bear.

We also took some great trips for the show. Canada, New Zealand, Africa. Africa was special because Karen came with me.

I killed a puff adder there with an arrow. Not a lot of room for error shooting that snake.

My favorite hunt in the States was to Hawaii, where I ended up stalking cattle—the Vancouver Bull. The story goes that George Vancouver, a British explorer, presented a dozen cattle to Hawaii's King Kamehameha I at the end of the eighteenth century. The king released the cows to the countryside and forbade

Puff adder, Namibia

anyone from killing them. The result was several thousand feral bulls and cows running amok on Hawaii some thirty or forty years later. They are mean creatures, able to climb steep hills, living and thriving in lava fields. They don't moo or bark, they groan. It is an eerie sound, especially when it comes out of the fog.

The first time I went into the outfitter's house, he took me into a room with a bunch of clothes hanging on the walls.

"What's all this?" I asked.

"Every hole you see was gouged by a bull," he said. He went on to tell me stories about the bulls overturning Jeeps and other vehicles.

There was no question at that point that I was getting one. And with a bow.

I love bow hunting. It's a huge challenge. You have to get close to your target, you have to be good with your shot, and you have to be ready to react. It's a test of intelligence and skill, and it has that immediate sense of adventure that I miss from the army.

We went out a short time later. It didn't take long before we spotted one of the bulls. He spotted us as well, ambling in our direction as if to ask, *You want a piece of me?*

I can shoot an arrow from seventy to eighty yards away, but the shot I took on that bull was from a bare eight yards. I was on my knees full draw, waiting for him to step into the opening where I was.

All I could think about was, *Which of these nearby trees am I getting into?* Because I'd been warned—every time one of these bulls was shot, it would charge the hunter.

So *boom*! I release. I drop the bow and *run*!

By the time the arrow landed, I was halfway up the tree. I glanced over and saw the bull running the other way.

He went a short distance and went down. I have his hide on the floor in my trophy den downstairs.

I joke that I learned to shoot a bow on my tour bus. There's truth in that; I got good on the road and during my hunting show, when some sponsors encouraged me to use their products. But I'd first picked up a bow years before in the army. I was stationed at Fort Polk. A buddy of mine lived off base out in the country. We'd go hunting and one day he showed me a bow and I started experimenting. It was quite a while before I got good enough to hit anything for real.

That takes practice, which is why I did it while we were on tour. I could set a target in my room at the back, get up front, and fire down the long aisle between the bunks while we were moving.

The guys used to holler that they were coming out so they wouldn't be hit.

Not OSHA-approved work conditions. But there have been no casualties.

We had a great run with *Craig Morgan: All Access Outdoors*. In 2017, though, I decided to take a break. The time commitments were huge and the show was interfering with everything else I had going. My timing was pretty good—not too long afterward, advertising and sponsors for all outdoor and hunting shows began drying up. Being tired made me look like a genius.

These days, the big sponsorships are in social media. That's a lot easier to pull off, and more lucrative. The show cost as much as a million dollars a year to produce, leaving slim pickings for profit. Post a plug on social media, and whatever you get is all profit.

I've never been as big into fishing as I am hunting, partly because the best times to hunt and the best times to fish are often the same, and of the two I'd prefer hunting. But ten years ago I did a trip to a deep-sea fishing tournament and caught the bug. It's an expensive hobby, which may be a good thing, or I'd probably end up doing it a lot more.

What I really love, though, is catching things like red snapper and your smaller fish, food to take home and grill. Nothing like a grouper you've caught that morning on the grill. Cook it very simply, and it'll be delicious.

I've come to appreciate the ideas of self-sufficiency and sustainability. Fishing for food that you're going to eat—whether it's grouper or freshwater bass, say—is part of that ideal. The same goes for deer, turkey, rabbit. Even squirrel. Having the ability to take care of yourself is so important—I'll always be able to feed myself and my family. I highly recommend it.

But back to fishing—it's something you can do with friends. Kind of like hunting—except you can talk.

RE-UP

In May 2009, the label came out with a reissue of *That's Why*, swapping out "Summer Sundown" and "Every Red Light" for "This Ain't Nothin'" and "Bonfire." We also changed up the order of the songs a bit.

Part of the reason for doing the rerelease was marketing. It gave fans and radio stations a new reason to pay attention to me before it was time to come out with a new album.

The other part of the reason was simple: the new songs were pretty good.

After *That's Why* was first released, I came in with a few new songs. The label execs heard them and their reactions were basically, "Holy $#@%! We wish those were on the record."

Which was a compliment, in a way. Kind of backhanded, though.

Nowadays we would just release the songs as new downloads, maybe put an EP out. But this was before downloads had really taken over.

"Bonfire" was released that May around the time of the album release and it took off. It quickly became a crowd pleaser and party song—especially when you're sitting around a bonfire at night during the late spring or early fall. Kevin Denney, Mike Rogers, Tom Botkin, and I wrote it.

"This Ain't Nothin'" was written by Chris DuBois and Kerry Kurt Phillips. Kerry, whom I'd written "Almost Home" with, sent it to me. That's another song that has a spiritual, or maybe philosophical, dimension. A TV reporter asks an old man how he's going to recover from a twister that's taken down his home.

The old man puts the loss in perspective, talking about real losses he's suffered—his dad, his brother, his wife. It's all about resilience, and keeping things in perspective, especially when the world seems to go to hell.

Good advice for today, I think. We'll get through it, whatever "it" happens to be.

GONE

In 2009, I learned what a difficult, nasty disease pancreatic cancer is. My mom was diagnosed with it toward the end of the year. In a few short months, she slipped from our lives.

I suppose the quickness was a blessing, lessening her struggle and pain. But it caught me, and the rest of the family, short. We always thought we'd have more time with her. I'd hoped to take mom and everyone on a cruise before she died. It was something she loved to do, and I imagined the rest of the family would have loved that time with her. But before we could even make the plans, she was too sick to travel.

My sisters took off work to help care for her around the clock. I visited when I could, but mom, being mom, was adamant about me putting my priority on the job.

"Honey, promise me a couple of things," she said the first time I visited her after the diagnosis. She was lying on the couch, fully alert, but you could tell she was in some pain.

"You name it, Mom."

"Number one, don't quit working. Schedule my funeral around your work."

I didn't know how that might even be possible.

"You can't change anything," she insisted. "You're not going to fix nothing."

"What's the second thing?" I asked.

"Don't fire your brother."

That's my mom, watching out for her kids.

My brother had been working for me as stage manager, and I

guess she sensed we weren't getting along all that well. Not that I was going to fire him—he was (is) my BROTHER. And he wasn't doing a bad job. But Momma did call it. Eventually we did split. The traveling life didn't really fit well with his plans to raise a family. He's done well since leaving, and we probably have a far better relationship now than we did then with all the business hassles and worries out of the way.

The next few weeks after my talk with my mother about her dying were heartbreaking. One day she was up and around, joking. The next, or so it seemed, she couldn't lift herself out of bed.

We were doing a concert July 3, 2010. I had just come off the stage when I got a phone call from one of my sisters. I knew what had happened from the tone in her voice.

Momma was gone. She was just sixty-three.

We had the funeral a few days later in Dickson. Her grandkids were the pallbearers. We laid her to rest in the Tennessee Veterans Cemetery over in Pegram, on property that my grandfather Poppy had once farmed.

She'd worked throughout her life, and kept going close to the time she died. Truth is, she didn't have to work, but she liked having a little extra money to get things for her kids and grandkids. The grandkids, especially. For her last five years or so, she was a cook at a rehab center in Nashville, helping people who were kicking addictions and trying to get on with their lives. That was who she was—a giver to the end.

EIGHT:
NOTHING CONSTANT
BUT CHANGE

GOODBYE SONY RECORDS

We were in the studio recording my second album for BNA and Sony when I heard the news—Joe Galante was retiring. That was a shock for a lot of reasons. He was a young guy, for one thing. And the label seemed to be doing well. There was no hint of conflict and the news seemed to come out of nowhere.

I wasn't too surprised two months later, though, when I got a call from my manager telling me that Sony was dropping me. That's the sort of thing that happens when the top guy leaves and a new person moves in; the label will fulfill its contract (or maybe pay you off to end it), but you're no longer their priority and can't expect much of a future with them. In my case, I think the new guy—for some reason I'm blanking on his name—looked at the signing bonus and everything and just decided they weren't going to recoup the money, so why not just let me go.

I was philosophical. Still am. This happens in our business. When you hang around as long as I have, you get used to it. What's weird, or maybe ironic, is that I was writing for Sony Publishing at the time. As I mentioned earlier, Maypop and its catalog were bought by Sony Music, and my contract came along for the ride. The deal was pretty good, but I knew it would come to an end when the contract ran out as well. So I prepared. As soon as it ended, I started my own company.

As I've said, the only reason a songwriter wants a publishing company—and is willing to share what may be a good chunk of their money with them—is for the publisher to pitch their music and get it cut by other artists. At that point, I was writing with some of the best writers in the business and was friends with plenty of performers. I'd be working with Blake Shelton and Tracy Lawrence and people on that level; I didn't need a go-between to reach them. Performers would talk to me about my songs directly. I don't generally need a plugger—what the industry calls a song salesman—but if there were to be an occasion where I did, I'd simply hire a freelancer. My royalty rights are administered by a company in town I hired. They file the necessary paperwork and handle the recording requests. I have a song I wrote and just played for Luke Combs; if he decides he wants to cut it, he'll give me a call and we'll go from there.

About publishing: Being an artist as well has a downside for a songwriter. Other performers don't want to cut your song because they're scared to death that someone will think the song was available because you didn't think it was good enough to put out yourself.

"Not good enough for him but good enough for me?"

You know what I'm saying? There's a lot to perceptions in this business.

To get around that, for a while at Sony I wrote under a pseudonym—a pen name or *nom de plume* or maybe *nom de chanson*, as the French might put it.

My own.

Yes, Craig Greer. So if you see a song credited to him—a number were recorded, though none burned up the charts—don't be surprised if it reminds you of something by Craig Morgan. The pseudonym didn't last very long. After a bit, I realized people in the business know I just write so darn much I can't record everything, so it was no use pretending.

The ups and downs in the entertainment world can kill you. That's one reason to take an entrepreneurial approach—branching out, having multiple revenue streams, starting your own companies. None of that's easy, but it's key to keeping food on the table.

Cut from Sony and the BNA label but still under contract, I finished recording the album I owed. It never came out. There's a Craig Morgan album somewhere in the archives gathering dust.

In the meantime, I looked for a new label. I had interest from a bunch, including Curb Records, at the time probably the biggest independent. Now they're so big I think everyone considers them a major.

I couldn't find anyone I was truly comfortable with until I met Gordon Kerr at Black River Entertainment. The independent had been started in 2007 by Jimmy Nichols, his wife, Tonya Cochran Ginnetti, and Terry and Kim Pegula. (If you're a football fan, you may be familiar with one of the teams they own, the Buffalo Bills. That's only a small part of their portfolio.) When I signed in 2011, they'd already had some hits with singers like Jeff Bates and Sarah Darling.

I liked Gordon quite a lot. The dynamic at my last independent, Broken Bow, had always been a bit weird for me—Benny Brown wanted you to know he was the boss; he was in charge. Which can kind of grate on a performer, or at least this one. Gordon was entirely different. He wanted you to know that he appreciated you as an artist, and he made it clear that without your success, they weren't successful. It was a 180-degree turn on emphasis.

Look, it goes both ways. The label and the artist have to be successful. And at Black River, I felt truly appreciated. I still consider Gordon a friend.

Gordon's vision for the label was strong, and I had the confidence that they would support me. And they did.

I went back into the studio with Phil and the boys and went to work. The album we came out with was *This Ole Boy*, which got its name from the first song and our first single, written by Rhett

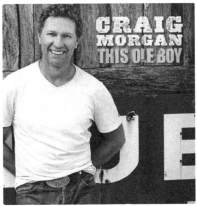

This Ole Boy, 2012

Akins, Dallas Davidson, and Ben Hayslip. The single came out in July 2011, ahead of the album.

Rhett tells a story about being on the road with me to write. He'd given me a demo and left me to listen to it. I woke him up around 5:00 a.m. in the bus singing the words. At that point, he decided it was the perfect song for me.

Rhett told the Taste of Country website that he thought the song felt like it fit me as soon as he heard me singing. He has the perfect songwriter's philosophy: songs go where they need to go. And that one ties in real well with the person I am. He nailed that, and also wrote in a way that fit my voice and singing style.

Can't argue with any of that. And I appreciate his generosity and creativity, not to mention that song.

"Corn Star" is on that album. An awful pun, but a fun pun. It's one of those songs you can't help laughing and singing to.

We released it as a single, and I thought that song was an absolute frickin' hit, and I still do. But the timing of its release was bad. There were a lot of things going on, and the time of year wasn't good. Chart-wise, it wasn't one of my better performers. But I love it. It's one of those songs that fans are going to either love or hate, tongue-in-cheek, don't take yourself too seriously listening to. But at that point it seemed like the world wanted serious songs.

"More Trucks than Cars," on the other hand, *was* a hit, as I knew it would be. The third single off the album, I wrote it with Phil and Craig Wiseman. It was a big response song for us. Even though it only reached twenty or twenty-five on the charts, it gets a huge response when we play it. More of the crowd'll sing along than on other songs that charted higher.

FAMILY

There was a four-year gap between *This Ole Boy* (February 2012) and *That's Why* (October 2008). Most of that was due to the business with Sony and just the amount of time negotiations with labels takes. The boys and I were also touring out the frickin' yang, and finding time to write and create the songs I wanted for the album took a heck of a lot of time. I had so many other things going on, professionally and with the family, that time to do *anything* was severely limited. It's funny— they say you can't rush creativity, but it's even more true that you can't rush life. Even hunting had to be rationed.

That's Why, 2008

The kids were growing up, getting ready for college and settling on life. I tried to spend as much time as I could with them, but it was a strain. Things got to the point where we all sat down and discussed the situation as objectively as possible: Should Dad continue what he's doing? It takes him away from home, but on the plus side, it makes it possible for the family to enjoy certain things.

It was a good discussion. In the end, I continued touring. But I also worked hard to be truly "with" Karen and the kids when I was home. A typical adjustment: We were homeschooling the kids at that point, with Karen doing most of the lessons. I pitched in more when I was around. My lessons included a lot of geography and biology—outdoors stuff that I loved, and that the kids could enjoy as well.

Raising a family is always hard. Fitting the kids in with a demanding job is tough, especially when you need to have two breadwinners. I'm not saying that Karen and I had it any harder than the average American. Once my music career took off, we had it easier in many ways. We were blessed with incredible opportunities and took advantage of many.

But we did struggle to figure out how to give our kids a normal upbringing, how to mix meeting Garth Brooks one day and doing well on the math exam the next. It was similar for me—do a concert Friday night and compete in Motocross on Saturday afternoon. Play for twenty thousand people Sunday and go food shopping at Walmart on Monday.

Ordinary stuff.

I was fortunate to meet some people before I really had a career who warned me what it might be like. Garth in particular with the idea of a stage name, but others as well. As things took off, my wife and I talked about it.

This ain't gonna be a normal life, we told each other.

As the kids grew, we kept trying to make things as "normal" as possible for them. Karen and I wanted them to appreciate the values that we'd grown up with—hard work, thrift, taking care of other people. But I'm sure they'll howl at this: We would occasionally stretch the truth when it came to money issues. At Christmas, we told them they'd get one thing—one largish thing—because we couldn't afford more. Which had been the truth not all that long before. And had been the reality that Karen and I grew up with.

Certain habits—and fears—of money and its lack hang around. Karen was an excellent budgeter. She kept money in envelopes to buy groceries and gas all the years that the kids were in school. And even when they were in college, she had envelopes. We taught them when that envelope runs out, that's all you've got.

As they got older, we went all Dave Ramsey on them, preaching a money-smart life with little debt and a "pay yourself first" approach to income and saving. Alexandra and her husband teach it now themselves. There were rarely moments of splurging. New clothes for school—there was a splurge, but a necessary one. Spending money? The kids got jobs.

Now having said that, as the time came for college, I told them all I would pay. I value education highly, and I felt responsible to provide the best possible for my kids. I wanted them to go into adulthood without any debt, or at least without the crazy debt college can rack up these days.

Again, we tried to be prudent.

"I'll pay for your college, but I'm not paying for everything else," I told them. "If you want to spend a bunch of extra money above the allowance that I'm going to give you, you'll have to work for it. I would rather you not have to work and concentrate on your studies, but I'm only going to give you this much money."

Some of this can come back to bite you. I insisted that the kids drive affordable used cars or trucks rather than brand-new, fancy ones. And when my daughter's car broke down on the way home from college, whose fault was that?

"Dependable" needed to be in that description.

The idea is to be humble, not cheap. One of the biggest compliments my sister has ever given me was this: "In twenty years of you doing this, I never really thought of you as rich. You don't carry yourself as a rich person."

Exactly.

We did shelter our kids early on. We homeschooled them through elementary and junior high, which was a lot of work for my wife. By the time they reached high school age, they needed more opportunities than they could get at home. Jerry went to a private school because he had dyslexia, but the others were at public school. Karen insisted they not get preferential treatment—positive or negative.

Negative? I hadn't realized that was a possibility until they were in school.

"We know your daddy's rich," kids would tell them from time to time, generally when they were looking for something.

Just because you hear me singing on the radio, doesn't mean that I'm rich. And just because you hear me singing on the radio, doesn't mean that I can snap my fingers and do a favor for you.

We talked to them about how people might think or treat them. We discussed the difference between what people thought was real and what was *really* real.

The kids would go with me to a show every so often, and that must truly have been an odd experience for them. My youngest would come off the bus with me and just about run back inside.

"What are all these people yelling at, Dad?" he used to ask.

"They just want to see me," I'd tell him.

Not sure how much of an explanation that was to an elementary school kid.

There were things that can happen to any family, famous or not.

After we adopted Jerry, Karen and I decided that we would tell him about the adoption when he was a little older, giving him the information in an "age-appropriate" way. We were still a way off when someone in church said something to him about being adopted and, well, the timetable changed.

You'd hope people would be a little more aware, especially at church.

Here's another thing Garth Brooks told me about fame: "It's not you who changes as much as everyone around you changing, expecting you to change."

I could never feel rich. I won't ever.

Look, I feel rich in certain aspects of my life. Absolutely. Like family. And I look at my children's lives and where they're at in their lives, with their careers and their kids, I say to myself, I am truly a rich man.

But moneywise? I never measured myself by money when I didn't have it. So I don't now.

It is a damn sight better to have it than not, though.

I mentioned that Jerry had dyslexia. I'd always wondered if I had attention deficit disorder (ADD), now known as attention deficit hyperactivity disorder (ADHD). At its most basic level, it means you have a hard time focusing on different tasks, start a lot of things but often lose interest, and sometimes mess up social interaction. Suspicious, I asked a doctor, who directed me to a website test. I had to answer a lot of questions.

Weird questions. Like, "You're in a room with twelve people, all of them talking. Who do you pay attention to?"

At the end, the test claimed I have ADD. I didn't really pursue beyond that, but if you're looking for an explanation about why I have so many interests in life, maybe it's there.

One way or another, I don't think it has seriously disrupted my life; it's just something I've coped with and possibly occasionally bene-fited from. It may not have helped me in school or in the army, but my *job* in the army, mostly revolving around short stints of high-intensity action, was perfect for me. And getting bored easily as a songwriter and performer means I have to keep reinventing myself for the audience—a requirement in the business rather than a drawback.

You get a lot of intergenerational connections when your extended family lives nearby. Grandkids connecting with grandpa, nephews with uncles, and so on. I grew up with that myself, and my kids had that advantage as well.

My father and Jerry, for instance, were really tight as Jerry grew older. They were also a lot alike—wicked senses of humor. Impossible to spend five minutes with either one without laughing about something. One day, Dad and my uncle Willie started talking to Jerry about fishing, and from then on there was a bond between them all, Dad and Jerry especially.

Fishing became something special for them. Jerry would hunt—Grandpa often subbed in for me when I was out touring—but fishing was what he really loved. No surprise, he got really good at it. It was one place he could really focus. He never took his phone out of his pocket—which is more than unusual for a teenager, especially that one.

Fishing with outdoorsman and good bud John Paul Morris in Missouri

My dad, Uncle Willie, and Jerry must've checked out hundreds of ponds, lakes, water holes—any spot they thought there might be fish. We had a place in the area near Kentucky Lake, Tennessee, just around two hours from Nashville, a bit less from us. They'd go up there and catch bass—or as my dad would say, *anything that'd be silly enough to bite.* Dad would be at the motor, trollin', Willie'd be at the bow with his rod, and Jerry'd be between them, most likely keeping them out of trouble.

They didn't have to catch anything to have a blast. According to my father, one of their best times was a day on the lake where their biggest haul was a bunch of sunk bushes near the shore, where all three of them managed to tangle their lines at once. One of them started giggling, and before long their little boat was just about swamped from all the laughing. How they managed to make it home dry, I don't know.

Looking back, I think I may have been a little too restrictive with the kids, especially as they got older. Having been through so much myself, I was very much aware of the dangers. I know Kyle loved the military and really wanted to join up, but I discouraged him. I didn't want him to get hurt. I felt I'd served enough for all of us. Natural reaction, I guess, but not really fair to him. Now he's turned out fine and he is a man every father could be proud of, but if I could go back in time I'd change a few of the things I said by way of advice.

Some of the moments that I've had and value most as a dad were due to my wife. There was a stretch of shows one summer when one of the kids was moving to school. I'd committed to helping them make the move—but I'd also committed to the shows.

Karen put her foot down. "You have to cancel the show. That's your child, and you're helping."

She was right. Family first.

FILM & TV

Doing videos for my songs kind of got me interested in seeing what I could do in television and film beyond the hunting and outdoor genres. But it wasn't until I was shooting the video for "This Ole Boy" and met Angie Harmon that my interest jelled into something real. Angie and I got to talking, and that eventually led to a chance in Hollywood.

Early in her career, Angie starred on *Baywatch Nights* and had a big role in *Law & Order*. Then came *Rizzoli & Isles*, where she played the police detective Rizzoli. The series was based on detective novels by Tess Gerritsen and mixed some humor in with its drama. Set in Boston, it featured two strong women leads, Detective Jane Clementine Rizzoli and Chief Medical Examiner Maura Isles, a forensics expert. The series was roughly two years into its run when I met Angie. We happened to talk about her show, and I mentioned I'd love to be on it.

She had some conversations with people, and the next thing I knew, I got a shot. I was a guest star in the season-three episode "Crazy for You," first aired in 2012, playing a Texas forensics expert. I walked into my first scene with a big black Stetson and a bit of a twang. My character, Dr. Ray, helped solve a murder, but my biggest scene was probably breaking up a fight, which as a deputy I had plenty of real-life experience with.

Best line?

"If you don't quit it, I'll whip you both so hard you won't be able to sit down for a week."

How many parents have said that? A lot, I'll bet.

Just before I filmed with Angie, I got a part on *Army Wives*. If Dr. Ray was only kind of close to home, my role on *Wives* was right out of real life. I was playing myself, Craig Morgan as Craig Morgan, giving a concert for army families. One of the big hooks for me was the chance to sing two songs, "This Ole Boy" and "Love Loves a Long Night," both from *This Ole Boy*, which had recently come out.

I wasn't exactly a TV virgin when I went Hollywood. I'd been doing hunting and outdoor shows for a number of years, and I'd had my own show on the Outdoor Channel. But acting as someone other than myself, following a script, interacting with other actors in a dramatic piece—those things were all new to me. I understood camera angles and that sort of thing, but I didn't know if I could actually *act*.

Turns out, I can. I'm not ready for my Oscar or Emmy nomination, but I'm working on it.

Your confidence builds after you've done a few shows. It helped that my early roles involved things I already had some knowledge in.

Having worked as a cop, I had more than a little knowledge about how a real one would be in a certain scene. So there were things I could relate to and build on.

For me, finding a connection to the character and the script is key, but not always obvious. In *After the Storm* (2019), my character, Sutter, is the older brother giving advice to a younger brother. That was my way into the role, thinking of my relationship with my own brother. I've been a big brother pretty much my whole life. I read the script and played the character I remembered my whole life.

I had a double role in *A Welcome Home Christmas*: on-screen as Col. Doug Cole, and off-screen as a military adviser, spending a few days on set making sure the look was right, people were in the right place, that sort of thing. I spent a day correcting uniforms, just like I was back in the ranks pulling an inspection.

Call me superstitious, but to me, I don't think I'm *in* a film or show until it actually airs. There are plenty of times an actor's scene will be cut out for one reason or the other. And in that business, so much goes on related to distribution and whatnot, that you never know. Until it's there and I see it for myself, I'm not banking on it.

I have ambitions—I want to do a big thriller, even a Jackie Chan–style movie, and do my own stunts. I can ride horses and motorcycles. So if you're a producer, get in touch.

But my biggest acting role to date had nothing to do with TV or the movies.

UNDERCOVER

I took a trip to hell in the winter of 2016.

There are many terrible places and situations in this world. One of the worst is to be an underage sex slave in Southeast Asia. The problem is pretty well-known. But for years, little was done about it. Even when international news media began to take an interest in the late 1990s and early 2000s, authorities in places like Thailand ignored the very obvious fact that whole blocks and tourist areas in large cities were devoted to bars where children were offered up for every imaginable sex act.

Then sometime in 2010, pastor Matt Parker and his wife Laura relocated to Thailand to head a ministry devoted to poor children in the northern stretches of Thailand. While in the process of reshaping a boarding school there, Matt learned about the problem, and the difficulties the police agencies who weren't bought off had in trying to use the law to combat it. Matt and some others came up with the idea of going undercover to provide evidence. It was a pretty bold move for a guy who'd never been in a strip club, let alone a brothel.

Within a few years, Matt and Laura's mission had expanded into an international effort to combat child prostitution. Working with local authorities and an army of volunteers, they shut down dozens of sex rings, and aimed for more. They called it Exodus Road.

Exodus Road volunteers pose as johns, going to places the local police can't, helping them develop information on the prostitute rings, and then cooperating in arrests. They work in teams, gathering and preserving evidence to make the arrests stick. That's the dramatic bit. The group also plays a big role in educating and rehabilitating the young girls—most are girls, not women—who have had the misfortune of being trapped as sex slaves.

I'd heard a little about the organization from a couple of friends, including Adam LaRoche, the ex-baseball player, and Nate Griffen, who'd been a Ranger back in the day. So when James King, who shot my video for "This Ole Boy," began talking about the photography he'd done for Exodus Road, I was all ears. James touted the group's cause and organization, and suggested they might be interested in any help I could give.

I guess I could have just written a check. But having been trained to work behind enemy lines, in dangerous situations, having been a law enforcement officer besides—writing a check seemed like the least I could do. They needed volunteers to work on the undercover teams. My skills pretty much made me perfect for that.

I wasn't too worried about being recognized. Country music is not all that big in Thailand. Plus, I grew a beard. On top of that—well, let's just say all sorts of people visit those places.

I had a meeting with the organizers. They told me about an upcoming operation. *Want to come?*

"Oh, yeah."

I made some phone calls to friends of mine who'd been in the service, including a Green Beret or two. We put together a small tactical squad of different experts who could handle the necessary jobs, which included communications and surveillance.

We landed in February, and one night made our way to the red-light district of Bangkok, Thailand's biggest city, and then over to an area where brothels cater mostly to Western tourists. While I was concerned for the women who are *actually* women in terms of age and (allegedly) free will, what was most heartbreaking were the younger girls who were being trafficked. And that's who our operation was focused on helping.

I should make this clear: everyone thinks prostitution is legal in Thailand, but it's not. And while there are some women and men who ply the sex trade freely and of their own volition, many, many have either been forced by others to do it or are so desperately poor that they have little choice. A large number of children are prostituted before they are even old enough to know what sex is. In some cases, families "give" young girls to prostitution rings because they can't afford to feed them. Selling the girl means survival for the rest of the family. It's an ugly cycle, and organizations like Exodus Road try to do more than just attack the symptoms.

And this isn't just happening in Thailand. Pakistan, India, other places in Asia and Africa—it's an epidemic.

We began our operation by scouting the area to familiarize ourselves. It didn't take too long to figure out what was going on in most of the places. We'd go into a bar and see some sixty-five- or seventy-year-old Westerner fondling a girl all of fourteen—say, sliding his hand up her leg and doing things too horrific to describe.

Of course, had he been confronted, he would have claimed he didn't know how old she was.

Bull.

One of the nights we were in a club where a group of service members from a particularly elite military unit came in for a big shenanigan party. It didn't take five minutes to figure out who the team leader was. I approached him and told him that they probably didn't want to be in there right now.

"*Who are you?*" he asked.

"It don't matter who I am. And I don't know who you are, but I know enough about what we're doing here to tell you that y'all do not want to be on camera tonight. Or any night."

"Thank you very much."

He gave a signal out and they went, the whole lot. Just to be clear—they were there for the drinks, not the girls, and had shown up at the wrong place. A bar run that could have gone very wrong.

Without going too deeply into Exodus Road's procedures, the idea is to attack the problem at its source. Our job was to locate the person who had brought the prostitute to the bar—the pimp or slaver. That takes a bit of work and a lot of hanging around. You can't appear too inquisitive, but if you never ask questions, you never get answers.

We would set up and get video of the girl, get video of the john, and then, eventually, video of the actual pimp.

Without any of that being detected.

The whole process can take months and involve several teams. Just by chance, we happened to have a case go from absolute zero to apprehension within a few days. Here's how it went down.

One night we went into a bar and got a table. Within a few minutes, a fellow comes over and asks us straight out if we wanted any girls.

"Young girls," said one of our team members. "These ones are too old."

"Come with me," said our guide.

We followed the guy outside and down the street. Now, this was a bit fishy—under other circumstances, I doubt any of us would have gone along, but we had plenty of backup on the street if anything went wrong. The man took us to another bar. On the way in, one of the bouncers gave me some grief because I had a buttpack with me, and I wasn't about to turn it over to him—it was carrying a camera and surveillance gear.

He insisted.

I objected.

He insisted some more.

Our discussion became physical. But there wasn't much to it, really—he was just a little bitty guy.

Unfortunately, the police were called, and I was "arrested"—which meant being taken outside and strongly scolded, warned never to return to that bar again . . . until the next day.

All of which may have helped our cover quite a bit.

The guy who'd brought us there came out after the hubbub and told us not to worry; he knew exactly what we wanted.

After doing a little bargaining, he took out his cell phone and arranged the meet.

"We go to the hotel now," said our guide.

He led us down the street. Here was the deal: for $200 per person (there were four of us), each would get one girl under sixteen years old for the night. They would show us IDs to prove they were under sixteen.

I have to admit, at least one looked like she *might* have been sixteen or even older, but her ID had her at fifteen. The others were all well underage.

I went into a hotel room with the fifteen-year-old. Once inside, she began rubbing my back. While my camera was rolling and I was recording the exchange, things were moving a little too quickly. We needed to set up a team outside and get the police in place. I had to stall.

"You need to shower," I told her.

"Already showered."

"No, you need to do it for me."

The girl went into the bathroom, turned on the water. Turned it off and came back out. Thirty seconds had passed, if that.

She wasn't wearing any clothes when she came out.

Reconnoitering and gathering intel in Thailand. Just to be clear, these young ladies were NOT engaged in anything illegal.

I texted desperately, trying to tell our outside team to get moving. It's amazing how slowly three or four minutes can pass when a naked girl is trying to get your clothes off.

Finally, the local police busted through the door. They arrested the girl, and me, putting me in handcuffs and carting me away—separately from her. The young lady, and all three of her friends, were taken to a sheltered home run by a church as part of a project to provide an alternative to the sex trade.

The police, of course, were in on the operation, and once the girl was gone, I was released. The man who had set this all up had already been arrested outside. He was prosecuted a few months later; I'm not sure what happened to him.

I know what *should* have happened to him.

BUSINESS IS BUSINESS

I didn't tell my managers, or really, much of anyone outside the family where I was going. They were a bit . . . surprised . . . when I got back and told them.

I guess from their perspective there were plenty of reasons why someone in the public eye shouldn't go undercover in a potentially dangerous place. But hell. Why should I tell them? It's none of their business.

I love my guys, but you know, a lot of artists become dependent on their managers and the record labels. Back in the day, the labels and management did everything they could to make the artist dependent on them. There are guys in the business, still, who have no idea how much money they're earning, because they leave all that to management.

I understand. All they want to do is sing and play and write and go tour. And as long as they can buy stuff while performing and recording, they're living their dream.

Not me. I want to know about every penny because it's a business. And not only is my name on the marquee, I'm the one writing the checks.

Not literally anymore. I'm not even sure we're using checks these days; it's electronic transfer this and Venmo that. But you get the idea. I'm the boss, and that means I have to know what's going on. And when it comes to managers—they work for me too. But they don't control my life, or tell me what I can and can't do.

I tell new artists to remember that. And know that if you don't make money, they don't make money. So of course they want you working.

But you need to keep up. There are a lot of little details to be mindful of. Just by illustration, say you're going to do a show where, because of capacity, location, time of week, year, etc., you get $30,000. Good money, especially if you're a young artist on the climb up.

What happens if the place is sold out? You still get that $30,000?

Heck no, not if the right person negotiated the contract. Promoters give bonuses all the time for sold-out shows (and under a lot of other circumstances). If you do a show for $70,000 with a $25,000 bonus for sold-out tickets—where does that "extra" money go?

If you don't know about it, there's a possibility it'll go into a pocket that's not yours.

The point is—it's a business. In my case, I'm the CEO. If they want to volunteer for the next undercover operation, then we'll talk.

But I'd be lying if I said it was easy to separate the business end from the personal. The hardest thing I ever did professionally was let go of my longtime manager, Faith Quesenberry. Faith had been with me since my Broken Bow days, and I can't say enough nice things about her, then or now. She was a hard fighter, and a lady with a lot of class and knowledge. She'd worked in a lot of jobs in the business before moving into management—she'd been a music publisher, a plugger, a publicist.

It wasn't easy for a woman then; probably still isn't. She navigated the sexism crap pretty well. I remember sitting in a meeting with her and the head of A&R for a label. (A&R, which is how it's usually styled, stands for Artists and Repertoire, the company division in charge of finding talent and taking care of artists; I'm going to conveniently forget which label and fellow it was for reasons that will soon be clear.)

The A&R guy looked at her after she said something and told her straight out, "Young lady, your job is just to look pretty."

I thought she was going to take off his head, or some other part of his anatomy. But she had way too much class for that. She just calmly looked at him and shut him up with a sentence: "I'm here to do both—look good *and* represent my client."

And she did. She worked her tail off. But as time went on and my career grew, we got to the point where I needed the resources of a bigger agency, one that could go beyond the music industry. She'd partnered up with Ken Levitan, who was pretty well-known in Nashville, but even that didn't bring things quite to where I needed them to be. We were doing so much, and the opportunities seemed boundless—imagine a string of marinas named Redneck Yacht Club and the possibilities there, thanks to that song.

And so one day in 2014, Faith came in and we sat down to talk. I think she had an inkling, but she was all calm and grace.

"Hey, look," I said. "I just, I think it's time for me to try to move on." I'm not good at beating around the bush, but I don't like to hurt people either, even if it is supposed to be just business.

"Thank you very much," was all she said. We could have been going over receipts, she was that professional and that calm.

Faith wrapped things up and I started interviewing some firms, looking for a company with a lot of resources, which took me to Red Light Management. I met with Gaines Sturdivant in his office in Nashville one day and got to talking.

"I'd love to work with you," he told me. "But I already have a bunch of acts, and I'm afraid I'd be taking on more than I could handle. But we have this guy, Bryan Frasher—"

"Bryan Frasher? Get him up here," I said. I recognized the name from my Sony days, when Bryan had been head of promotions.

We settled on an arrangement where Bryan and Gaines would work together. They have different styles, different ideas, different strengths—and I love that. Bryan is the yin to Gaines's yang, and vice versa. Gaines tends to be more of the quiet professional; Bryan's the passionate bull in the china shop. I figure I have the best of both worlds. The back-and-forth—even one guy saying yes, another guy saying no—has given me a lot of opportunities and broader ideas.

Not everyone's like that in business—some artists and execs get threatened by differing opinions. I like the give-and-take, whether on the creative side or the business side. If you're sure of yourself—and, more importantly, sure of the people you're working with—it's all good.

And they all know, once I make a decision, that's what we're doing.

WHOLE LOT MORE TO ME

My second album with Black River Entertainment was *A Whole Lot More to Me*, which debuted in the top twenty of the country albums charts when it came out the first week of June 2016.

I love that album. Like the title says, I feel it shows a side of me that fans hadn't seen before. The R&B influences came out more in the songs than those from the earlier days.

When I say R&B, I mean everything from early soul music to today's pop. Lionel Richie,

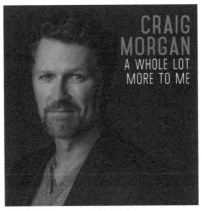

A Whole Lot More to Me, 2016

Luther Vandross—they were influences on me I don't suspect many fans know about. I sing country because I'm a country boy, but I'm a *soul* singer—there's a lot of passion, a lot of emotion in my music. I felt that on that album, we found country songs that were very soulful—super sexy.

There's a range of songs—"Living on the Memories," which I wrote with Scott Stepakoff and Josh Osborne. That was the first song I did with Josh, a very talented writer who's been nominated for a couple of Grammys.

"Hearts I Leave Behind"—I sang it with Mac Powell, who ended up touring with me on my American Stories tour. There's a lot of truth in that song: The singer wants to be his own man, a person who lives by his conscience, who does the right thing and is known for it. He has a strong relationship with God, and he has values that maybe some think are old-fashioned today, but I feel were baked into me as a child. Like the song says, I want to make my mark in the hearts I leave behind: my family, my army buddies, our neighbors.

"Nowhere Without You." That was written by frickin' Michael McDonald and John Goodwin. Doobie Brothers Hall of Fame Michael McDonald. The demo I heard on that song was just Michael singing alone on the piano, real rough and unpolished, but I loved it right away. We didn't release it as a single, but it could have been.

"Remind Me Why I'm Crazy"—Karen loved that song, and that's why it's on the album. I think that was the first song I ever picked for an album because of her.

I remember meeting with the label execs and telling them I wanted to put it on.

They hesitated. The argument against?

"It's too country for country radio."

Ironic, but I know what they meant. Country radio had become very pop-oriented, and the song has an older feel. But it was my wife's favorite. It was going on.

Phil and I wrote it, with Jim McBride.

I got your memory . . . It's a heart-grabber.

The thing is now—I forget a lot of the songs if we're not doing them in the current show, or if they weren't big hits. There are just so many. Some guys are the opposite. They can remember every song they've ever done, where it was recorded, what the weather was. Me, I've never been one to look back. I'm thinking of the next song, and the one after that.

The album opens with "I'll Be Home Soon," which Justin Ebach, Steven Dale Jones, and John King wrote. I think everybody that has to spend any time from home for any reason can relate to that song. The scenes in the music video were shot in Dickson, which is always on my mind when I'm on the road.

The guys are my family when we're touring. We travel in one or two buses, and living close together like that, you have to be a family. I do run a pretty tight ship. There is NO drinking before a show. After a show, after we're packed and everything's good, that's different. But people expect us to be at our best, and we don't purposely do anything that might prevent that.

I think I've loosened up over the years, though. When I started, I was very, very strict. Probably a holdover from being in the military.

How strict?

I hate tardiness. Absolutely despise it. You know, in the military, being on time means being where you're supposed to be five minutes before you're supposed to be there. At least. I fined my guys for not being in the bus at the assigned time. The fine was calculated on the band members' per diem, and it was not a light fine. I remember it being twenty-five dollars a minute at one point.

Jerry Hines came to the bus three minutes late one day. He reached into his wallet and paid up.

Gladly, he claims.

I'm not so sure I remember that part, but we'll take his word for it. Especially since he is my sergeant major/road manager and has been for going on seven or eight years—more by the time you're reading this. He must have a little command sergeant major in him because he has a knack for getting and keeping the show organized and smooth.

People ask how to get into the technical end of the business. Jerry's story is probably typical for a lot of the guys and gals who star behind the scenes, so let's let him tell how he came to work with me.

> *I was in college to be a music engineer. I'd had a job as a dental technician. It was good pay, but I didn't like it. I wanted to be in the entertainment field. So I worked my way through school. Before I graduated, I was supposed to write an essay about what my goals were, why I'd gone to school, where I wanted to work. I listed working in a studio and traveling and working with a couple of artists—Garth Brooks and Craig Morgan in particular, those two guys. That's what I wrote down.*
>
> *I couldn't get a job right out of school, not in music. I was working with my stepfather on a construction crew. My wife had just found out she was pregnant. So life was crazy. I was on top of a building in Dickson, nailing down some shingles. And I got a phone call from Brian Tapley, Craig's road manager at the time.*

*"Hey, I got your number from your instructor in college,"
he said. They needed some help as the monitor engineer on the
road—but he didn't say who the artist was. As a matter of fact,
all he told me was where and when to meet the bus.*

"I'll be there."

*It was a Walmart parking lot. I showed up, got on the bus,
met Brian, stowed my stuff.*

Still didn't know who I was working for.

"Craig's here," said Brian.

I was like . . . Holy—

*That would have been 2004. I've gone from monitor engi-
neer, to front of the house, to production manager, and then tour
manager. There's not an aspect of Craig's tour I don't know or
can't do myself. I could probably even play guitar—badly. Very,
very badly.*

I wouldn't be surprised if he could play, and a lot better than he
thinks.

There have been some . . . incidents on the road. Crazy, crazy
stuff. Like the time a band member—who shall remain nameless to
protect his guilt—came back into my room and proceeded to pee
on the bed.

With me in it.

I woke up and started shouting at him. Then I started laughing.
He'd mistaken the room for the bathroom, obviously due to the fact
that he was less than half-awake.

He did stop right away, and it hasn't happened since.

Then there was the band member—again, we'll protect the guilty—
who decided to commandeer some of my bourbon without permission.
I had Jerry read him the riot act and put him on probation for a month.
In the process, Jerry made it clear I was angry as all get-out, as mad as
I get, probably never to calm down for months. Homicide would be
possible if the guilty crossed my path.

Stern stuff.

Jerry checked on him later in the day, asking where he was.

"I'm having lunch with Craig. He said he needed a ride and invited me to lunch."

I'm not sure whether that violated the terms of his probation or not. Anyway, there were no more misappropriated libations, and the band member's still with us.

I broke my hand racing in 2005. I had to cut the cast off before the shows. The doc seems not to have liked that; when I went back to get a new cast the third time, he gave me a pink one.

If I was as angry as alleged, I seem to have gotten over it pretty quick.

Maturity.

That June, not too long after the start of summer, just as *A Whole Lot More to Me* was going to be released, our daughter, Alex, had a baby boy. So now there really was a whole lot more to me—I was a grandfather.

It was unexpected joy. Nothing I'd worked toward or practiced for, just a shining moment that occurred with no input from me.

I called my grandfather Poppy. My kids called my dad Poppy.

And now, I'm called Poppy.

Makes a man proud.

Me and the family: Karen with baby Cruze, Ryan, Alexandra, Wyatt, Jerry, Kyle, Chelsea

NINE:
JULY 10, 2016

It was an awesome day, gorgeous beyond belief. The kind of day God grants rarely. Azure sky, warm but not oppressive. Perfect July weather.

Perfect day.

July 10, 2016.

My son Jerry and a friend went out on Kentucky Lake to do some tubing. Nineteen years old, in great health, Jerry was looking forward to starting college in the fall. He was a big kid, athletic, an incoming freshman at Marshall University, where he'd be playing football as well as hitting the books.

They hitched a tube to a motorboat. Jerry was in the tube. He was a good swimmer, but he wore a life jacket anyway.

The boat sped forward on the lake.

It was an awesome, dreadful day.

TEN:
LOSS & REMEMBRANCE

THAT DAY

Jerry had called me earlier the week before and let me know he'd be coming home from school on Friday morning, earlier than he'd planned. He wanted to surprise his momma, and I agreed not to tell Karen that he'd be in early.

Wyatt, Alexandra, and her son were in that weekend, and we were all sitting there in the kitchen that morning. There was a knock on the door, and I went to answer it, knowing who it was. Karen's back was turned, and she couldn't see.

"Turn around," I told her.

"Who's here at six in the morning!" She was indignant.

Finally, I got her to turn around and Jerry had the fun of his surprise,

Jerry as a baby

stepping in and hugging his mom. He let her know how special she was to him, a thing he had a knack for. He'd absolutely beefed up in the few weeks he'd been gone, getting ready to play football for the college team.

That night, Jerry went with me to the Grand Ole Opry, where I was doing a show. The hour it took to get to Nashville was my hour with him; we talked and we joked. I don't know if you remember, but at the time there was a bit of a craze over a dance move called the "dab." There's not much to it—you turn your upper body slightly, slant your left arm upward and tuck your head behind the right, as if you can't bear to look at what the left arm is angled at.

"You're too old to do that," he told me.

Really?

I called him out on that—onstage. He was over in the wings, smiling his big Jerry smile. He came on out and we all had a great laugh over it.

I believe the audience sided with me: I was and remain capable of doing the dab.

Afterward, I had to hop on the bus to do a show Saturday. I hugged him and kissed him, told him I loved him, and left.

I've thought a lot about that. Maybe I could have been there, that Sunday. You think about things you might have changed, you might have interfered with, as if there were a way of getting the better of God, or Fate.

It's a foolish thought, but it's always there.

Sunday I was back home and out back at our pool, enjoying the sun with Karen and our guests. Jerry and I texted back and forth; I didn't want him to go back to school without spending a little more time with us.

"We're just about to get out of the water," he told me. "We'll have something to eat and then come down to the house."

Not too much later, around four o'clock, I got a phone call from a friend of mine in law enforcement who told me there'd been an accident on the lake. Jerry had gone under, and they couldn't find him.

We all got in the car and headed there, probably doing a hundred miles an hour. Part of me was sure that Jerry was on the shore somewhere, playing a good joke on his friends.

But another part of me, a deeper part, knew he was gone from us. Karen felt the same.

It was a circus when we got there. Media was camped out around the lawn, which happened to border state property. Eventually we went out in a boat and joined the search; by that time, it was pretty hard to think Jerry might be doing any of this as a joke.

I'd been involved in searches before. I knew how these things went. My main hope was that he didn't end up in the river, where his body might be taken Lord knows where.

I also knew that I was causing a distraction. Because of who I was, so many people wanted to help or gawk, which made it difficult for the actual search. I talked to the sheriff, whom I knew from back in Dickson—and made a deal: We'd leave, which would make things easier for him and his people. When they actually found Jerry, they would let me know and allow me and Karen to be there when he was recovered.

"You have to promise me," I told him, "that I take him out. I'm his daddy, and it's my responsibility to get him out."

The sheriff agreed.

By the time we got back home to Dickson, the kids were on their way or had already arrived at the house. We sat and waited and prayed and thought endlessly about whatever little thing we could, always coming back to the shock of grief and the prayers to God.

Then finally the call came that we'd dreaded but knew was inevitable.

The sheriff sent an ambulance and some of his people to part of the lake; the media saw that and headed there, but it was actually a decoy to give us a little space.

Karen and I went to another cove. I went down in the water. Jerry's hands were clasped and he had a peaceful look on his face. He gazed upward, as if glancing toward heaven.

Karen kissed him on the head. We placed him in the ambulance and said our goodbyes.

I don't remember much of the funeral. There were so many friends, country stars, people whom Jerry had inspired somehow . . .

Karen spoke. Not only did she speak, she inspired, talking about the power of faith, reminding us all of the opportunity faith provides not just for salvation but for meaning. Her confidence that Jerry was with God filled each one of us with hope for ourselves.

There are still days I wake up and think he's there. I still take private moments to cry or get angry, going through the different phases of grief.

We've struggled through. My son Wyatt said it best: "We live with the suck."

I think about Jerry as soon as I wake up, and he's the last thing on my mind when I go to bed. I knew from the moment I saw him that there was something special about him. I also knew that there might come a time when we had to give him back. I didn't realize that it would be this way, at this time, at God's direction, not Social Services. But I'm very grateful for the nineteen years we had him.

Karen, me, and Kyle at his wedding, shortly after Jerry died

SPOONS AND REALITY TV

I took some time off after Jerry died. We all did.

I didn't shut down, but I didn't give myself the effort that I should have. I didn't stay in shape. I didn't go work out. I didn't eat properly.

I might go three days and not eat a bite. And then gorge on food for two or three days. My mood just went up and down.

I shouldn't have done that. I could have worked harder to keep my physical and mental health in order. Whatever I did or didn't do, my son was dead. That wasn't going to change.

One day I was out in my shop, just hanging out, grieving unconsciously. I had a piece of wood and I started messing with it, shaping it down with a lathe and some other tools. I'd fiddled with wood since I was a kid in my dad's cabinet shop. Summers I worked for Dad and he did some beautiful, artistic stuff, but that was him, not me. I've piddled to some degree, but the things I made were like bookshelves or tables, everyday things, and that was back when I was younger, just starting out. We couldn't afford to buy those things, so I'd make them. Nothing super fancy, just something to be used.

That day, I made a bowl. A simple bowl.

Then I made a spoon, and suddenly I started making a lot of spoons. I hadn't set out with a plan, and I hadn't really thought about bowls or spoons. I began noticing that there was a beauty to their simplicity. The curve of the wood. The grain. There can be art in a spoon.

I made some more.

Then came charcuterie boards—wooden boards where you lay out cheese, prosciutto, salami, and other things to nibble on at a party. The boards can get very elaborate, but mostly what you're doing in all of these is letting the wood speak. You're a sculptor, finding Nature's art hidden behind the bark or the years of wear and weather.

The woodworking was therapeutic. There's something about using your hands and making things that gives you purpose. It's as if you set your sights on something beyond you—like a military mission—and you forget about your cares and troubles to achieve that goal.

The woodworking also taught me patience. I'm a do-it-and-get-it-done kind of guy. Still am, but I used to be far worse. Things were good as long as they were done. That's not true when you're making something from wood. Even a spoon. There are stages you have to go through: finding the right piece, making the rough cuts . . .

Join two pieces of wood for a board? You glue them together, then you let them sit for twenty-four hours, at least, before you can go back and cut out the design. That's patience—and learning to progress in steps.

Thinking about it now, maybe that's had an influence on my recent career. Starting out, I approached music like a military mission—mission accomplished, move on. Now I have a longer view—and I'm more aware of trying to stop and look around and enjoy the moment. Which ties into life. I love what we've done with our kids, but if I could have found a way to enjoy them just a little more, that would be a bonus.

But I was talking about spoons.

I had a bunch, along with bowls and boards, when Alexandra decided it'd be a good idea to sell a few on Facebook as a kind of family business.

It took off.

Wooden spoons

Charcuterie boards

One day not long after we'd started, Karen, Alex, and I were driving in downtown Dickson. Alex spotted the corner Dickson Furniture building and realized it was empty.

"We should see about getting that building," she said.

Her idea was that we would open up a physical store.

We started talking about it as a family. I could see the value of a physical store, and I wanted it to be in Dickson because we were proud of what was going in town. COVID aside, it's gone through a bit of a renaissance over the past few years or so. I'm prejudiced, but I think my hometown is a fun place to visit and an even better place to live

Downtown Dickson, before my time . . .

I share a lot of memories with the place. There's the old hatchery building, a performance space since I don't know when—before my time, certainly, because I did shows there in the very early days. There's Lugo's, a five-star restaurant where I'll take my wife for a special occasion. (Save room for dessert.) Fussell's, where all the boys in town go for their prom tuxes.

Our idea wasn't just to sell the things I was making, though that was

a big part of it. We would sell things from our farm, especially our honey. We would also sell crafts from other family members, along with a few things from local artists and craftspeople. Some would be made from recycled or repurposed material like old wood. The general theme would be organic or handmade, somehow in tune with Nature. I see reusing old wood or growing your own vegetables or things like that as an expression of self-reliance. America was built on that spirit, and it's still deep in our bones.

We weren't selling bowls or spoons—we were selling art. Paintings. Candles. And the stories behind that art. Pieces made from an old barn or a Christmas tree. Pieces that would have new stories, and new meanings for the people who bought them.

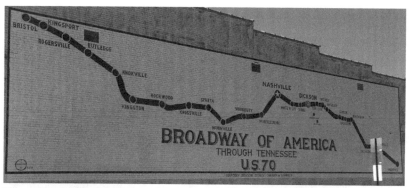

The mural on the side of the Gallery at Morgan Farms building shows just how connected Dickson is to the rest of Tennessee.

Located at the corner of Main Street and College Street, pretty much in the middle of the historic business district, the building my daughter spotted—123 North Main—was a fine old 6,550-square-foot building that unfortunately hadn't had a lot of attention in recent years as people's shopping habits changed. It needed a lot of work. We ended up getting a good-enough price to buy it, and went about renovating

We're not sure who the young lady is, but the old sign behind her confirmed our suspicions that people had shopped there whether they were coming or going.

it, cleaning it up, shoring it up, and generally bringing it into the twenty-first century.

We made a few discoveries along the way. One was a sign on the outside that declared it was the Dickson Furniture and Undertaking Company. They had customers coming and going.

The businesses were owned by separate families, though they must have been pretty close. Both did well enough that the undertakers moved to a new building a short walk away in the 1940s. The upper story was renovated, adding a floor to what had been a mezzanine in the middle of the building as they expanded. In the 1980s, the family that had owned the building got out of the furniture business and leased the

The Morgan Farms logo

space. It was everything from a dress shop to an antiques mall. Along the way, walls were added, coats and coats of paint applied.

We tore most all of that away. I went to work with my jackhammer, tearing off the old plaster to reveal the hundred-some-year-old bricks.

I was stoked, working that jackhammer.

We got it all done and opened the Gallery at Morgan Farms in September 2017.

In the meantime, the family was working on another project—a reality TV show.

I'd been approached a few times about doing a reality TV show that would focus not just on me, but the family and all that we do. The timing hadn't been right, but just before Jerry's accident I'd had a new offer.

Jerry's death put that on hold, but now I thought it might be a good idea. There was some opposition—Karen really was reluctant. But we took a vote, and the majority were in favor.

Having the physical store would give the show a lot more focus. There'd be something specific to focus on instead of just filming our

Morgan Family Strong, 2018

family in different places. The store was something about us all trying to do something together and deal with Jerry's death.

I'm a big advocate for the idea that you have to stay busy to deal with misfortune and grief.

The show was *Morgan Family Strong*, and it ran for five episodes on UPtv, beginning in March 2018. The episodes included everything from me recording a new song to a party for my two-year-old grandson Cruze.

The first episode caught viewers up on some of who I am—a little touch of my military background, some nice snippets of the family. I'd decided to take them with me on the road for my American Stories tour, and the crew filmed us doing a typical concert with the band. My producer/songwriter/good friend Philbilly joined us for a bit, along with some other friends from the music business and the military. Of course, my road manager and "lean-on," Jerry, was there, ushering us all into order. They even caught a little bit of me in my mobile woodshop—the back of one of our trucks, outfitted with some basic woodworking tools.

True confession: Karen hates being on the road, but we had a secret weapon—we brought Cruze, which made it impossible for her to refuse. Karen may even have liked being with him more than being with me.

The one person who was with each one of us the whole time was Jerry, son and brother, uncle and friend. We made sure to have a picture of him alongside us when they took a shot of the family. His spirit was strong with us, onstage and off.

It's a little amusing hearing the media try to describe me, as they have to preview or talk about shows like that. *Country star. Eighteen top-ten songs, three number-ones. Soldier.*

Add family man to that.

Father. Grandfather.

Husband. Man of faith.

Someone mentioned, *Guy next door.*

I'll take that.

The TV show followed us around as I performed, as we got on with the store, and as we worked on new music. They even included me doing some dad stuff, like trying to get one of the kids to budget his money.

There were visitors, fans, neighbors—a slice of life, every show. The times when people would come in and talk about the loss of their own family members was really heartwarming. Talking about how much Jerry means to us, how he'd changed our lives every day when he was alive and was still enriching us—I nearly always teared up.

It was amazing how much of an impact Jerry had on other people, and still has. He was just a happy, giving kid. Dads are supposed to be models for their boys, but I am sincere when I say he's a model for me.

UP's finale showed Alex debuting at the Grand Ole Opry singing with me. Alex has a real talent for songwriting and singing. I didn't want to be the dad who pushed his kid too hard or unfairly, but I believe in

My daughter and me during an interview for our show in 2018

Kyle, Alexandra, and Wyatt on *Morgan Family Strong*, 2018

her, and when the opportunity came up to have her perform with me at the Opry, I was happy she accepted. Alex told the camera backstage that she was worried about walking out there, opening her mouth to sing—and having nothing come out.

No need to worry. She came out and absolutely nailed it. As far as making music a career, though—I think she's been so busy being a mom and raising a family that it's one of those things that's not really on her radar, at least at the present.

That same night at the Opry, I called my friend Josh Ferguson and his family out onto the stage. Josh was a local boy. He'd been in the military for twenty years. While he was in Iraq, he was severely injured by an IED, or improvised explosive device.

The explosion cost him his lower leg, but Josh and his family have persevered. I'd met him at the store sometime before. Myself and a few other veterans would gather once a month to talk about different things—not just military service or ailments, though if you had something you needed to talk about, it was the perfect place. It was all informal, with just a dozen or fewer guys coming around and hanging out. It may have been therapy for some. It certainly was for me, talking about some of what happens as a soldier that people who haven't served or seen combat may not be able to understand.

I had been working with a group called Operation Finally Home that honors veterans by building them houses. I knew Josh would be a perfect, deserving person to honor, and we surprised him and his family after I brought him out onstage to have the audience thank them for his service and sacrifice.

There wasn't a dry eye in the house.

Except for Josh's. He told us later he was so overwhelmed, it was like a dream.

That last episode was packed with highlights. One was Cruze's birthday, which was filmed while I was on the road in Florida. Even though I missed being there, I was not only able to FaceTime the family to join in the celebration, but I got the crowd I was performing for to sing happy birthday too. He may not remember it, but I will.

Retail's tough, but the pandemic in 2020 made it impossible in a lot of places, including downtown Dickson. The whole area basically shut down for two or three months. There was hardly anyone on the streets. I don't know how any of the places down there survived.

At that point, we decided the Gallery at Morgan Farms as a physical location had run its course. We were trying to sell art at a time when people were worried about necessities. With all my other commitments and everything the family had to do, it had just become too much. So we sold the building and moved the online and mail order part of the operation into the back rooms.

We also do custom pieces: Let's say there was an apple tree that someone's grandfather planted, and now it's died. We can take a log off of it and I'll make something special for them.

Me, personally.

Spoons remain big. Bowls. And charcuterie boards. Even without a physical store, the demand for things can get ahead of me. Which sometimes means the separation between things I do for us and the things I do for other people becomes a little less separate. I had a beautiful, big charcuterie board made out of a one-inch slab of black walnut. It had nice marbling. We had it in the house and we all liked it. But we were running low on stuff. And Richie, our store manager said, "Hey, if you can bring something down . . ."

So I have to make another one sometime.

THE FATHER, MY SON, AND THE HOLY GHOST

Surviving after loss is often called "healing," but that word implies a process where a wound is made whole and disappears. In my experience, that's not what happens.

Oh, you heal a bit. But it's not like you replace the pieces you've lost. New limbs don't grow. The hole in your soul doesn't get replaced.

Jerry had been gone almost three years in January 2019 when one night Karen and I lay down to go to bed. I kissed her good night and she started crying. I knew exactly why.

After you lose a child, any sense of joy or love you feel comes along with a sense of guilt. You feel like I should not be happy because you've lost a child.

I should never be happy. Jerry's gone.

It's a tangle to struggle with. I know Jerry wouldn't want us to be sad. He was all about making people happy. That's what his love was. He had so much of it.

But the sadness doesn't go away.

I struggle to find a balance. There are days of suffering, and others where I know it's OK to feel the joy just in life.

That night, when Karen hugged me, she cried out of the suffering. I felt it, too, but I kept my eyes dry. I didn't want to hurt her any worse, and I knew my crying would do just that. We went to bed, falling off in our own cocoons of grief.

I woke up early—I'm an early riser anyway, but that morning it must have been 3:00, 3:30 a.m. when my eyes opened and my legs said, time to go.

I gave Karen a kiss and made my way to the kitchen. I poured myself a cup of coffee, my mind riffing on the idea that it was a cup of get-me-up rather than a dark liquid from roasted beans.

There was a lot of emotion in me, from that moment with Karen the night before, and all our months moving through the pain. I took the coffee and walked out to the living room with my guitar.

And something just happened. That emotion and a tune, words—it was more my emotion coming into a song. God talking through me, in a way.

Now, I've woken up with ideas or a melody before. I've felt like I dreamed something in a song. I've written it down—I have a pad by the bed for notes, though with the technology now, it's just as easy to grab your phone and hit record, mumble, tell yourself to finish it in the morning.

There was something about this, though, that made me feel like I had to keep going. I needed to get the whole idea down.

I kept working on it. I was afraid if I stopped, I might forget. I *would* forget.

I recorded the lyrics as they came to me.

I know my boy ain't here but he ain't gone . . .

Some of the words are exactly what I did that morning, right out of life—poured myself a cup of "wake-me-up." And some are from every day:

My God.

He gave me hope . . .

It got to be six, six thirty. Karen was up by then, but I guessed she'd heard me and didn't want to disturb me while I was working. I went upstairs and found her in the bedroom. I told her I'd just written a song.

"Are you all right?" she asked.

"Yeah, yeah."

I didn't say I wanted to play the song for her. She didn't ask, so I didn't. Writing a song is pretty much a regular occurrence in a song-writer's house; nothing special. And I wasn't sure I was ready to play it for her.

I called Alex and told her I wrote a song and she asked to hear it.

"I don't have even a work tape. Just what's on the phone."

"Well, go ahead and send that," she told me.

I sent it. She called back in a few minutes, crying. "Oh my God, Dad. This is great. This is big. You need to record it."

I didn't know that I wanted to do that. It was too personal, too raw.

A few days went by. I went back on the road, to do a show in Colorado. I played it for my bandleader Mike and I think Jerry, my road manager.

They liked it. A lot.

The other guys heard it, and we worked it together a bit. I played it that night for a smallish audience, a private show.

I couldn't finish. I don't know how far I got, but I was so choked up I just couldn't finish.

That's never happened to me. But those people were great. They stood up and started clapping. I think that ovation lasted a good five minutes. It felt like forever.

We finished the show. Afterward, a couple came up to me with tears in their eyes and thanked me. They'd lost a son themselves. The music had touched them in a way they'd never felt.

"It gives us so much hope," the wife said to me.

A month or so later, we were back in Nashville. I had a show at the Grand Ole Opry, and I decided to try singing it there.

Truth is, I didn't know if I could. My heart hurt so bad when I sang those words. There's a lot of hope in that song, a lot of love—but it hurts to get it out.

I told Mike I wanted to try it. The band was up for it.

Lights are shining bright
as always downtown on the road
I have friends that come from outta town
Asking me to go
They say, "There's so much going on
Why don't you come along and show us around?"
I tell them Karen's not feeling well

So I probably shouldn't go out
Besides I've got a fix-it list of things
I need to do around the house
Then I hang up the phone
Turn the radio back on, and sit back down
I know my boy ain't here but he ain't gone

In the mornings I wake up, give her a kiss, head to the kitchen
Pour a cup of wake-me-up and try to rouse up some ambition
Go outside, sit by myself but I ain't alone
I've got the Father, my son, and the Holy Ghost

I've been beat up
I been pushed and shoved
But never ever really knocked down
Between Mom and Dad, Uncle Sam and friends
I somehow always pulled out
But the pain of this was more
Than I'd ever felt before, yeah I was broke
I cried and cried and cried
Until I passed out on the floor
Then I prayed and prayed and prayed
Till I thought I couldn't pray anymore
And minute by minute, day by day
My God, He gave me hope
I know my boy ain't here but he ain't gone

In the mornings I wake up, give her a kiss, head to the kitchen
Pour a cup of wake-me-up and try to rouse up some ambition
Go outside, sit by myself but I ain't alone
See, I've got the Father, my son, and the Holy Ghost
I hope, I love, I pray, I cry
I heal a little more each day inside
I won't completely heal till I go home

In the mornings I wake up, give her a kiss, head to the kitchen
Pour a cup of wake-me-up and try to rouse up some ambition
Go outside, sit by myself but I ain't alone
I've got the Father, my son, and the Holy Ghost

One day I'll wake up and I'll be home
With the Father, my son, and the Holy Ghost

We did it, and I kind of got through it—I was pretty choked at the very end.

I walked off the stage and Ricky Skaggs grabbed me by the shoulder. There were tears running down his cheeks.

"Son, that's beautiful," he said.

"I'm glad you got to hear it," I told him. "Because I don't think I'll ever do it again."

Ricky pulled me close.

"You have to do this song," he told me. "You have to. There are people who need to hear this song."

I'll never forget those words or his face, so full of conviction. I sent the tune to my good friend Blake Shelton and a few other friends. Blake had lost a brother, and I wanted him to hear it. I wanted his thoughts—Blake is one of my best friends as an artist. As far as singers go, he's probably my number-one call. We've been friends for fifteen, eighteen years; if I need an opinion on anything, he's top of the list.

But he didn't say anything.

My managers, on the other hand, insisted I record it. So I got the guys together and I called up Sonya Issacs, who's such a great singer, to come on in and help.

We did it up. When Sonya was done, she started talking to me, and mentioned that she'd lost a child herself.

Damn. I knew that. I hadn't thought about it. I felt like . . . an idiot. But she was gracious, generous with her spirit as well as her voice.

It was recorded. What was I going to do with it, though?

The answer was put it on an album. It happened that I was working on a new one for Broken Bow.

Yes, the same Broken Bow I had left a few years before. It wasn't the same label though. The people there were mostly different. Benny Brown was gone—and again, despite our differences, I have to say I owe him a lot. But now there were newer attitudes, different ways of doing business—positive, future-oriented ways. The people there wanted me and appreciated what I could bring. Broken Bow was also now part of BMG, a global publishing and recording company, which could offer me a number of different opportunities. So things had sort of fallen into place when I decided to sign a deal with a new label.

We'd worked hard recording the new songs over the past several months. The release schedule had already been drawn up.

Those plans got ripped up when the label heard the song. They scrambled to release it as a single and in the meantime reshuffled the album.

Fox & Friends very generously invited me to perform the song the same morning it released. When the show was over, I bid my goodbyes and figured my work was done. I flew to Alaska and went off the grid.

ELEVEN:
PEACE & POPULARITY

ALASKA

I've been going up to Alaska for twenty-five years. If you like the outdoors, if you like hunting, if you like fishing, if you like testing yourself against Nature or just communing with it, Alaska can't be beat.

I had a friend I'd met while performing up there years back, and I told him I'd be happy to do a show anytime—as long as he got me hooked up for a bear hunt. Sure enough, I got a call almost right away. "We got a bear hunt," he told me. "You do this little acoustic thing for us, and then we hunt bear."

I was there.

Visiting every so often to hunt wasn't enough, and eventually I decided I wanted a place. It had to be far up, located for good fishing and hunting, and not too expensive. It also had to be a place I could bring the family.

I guess I had high expectations, because it took about a year and a half of looking before I finally found something suitable. Fifty acres. It had a little cabin and was right on a lake.

Salmon fishing with NBA great Karl Malone in Alaska

I bought the place the year before Jerry died. I was sure he'd love it. He was at a summer camp and I FaceTimed him to show him the whereabouts. Just about everyone else in the family liked it too. Wyatt was the exception. He doesn't like the cold. Funny thing is, he's moved to Minnesota now, where it is freaking freezing in the winter.

When I say the Alaska place is off the grid, we're definitely talking off the grid. It takes an hour flight in a small plane out of Anchorage to get to a place where you can either fly for another forty-five minutes or drive for three hours, then hop on snowmobiles for a half-hour trek to the cabin.

The kids say that last stretch is more like an hour, but they move slow.

The place came with a tiny cabin perched five or six feet off the ground. I decided I wanted a larger cabin where we could fit the whole family and whatever friends we had brave enough to visit with us.

I also decided I'd surprise Karen with it.

We planned a full family trip—with the crew from the TV show along for the ride. Karen had no idea until she walked over the threshold that it was ours.

It's not huge, but it's a nice size for a log cabin, twenty-two by twenty-four feet, with a loft, and even has indoor plumbing. Of a sort. The indoor plumbing consists of a compost toilet, since there's no running water. (Water runs plenty at the lake; you just have to fetch it.) The only downside to the facilities: It's pretty easy to hear what's going on in there. You have privacy as far as visuals go, but sounds are another matter.

We're planning to put on an extension, and add another cabin as well—plenty of room for the family or friends when they join me.

One of my proudest accomplishments was getting Alaska to name the lake Jerry Lake after our son. The neighbors had agreed, and now it's a permanent memorial to him.

We get some good snow—high enough to cover the porch, several feet off the ground. The family and I go up there and we get away from everything. There's no electricity, no cell connection, no communication with the outside world without doing serious traveling. Karen will hang out and cook, do a little quilting, knitting, and whatever. I'll do a little fishing. I don't do much hunting when she's up there with me because that can take me away from her for days at a time. Especially if you're hunting a moose. Even with a

Paddleboarding on Jerry Lake, 2020

scout, how long it takes to find the trail and catch up with your prey depends a heck of a lot on the moose.

I like the self-sustainment aspect of being far north in Alaska. Hunting or fishing for food, cutting wood for fuel. I love knowing that no matter what happens—for the most part anyway—I can survive. And I can take care of the people around me.

Our family, Alaska, 2017

Karen and me in Alaska, 2017

A HIT BEYOND ALL HITS

The trek back to the rest of the world takes longer than the ride away. You know you're getting close when the cell phones once more pick up the towers.

My phone didn't just light up on that trip back—it practically exploded. Usually there are bunches of texts and voice mails from friends and industry people. This time there weren't bunches, but hundreds.

I started checking my voice mails. Management wanted me to call ASAP. So-and-so needed an immediate callback. And on and on. I gave my road manager, Jerry, a call, to find out what was going on.

"Dude, you're not going to believe what's going on with the song!" He was just about shouting.

"Huh?"

"Dude, you're number five, most downloads in the country. And it looks like it's going to be number one."

"Great."

To be the number-five download in country music on iTunes is truly great. To be trending toward number one is even better.

"You don't understand," added Jerry. "Number one in everything. The most downloaded song in America. All genres. EVERYTHING!"

"The Father, My Son, and the Holy Ghost" had blown up and gone viral.

My performance of the song at the Grand Ole Opry had been recorded and had been making the rounds among other musicians and fans even before we went into the studio to formally record it. Word of mouth—and social media—was phenomenal, boosting it up and raising anticipation for the download.

My friend Blake Shelton kicked up a firestorm by tweeting that country radio should play "Father" instead of his songs. An incredibly generous statement, given that he had his album *Fully Loaded* and its singles out at the time. To say nothing of his earlier songs.

Then Blake got other friends to tweet. Gwen Stefani, Ellen DeGeneres, Kelly Clarkson—I have no idea how many of his personal contacts took up the torch, but they started a bonfire. There were other tweets from friends, musicians, singers, and thousands of people I'd never met. The song touched them in the way it touched me.

The song got attention in other places like Facebook, liked and forwarded and copied and just in

Sharing some wine and laughs with Larry the Cable Guy in 2018. (The comedian, not the fellow who messed up your TV.)

general passed on. I always talk about writing from emotion. In this case, I'd gone so deep that I had tapped into an emotion way beyond my own.

I called Blake. "Dude, what have you done?"

"Nothin."

"You blew up my song."

"When did you write this?"

"I sent it to you a month ago."

"This is the biggest song I've ever heard in my life. Wow. This song deserves to be number one forever."

"Well, man, thank you."

"Where are you?" Blake asked.

"I'm in Alaska."

"You better get home. All hell's breaking loose."

We'd planned to spend another few days before coming back to Tennessee. Was it really worth coming home early? I called my managers.

"Can you come home right away because so-and-so wants you on their show."

I forget which show they meant, because there turned out to be so many of them. *The Today Show*, *Ellen*, and shows I'd never heard of. Everybody so graciously and generously wanted to invite me on to sing the song. The only one thing I could say was, "Hell, yes."

I accepted a lot of the invitations, but I had trouble with that song at every performance. The hardest may have been on *The Kelly Clarkson Show*, when my knees started shaking before I was halfway through. I started to feel a little light-headed and I almost passed out.

It takes so much energy to keep my grief tamped down while I sing that one. It's physical—a little like popping a rib, or taking a hard shot to the side. It hurts to breathe, let alone sing. I don't do the song at every concert; I can't. I couldn't. Even in a place like the Grand Ole Opry, where I feel at home and comfortable, the song just pulls so much out of me that I feel like I need a blood transfusion when I come offstage.

But I keep singing it.

I've learned to be careful where I look. If I see someone tearing up in the audience, my own emotions get riled, so I fix my gaze somewhere else.

The song remains popular beyond belief. As my tour manager Jerry had predicted, it hit number one as most downloaded song across all genres. Just the official video on YouTube has over two million views. The statistics jump up every day.

But I very quickly came to realize more's going on than the numbers capture. I had no idea that morning when I tried to rustle up some ambition that God was doing this to help other people who are dealing with grief. The first hint came on the flight home from Alaska when I scrolled through some of the comments people were sending or leaving about the song. It took just about the whole flight to go through them all.

"What's wrong?" Karen asked at some point over the Rockies.

"Nothin'."

"You've been cryin'."

"I'm not."

I reached to my face and realized she was right; the tears were rolling down.

The comments were shaking me up so badly that Karen finally told me to put the phone away, and not read them.

"Don't put yourself through that," she said, knowing that every time I read a comment, I thought of Jerry and felt his loss.

"I feel like I'm supposed to. People took the trouble. They want somebody to read it."

Ninety percent of the comments started with words along the lines of: "I don't know if Craig will ever see this, but I felt as if I had to write and tell him or someone what this song has done for me . . ."

I've had other songs that have strong emotional responses. "Almost Home," for example. But nothing comes close to "Father" in volume or intensity.

We played the Washington State Fair one year. Nice show. Big audience. After the performance, we had an album signing. As people lined up with their CDs, I spotted a young man kind of hanging back to the side. I could tell from the way he stood that he had a prosthetic leg. I motioned for him to just come on over, but he shook his head.

Finally at the very end, he walked over and handed me a CD to sign.

"I just wanted you to know your music saved my life," he told me. "Twice."

"Twice?"

"I was in Iraq and we were driving down the road in a Humvee, listening to your music on a CD player. I set it down. 'Paradise' was playing."

"The first single I got on the radio," I said.

(For the record—"Something to Write Home About" was actually the first; "Paradise" was the second. But "Paradise" was apparently on my mind.)

"I was listening to it and it skipped or something. I reached down to see what the matter was and a bullet shot through the window."

The bullet would have struck him, had he not ducked down.

"Holy cow." I didn't know what else to say. "Well, on that, wasn't my music or me. That was God."

"Yeah. But I was listening to that song."

"Fair enough."

"Fast forward to 2000," he continued. "I was at my house. I was struggling bad. I had picked up my pistol. I had pulled the hammer back on it. I'd stuck it up to my mouth. And then this song came on the radio called 'Almost Home.' I listened to it. And I put the gun down."

Couldn't really say much after that.

"That was God," I told him.

"Yeah, but God used your music to save my life twice." He didn't say anything about his missing leg, though I'd guess that was why he'd been in despair.

"I just wanted you to hear the story." He let me know God must have some special assignment for him, keeping him alive as he has. "Will you sign my CD?"

"You bet."

We took a picture.

"The Father, My Son, and the Holy Ghost" has been like that, only more. The stories go on, over and over. There are people who hear the song and react to it, not because they lost a loved one, but because they feel a struggle with their faith. I had a man tell me he hadn't prayed or gone to church in years and years.

"I dropped my daughter off at school," he said, "and I heard this song. I pulled over to the side of the road and cried. Then I prayed."

He said he's been praying and attending church regularly since.

Every time I sing the song, it takes a little more out of me. But I think of those people, and I think of God, and I think it's just my job to go back out there the next night and do it again.

There's a difference in delivering a song like, say, "International Harvester," and singing a song like "Almost Home" or "The Father, My Son, and the Holy Ghost." I love "International Harvester," and people love it; it's fun and it's certainly meant a lot to my career. But it doesn't move me emotionally the same way as "Almost Home," let alone "The Father, My Son, and the Holy Ghost." I do them both because those are different parts of who I am.

We're all like that, maybe. Happy and deeply sad, fun, and more than a little down—it's the human condition. That's why certain songs touch people so hard.

The funny thing is, "The Father, My Son, and the Holy Ghost" didn't get a whole lot of airtime on terrestrial country radio—the radio stations you tune to, or used to, in your car or at home. I think they might have thought that it was a bit too sad—I can understand that. A lot of people, including Karen, criticized them for that. Honestly, it wasn't that big a deal to me. I understand it's a business, and the stations have to make their decisions based on what their perception of their audience is. I'm just truly thankful that the song did get a lot of airplay elsewhere.

We shot the video for the song at Morgan Farms. The piece is very simple visually, very bare bones, like the emotion that flows from it.

Morgan Farms fire pit, made by a friend, Dickson, Tennessee

In the opening sequence you can see a stained-glass window as I walk down the steps. The image is of St. Michael the Archangel. (Technically, Michael is an archangel not a saint—saints are human; angels are not—but most Catholics refer to him that way.) There is a long tradition of Michael as the head of God's army fighting Satan, and of protecting people. Many Catholics wear medals or symbols of St. Michael the Archangel and call on him for protection in difficult situations. Not coincidently, he is considered a patron or special saint of police and firemen.

The glass that was seen on screen was a window for the chapel we were constructing in Jerry's memory. It's a beautiful Catholic-style chapel, located on a special part of our property. The architecture hints at classic medieval cathedral styles, but the scale is personal, so the space feels not only holy, but comforting. I didn't build it, but I did make the doors and pews, which I modeled after an actual church pew I had. Taking that pew apart so I could use the pieces as a pattern for the others may have been the hardest part. Took me several days to do—I had to be very careful; anything broke I wouldn't have a pew or a model.

I made a font for holy water too. Catholics dip their fingers into holy water on entering a church or chapel, then make the sign of the cross, symbolically asking God to bless us and protect us from evil. There are a lot of other little personal touches. Jerry's favorite number was thirteen. The overhang on the roof—thirteen inches.

The chapel stands at the edge of a sharp rise if you approach from the direction of the road. To make it easier for people to get to it— Jerry's friends have an open invitation, and often visit there—we built a set of steps into the hillside. Karen goes down there and to his grave site every day when she's home; I join her when I can.

FAITH

I've made a few references to Catholics because my wife and I are of that faith. I'm not here to preach or proselytize, and this isn't a book about religion. But God plays an incredibly important role in my life, most especially since Jerry died. So let me offer just a few words about our personal faith and relationship to God.

I grew up a Baptist. My parents were pretty regular churchgoers, and that's how they raised us. As I got older, faith remained important. I was a typical Protestant, I think, in that I thought the Bible was the be-all and end-all. Anything in the Bible was sacred and important; you didn't need anything outside it. Nothing. Just the Bible.

I still believe the Bible is important, but I've come to see faith and religion as a living thing. Jesus Christ came to us as a human, living God. The confidence that we have as Christians comes from the knowledge that our God is not in the past, or strictly in the past, but in the present and the future. There are a lot of religions that support great morals and values. Christ being alive makes the Christian faith one of love and action, not just rules and certainly not hate.

My darling granddaughter Winnie and me in 2019

Now there are a lot of people who claim to be good Christians while preaching hate, but that's a different matter. The core of Christianity, of Christ's message to us, is to love God and to love our neighbor. Specifically as a Catholic, I have to live that love by helping other people. My actions have to do something positive, make the world a better place. Maybe only in a very small way, but it makes a difference. I have to do what I'm capable of. It's not enough to think good thoughts. I have to live them. The idea of *action* leading to grace fits in with exactly who I am. Who I have always been.

What I've learned of late—and where I think being Catholic rather than Protestant comes in as well—is the importance of God's church. Before there was a Bible, there was a Church. God's word is true, but there is more. The Church teaches that. It can be the tool for us helping others, the conduit for our good acts, or the prod for them. It can help us find the truth, and to help others.

Helping others. Good works. Service. Those are important things for a Catholic. I believed that before I found the faith. And you do those things without expecting or wanting recognition. That's a difficult thing, but you should offer in that spirit.

I believe in the Trinity, the idea of the Father, the Son, and the Holy Spirit as one God, yet conceivable by us as three instances. I know the idea can be difficult for somebody who doesn't understand Catholicism or Christianity. I understand. It's difficult to fathom that God came to earth in the flesh as Christ. And if it hasn't happened to you, it may be hard to understand how the Holy Spirit fills our hearts with grace.

I came to Catholicism through Karen, who had taken the time to do a lot research and study before joining the church. I know I'm not a perfect Catholic. But I also know that whatever my faults, whatever my sins, I am loved by God. I do my best to be worthy of that love.

GOD, FAMILY, COUNTRY

Returning to Broken Bow was a bit of a homecoming, but also a new adventure—different people, different attitudes, much different marketplace. The album *God, Family, Country* reflected that. We decided it would include some of my older music as well as some of my new—a new beginning that still paid tribute to my roots with the label. I wanted the album to sum up my life, but also to point the direction forward.

God, Family, Country, 2020

But selecting the music was not a journey through greatest hits. I wanted the sound to suggest my full range—you can hear a little blues, maybe, and hints of gospel. And the songs I chose are not songs "stuck" in the time period. I wanted, and I think we got, a timeless sound, something enduring, and as relevant lyrically as the day it was written.

"The Father, My Son, and the Holy Ghost" obviously had to be included in the new album. The other songs all fit in somehow with the title song, "God, Family, and Country," which had been on my first Broken Bow album, *I Love It*, almost twenty years before. I think the song not only sums up the album; it totals up who I am and what I am about pretty well.

I wrote that song with Craig Morris of 4 Runner, but because it had come out during the early stages of my career, it wasn't that well-known. It made sense in a lot of ways to remix it and bring it back.

Another of my favorites on the album is "Soldier." Every line means something to me. Gavin DeGraw wrote it. I thought maybe his brother Joey, another very talented writer, had a hand in it as well, but it doesn't look like he's credited on this one. The funny thing is, as far as I know, neither one of them served in the military. Gavin's a pop singer, but when I heard that song, I thought it caught the deep truth about our men and women in uniform. To me, it really describes the heroic attitude of all the people who serve in the military. They have that ideal of service, an attitude of selflessness. At the same time, the song uses "soldier" as a metaphor, so it has meaning for anyone who has that same ideal, a person who'll stand beside his loved ones or friends no matter what. You don't have to be in the military to feel it's speaking to you. There are other reasons I like it. It's a great song for me to sing, especially. It's got a big range—it's a bit of a challenge, a tough song to sing. I like that.

"Going Out Like This" is another that uses my whole range, or a lot of it. That's one of mine. My band members Mike, Corey, and Sam had been working on the song and let me hear what they had. I loved it so much I took it and finished it. It's a positive take on a negative situation. That last verse, I wrote the words with them sitting there— it just runs out of me, you know? The words just come.

Sometimes.

Then there's "Whiskey." I love it, but it is a bit dark. Anthony Smith

USO tour, 2017

was one of the writers. He'd written it with Sarah Beth Terry, and it was Sarah who turned me on to it. Anthony had posted it on Facebook; she had me listen to it there, and I immediately got a hold of him and told

him I was going to record it. We had it on hold for a year before we found the time to get into the studio and lay it down.

"Sippin' on the Simple Life" is another special song, with a personal meaning to me. Back in 2016, I was in Washington, D.C., for the USO's seventy-fifth anniversary when two Rangers came up to me backstage and asked if I'd write with them. I get a lot of requests like that, but these guys had so much energy, I asked them about their song ideas. I stopped them when they got to "Sippin'

USO tour, 2018

on the Simple Life." The Rangers were Captains Andrew Yacovone and Justin Wright, who perform on the side as Interstate 10. I got Mike Rogers to help shape the music, and we pretty much had it figured out right on the spot.

If the themes and the music sum up who I am, the release itself pointed to the direction the industry is taking. Most everyone who listened to the music got it through downloads or services. CDs, like vinyl records before them, have become an endangered species. The business of the business has radically changed.

Which is one reason I've kept busy with TV and its many different permutations. In 2020, COVID and all, we premiered *Craig's World* on the Circle network, a channel dedicated to the country lifestyle. The network features an array of classic entertainment as well as new material.

My show documents some of what I've done in the past as well as capturing me in some day-to-day activities. We've had a lot of fun with it—viewers have seen me playing

Singing at the Grand Ole Opry

with my grandson as well as performing at the Grand Ole Opry and even doing the national anthem for the Nashville Predators. (You didn't know we had hockey in Tennessee? Shame!) I even ran a half-marathon with my son-in-law. But there have been serious moments, and a chance to do some good and spread the word about others doing good. One of our first shows featured Taya Kyle, widow of American Sniper Chris Kyle, visiting to help surprise a dear friend with the help of Operation Finally Home.

I guess I ought to mention that I shaved off my beard before someone asks why.

Vanity.

It had started to go gray after my son died. So I shaved it one day, and I thought to myself, let's see what the reaction is.

"Oh man, you look like you're twelve."

"You took twenty years off of your life."

And then it was time for a new photo shoot. So rather than try to grow a new beard—and maybe search out some secret age-reducing formula—I kept it shaved.

That did lead to a bit of a story with President George W. Bush, our forty-third president. My wife and I were invited to an event at Johnny Morris' Wonders of Wildlife National Museum &

Me and President George W. Bush, Missouri, 2017

Aquarium. The president made a beeline through a mob of industry hotshots and entertainment stars to grab my hand.

"Last time I saw you, you had a beard," said the president.

My wife looked at me kind of funny.

"When did you meet George Bush?"

Answering would have required me to fill in what I had done, so I let it pass. Some things are destined to remain secret.

TWELVE:
MOVING ON

BUSINESS AND PANDEMIC

A little story about the business of the business, with a nod to my business manager.

I was looking at opening up a coffee shop in Dickson. So I asked her to crunch the numbers.

"I'm happy to," she replied. "But first, why would you want to do that?"

"It'd be fun," I told her.

That clearly wasn't good enough.

"I'll hire veterans to run it and take care of a bunch of veterans in our area," I added.

"And?"

"It'll be fun."

She worked out some numbers, and in the end told me we'd possibly make $40,000 a year, with a lot of work. Note that word, "possibly."

And to make that amount of money, I'd have to miss a bunch of shows. So as a business venture, let's just say it wouldn't have made the best sense. Now, I don't and won't take on a venture just because I like the numbers. And I don't expect my business manager to understand all the things I want to do. But I have to concede, business is business. And business decisions, whether they're about pouring coffee or doing a show, should make sense dollarwise.

Writing a song is different.

To me, songs are not about the money. Yes, the idea is to sell them as well as sing them, and I'm always hunting for a hit. But I'm *not* think-ing about money or charts or downloads when I write.

You can't. You have to think, *I'm writing a great song. I'm hitting this emotion. I'm letting something important hit me and communicating it.* You can't write for a dollar sign.

Business does have to come into what I do, because this is what I do for a living. Book-ings, COVID aside, are a major part of the business. But there's more to a booking than how much the band and I are going to get paid, or even what our expenses will be getting there and playing. Who's the promoter? What are the ticket prices? How big's the venue? What are the expec-tations going to be?

Photo shoot for *God, Family, Country*, 2020

Obviously, I have a certain amount of money that I have to make on a show or I won't do it. But I also want to make sure that the promoters are not going to lose their shirt. On the other hand, if they set the prices so high that instead of ten thousand people they get thirty-five hundred—well that doesn't look good for me.

Starting out, I would play just about anywhere—run and gun. The idea was, make your money while you can, because this fame thing isn't going to last.

Now, I know better.

There were years when I did one hundred and fifty shows. I wouldn't do

Boar hunting with Al

that now, even if COVID magically disappeared. I don't want to be away from my family quite as much, and I have too many other things to do, professionally—TV, movies. And there'll always be hunting, fishing, and chores to get done at the farm.

Right as I'm working on this, we're still dealing with the fallout of COVID. Touring was practically shut down for a year and more. While I had alternative income streams, a lot of musicians, including guys who work with me, don't. It hurt us all pretty bad. If you're an entertainer who thrives on live shows, you can't really work at home.

Well, that's not entirely true: I did have a lot of success with some streaming projects, especially my

Turkey hunting with my cameraman, Al Lambert, Texas, 2021

homegrown "Fridays at Four" livestream, which were pretty much what that sounds like. One of the surprising things about those—to me, anyway—was how they affected merchandise sales. Those went through the roof. I don't know why. Maybe people wanted a connection to the music and decided to use a little of the money they saved by not going to shows to get that connection. Certainly, I'm grateful.

Full disclosure: I can't take too much credit for the merchandise. We use designers who know the artistic stuff, and my managers know the market; I just say go for it. I don't need to know what the most important color is, or what shirts should be in what size.

Having said that—when they tell me something, about one out of ten times I'll start asking questions to find out if they really know what they're talking about, or if they're just guessing like everybody else.

So far, the answers and results have been good. Gotta keep them on their toes, though, right?

There's been a lot of guessing due to the pandemic. Are meet-and-greets a good idea? Are outside shows better than inside shows? How much do online remote performances make sense? How many should a performer do? It's a different world now, but it always is. We'll all figure it out eventually.

The virus caught up with me early on while I was doing a concert offshore, even though we'd followed the specified protocols, been tested and quarantined and all that. I was one of the lucky ones—I probably wouldn't have known I was sick without the repeated tests. I got home, kept to myself, and recovered. Credit that to God, good living, my wife's gentle nursing, or a strong constitution—or maybe all of the above.

One of the things I had to give up because of COVID—temporarily, I hope—was my ambition to do a triathlon. I'd started training a few months before everything got shut down and the competitions canceled. Even as an amateur, there's a rhythm and pattern to your workouts you have to maintain, building to a peak right in time for the competition. That's difficult to begin with, and in my case hard to maintain with touring and everything else I'm doing. I'm not sure when I'll be able to aim at one. It's definitely on the bucket list, though.

I do run when I can, especially while we're on the road. All that PT we did in the service gave my legs and lungs muscle memory. If nothing else, aiming for a competition at some point means I'm taking better care of myself than I have at times in the past.

We were busy despite the quarantines, and not just with the video and social media stuff. We worked up an entirely new show and presentation for 2022, including a set list that brought back some old favorites as well as mixing in my new stuff. And of course, I was writing.

There's no magic formula for what I play onstage—well, no wait, there is:

WIN.

That means making sure the fans get what they want. It's all about entertainment. You gotta make them laugh, you gotta make them cry. You gotta make them feel good about having been there. The people in the audience have to know that the performer is sincere. And if they aren't convinced of that—even if in your heart you believe you are— man, that is trouble.

There's probably an algorithm for all that these days. Being old-fashioned, I guess, I just go by people's reactions, and what I feel in my gut.

Things are changing in the music business every day. Social media is having a bigger and bigger impact. And so is technology. I listen to kids who are producing music on iPads and sharing it on TikTok, Instagram, whatever. It sounds very good. Outside of the technology, there are a lot more singer-songwriters in the business, these days. That was one of my business strategies early on—have those different revenue flows.

Given what's going on with downloads, it's possible I'll reach a point in my career where even a record label is no longer necessary for me to stay in the game. You could argue that if they're not getting my music in the stores or played on country radio, there's no need for labels. Every artist is thinking about that. When you reach a certain plateau, you may no longer need them to maintain that level. Or take a group that's reached a high level and started to decline a bit. If the label isn't going to do anything to bring them back up, maybe they don't need the label at all.

One thing about country radio that hasn't changed is the fact that they can only play so much. There are only twenty-four hours in a day, which means there are only so many three- or four-minute songs that can be aired. And because of that, some songs and some artists will not get as much playing time as they deserve. And certainly not as much as they may *think* they deserve.

I respect this. I'm not like a lot of artists who get all twisted because country radio doesn't play as much of them as they used to. I think,

There's a new artist coming into the business and people want to hear some new stuff. Meanwhile, new artists probably look at people like me and say, "Shove over. I deserve a chance."

And maybe they do.

New music can be a double-edged sword for established artists. They may play your *old* stuff, because it's popular, but because they already have that on, they may not want your *new* stuff. I'm fortunate—golden—in that area because I was lucky to establish my career on a lot of big hits. But even I have to reckon with the realities of the business.

And that reality is—country radio is not as important as it once was. "The Father, My Son, and the Holy Ghost" was popular because of social media and television; as I mentioned, it hardly played on the radio.

I used to say that radio will go away, but I don't think that anymore. They're just going to change the avenues in which they're reaching their consumer. Maybe they will no longer be on the AM/FM dial. They'll be on satellite and the internet. You'd still be able to listen to, say, WSIX, WKDF, WSM—great Nashville country stations—and maybe plenty more, but you'll listen to them on satellite.

I'd bet most people are doing that now. And not just in the Nashville

AOL session, 2013

area, since with a satellite or the internet you're not limited to what the antenna at the station can put out. That's where it's going to go.

You have to stay relevant in this business—if you're looking at it as a business. If the way of listening to music changes, you change with it. To a point. I'm not going to keep fighting if I'm no longer relevant. If no one wants my downloads, if I do shows and only fifty people come by—well, that's judging me as not relevant. There are guys who will play for those fifty again and again, in hopes that the next show there'll be a hundred. That's just not me.

Playing for thousands in an arena is way different than playing in a small club, but no matter the venue, I'm aiming to entertain every person in the audience.

I've played for eighty thousand people. I know what that's like. I've also played for three thousand. Heck, I've played for fifty, and we all had a heck of a good time. But if my career gets to the point where it's down to fifty when I was expecting thousands, and that's the trend, I'm not going to hang on to it.

I don't want anyone to misinterpret and think that I only play for money or big crowds, or that I'm not grateful for my career. I am damn grateful. I love what I do. But it is an occupation and there are things that I love more. My family. God.

I've said many times that I don't deserve what I've gotten career-wise nearly as much as a guy like Blake Shelton. I don't merit my success nearly as much as many other artists who only want music. I want more than music. That's made it a lot harder for my management and the record labels. I probably keep some of them up at night. I'm racing motorcycles. I'm jumping out of airplanes. I'm doing hunting shows and giving them all sorts of headaches.

And I'll keep on doing all that until it's no longer fun, or I'm no longer getting on with the audience.

What will never change is the gratitude I feel when I look out at the audience. I'll probably always get emotional sometimes because, deep down, I still believe I don't deserve their cheers.

BEYOND THE EDGE

Last fall—that would be September 2021—I got a chance to go back to Panama. Not as a military adviser or even a civilian tourist. I

was a ringer on the celebrity talent/survivor show *Beyond the Edge*, a CBS production.

Not a "ringer" exactly. After all, it had been years since I'd been in the jungle, and the producers did know about my military and outdoors background. As a matter of fact, even though I'd initially been screened to do the show, I

Beyond the Edge, 2022

hadn't been selected as a final contestant apparently because there was some thought that I wouldn't be awkward enough to make good TV.

A last-minute dropout due to illness changed that thinking.

I arrived in Panama not knowing much of what was ahead of us. It happened that a friend of mine—Mike Singletary, former NFL coach and Monster of Midway linebacker for the Bears—had been selected as another contestant. We met up at the hotel for dinner and an intel session, but neither one of us came close to predicting what lay ahead.

A dozen of us were taken out into the jungle, pointed toward roofless huts, and told we would have to live off the land and compete for luxuries like bedding. There were other incentives besides simply surviving—the producers split us into teams for various competitions, with money going to the charity of our choice.

The first day we arrived, I surveyed the situation.

"Most important thing we have to do," I said, "is get some roofs on the huts."

"That's more important than food?" said Ray Lewis, another former football star, who played for the Ravens.

"We can live for three days without water. And three weeks without food," I told everyone. "I guarantee we won't make it through the night without shelter."

Thinking back now, Ray's so big he might not have made it three days without food, but at any rate, we got some tops on the huts and even managed to make some crude bedding. The real aim of the show was to demonstrate that people from diverse backgrounds who are not used to roughing it—let alone living in a jungle—can work together to survive.

I think we accomplished that goal, despite the howler monkeys and some of the worst downpours Panama has ever seen. I managed to raise a good bit of money for Operation Finally Home, which I'm sure will put it to good use.

And I have to be honest: I'm not saying it was easy, I'm not saying every minute was fun, but good Lord if that wasn't one of the best vacations I've had in years. I made some good friends there, including Ray. As a matter of fact, I recently sent him a present of ninety pounds of bananas—after hearing him complain that he'd eaten so many bananas for the show that he was sick of them. I can't wait to see how he retaliates.

Me and Jodie Sweetin in *Beyond the Edge*, 2022   In Panama for *Beyond the Edge*, 2022

Spouses and significant others weren't invited. I don't think Karen would have come if they had been, even if the lodging had been a fancy hotel. She's not big on joining me on the road, and for the most part, she's always kept herself separate from business decisions. She'll give advice when asked, but by and large she's happy to let me concentrate on that end of my life. And she's certainly not one of those women who "wear their husband" as she puts it—using whatever fame their spouse has to get a certain status or bragging rights. If anything, she's the opposite.

She's not starstruck either—usually. But then came the day she met Kris Kristofferson. I'll let her tell on herself:

> *Kris Kristofferson walked in and my friend Carol asked, "Would you like to meet him?"*
>
> *I said, "Sure, it's Kris Kristofferson."*
>
> *And so we go up to meet him and she introduced Craig and then she introduced me.*
>
> *I said . . . nothing.*
>
> *I said . . . more nothing.*
>
> *Oh, I tried. My brain was absolutely screaming but my vocal cords were just not moving.*
>
> *Nothing came out. Nothing.*
>
> *I stood there with a stupid smile on my face, embarrassed.*
>
> *Finally, he just laughed and said, "It's OK, honey."*

It must happen to him all the time. Starstruck laryngitis. Gracious man, though.

We all have our personal heroes and untouchable stars. Some of the band and crew members have had similar experiences—I remember Jerry stopping in his tracks and going numb when he walked backstage on one of our military tours and saw Merle Haggard and George Strait tuning up. Couldn't even remember what he went backstage for.

He recovered quickly and sufficiently to tell the story on himself many's the time, usually concluding, "Who else has a job like this?"

Not many.

I can't recall being voiceless when I've met anyone, but I swear Willie Nelson is the only man I've ever met who had an aura around him. And I was awed one time when Kevin Costner—*the* Kevin Costner, movie and TV star—opened up for me with his band. A lot of people don't know that Kevin has a country rock band, Kevin Costner & Modern West. They've released three albums and a bunch of singles, with some success. I love the way he works stories through his music.

The more famous people you meet, the more you realize they're just people. A few are jerks; a few have let things go to their heads, but by and large . . . just people.

The flip side of all this—I'm not going to call myself famous, but people do know who I am. And that's made it easier for some old friends to connect. I've been able to keep in touch with some of the soldiers who served with me during Panama and other points in my career. Some of my army guys got together with me recently to fish and share some stories, a few of which ended up in the book. A lot of times while I'm on tour I've been lucky enough to hook up with them and visit for a few hours. Not all of them are country music fans, but we have a great time catching up and commenting on the current state of the world.

Sometimes I get asked about my voice, where it comes from, how it does what it does.

The answer is easy: I don't know.

It's an instrument, I guess, but it's not one that I can take apart and analyze. It's so much a part of me, and has *always* been a part of me, that I just accept that it is what it is.

I'm doing this kind of song, so I have to sound like so . . .

Whether I write the song or not, I sing what fits my voice. I try to find a place in the song that I belong. I worry about two things, pitch and meter. I want to be in the right key, and I want to be in time. As long as I'm doing those two things and conscious of them while I'm singing, everything else will work out.

I use my keyboardist as a pitch reference. It's always right. The fiddle may not be one hundred percent on, and the guitar might be gently off. So the keyboard is my primary reference.

I have a click track in my ear when I'm performing, which helps me and the rest of the band keep time. (A "click track" is a kind of virtual metronome, keeping a steady beat.) A lot of people will say that when you play to a click track, you lose emotion, but I haven't found that. What I lose is bad timing and poor synchronization with the rest of the band. Click tracks make it easier to concentrate on the other parts of singing. If anything, they let me put more emotion into my singing.

Singing is physically demanding. If you sing with intent and intensity, if you throw all your emotion and energy into a show, you will be physically exhausted at the end of the night. Some nights I feel like I just ran a half-marathon.

Other nights, it's more like the whole 26.2 miles.

Depending on the venue, my shows run sixty to seventy-five minutes long, or seventy-five to ninety. The set list is arranged that way—I know that if I do every song on the set, I'll be right at seventy-five or ninety.

With the longer sets, I know that I can pull three or four songs out to get to the earlier mark. If I walk in and feel fricking wonderful—my energy is really good and I don't feel tired—everything stays. But if it's been a long day and I've had to talk a lot or my health is running a little low, then the show may be on the shorter side. Or I may skip an early song because my voice isn't quite warmed up yet.

That's why sound checks aren't just for the equipment. They give my vocal cords a chance to loosen up and stretch.

There was a time when I didn't warm up before a show. Then I got older and wiser. Now I usually go down about three hours before

My Old Tattoo Cabernet Sauvignon with Lot18.com, 2017

showtime for the check, and shut my mouth down after that.

As any singer will tell you, your voice is like any muscle; you have to exercise it. Performances, songwriting, recording—it has to be used on a regular basis. But otherwise I have no secrets, aside from drinking a lot of water and enjoying the fruits of a good cabernet.

There are nights when . . . stuff happens. But sometimes it works out. One night I forgot the words to one of the songs and the crowd just went crazy, helping me out. I got such a big response that I worked it into the act for a while.

Then there's the time I told the band we would play one song, and I started to sing another.

Maybe it's happened more than once. You'll have to ask them.

I like talking with the audience. I want to make them laugh at least once between the songs. I want them to have a good time. And I want them to remember the night.

My favorite shows are in really old theaters in small towns, places that may not get a lot of attention because their venues are on the smaller side. Admittedly, the business calculations can be tight, but that stuff aside, I love performing in places where basically I'm dialoguing with the audience. People want to hear the lyrics. They want to inter-act. Even though they don't physically talk to me—some yell at me, but in a good way—we do interact and communicate. All right, there's nothing like playing before eighty thousand people and hearing them roar applause at the end of a song—but the applause in the smaller local theaters is just as sweet.

A different animal.

A lot of guys won't do a show if the venue doesn't seat at least twenty or thirty thousand. I understand the business side of things, but I resist, at least to the point that I can.

I expect a call from my managers when they read that.

Here's another thing that gets under my skin: there's nothing worse than watching the entertainer turn his back on the audience again and again to talk to his band. All right, once or twice, or to cover some sort of tech glitch, but after every song?

I do have a little mike I can use to talk to the band if I need to. But I try to avoid that too.

There was a time and place where turning my back on the audience could be deadly. When we were traveling in Afghanistan and Iraq, I'd regularly scan the place, keeping my eyes open for anything threatening. That isn't even a bad idea here in the States, given what happened in Vegas a few years back.

My uncles and my dad tell stories about fights in the places they played. With maybe the exception of some of the festivals we play where there is a good amount of drinking before the show, that isn't generally a problem. But yeah, I've stopped the show for a fight or two. I mean, if there's two guys punching it out and they aren't going to hurt anybody else, well, that's their business. But if they're going to shove into other people, or somebody is hitting a woman, I'll end it myself if I have to.

NEXT

I have a few souvenirs of my past, but I'm not the kind of guy who keeps a scrapbook and pages through his "good ol' days" every so often. You'll find a number of musicians will collect guitars and other instruments as valuable pieces of nostalgia and even investments, but that's not who I am. To me, guitars are the tools of the trade, nothing more. I never put a lot of emphasis on them, for some reason. They sound good; I use them.

I do have a good one I keep at the Grand Ole Opry in a locker. Otherwise, they're solid, dependable, but not beyond replacing. My life on the road's a lot different than when I started out, with people to take care of our instruments, but I've always had that feeling that if something breaks on the road, you want it to be something you won't feel too bad about.

OK, there is one guitar that's special to me: a 1962 Gibson Les Paul with the original pickups. One of my uncles happened to work for Gibson and he gave it to me. It's special as much for him as for its uniqueness. Brad Paisley would probably trade a bus for it. I don't play it much; it hangs quietly on the wall of one my offices.

I guess the closest thing I have to a memory book is the array of deer and other animal trophies hanging at the house. They were mounted by some incredible taxidermists. Looking at them doesn't make me nostalgic—it makes me want to get back out and go hunting again.

So, no. I'm not looking back. I'm looking forward, to what I can do next.

I used to have an issue with calling a singer an artist. Because to me, artists are people who create something tangible, in the sense that I can touch it. Now, having done music for so long in my life, I appreciate that it is an art. And I respect that a song can have the same impact that a book or a movie or a painting can.

But when I write a song, I don't think about any of that. It's closer to . . . well, when you're put in a dilemma, you have a situation where you've got to figure something out. It's like problem-solving.

Take today. I have some of the boys coming over and we're going to lay down something we started on the road. I've had this piano tune in my head, but I can't really play the piano well enough to fill this song out. So I took what I had and gave it to one of my musicians. We talked and had a few ideas that drove me lyrically to do some cool things. Today we'll work on it some more, with a friend on the fiddle—I know it needs that. We'll see what happens next.

I've always loved songwriting. When I first started taking it seriously—I'd say around the time we were at Fort Polk or maybe Panama—I learned to let the song take you to a place that's emotional, that's you, that's what you're feeling. I could feel things like missing my family and let that come into the words and music. Panama put me in a place mentally that forced my brain to think about those emotions and want to write. That was my outlet, writing, I guess, and it grew from that seed.

I have other outlets for creativity, so I can feel creative without having to write, but I always come back. Those other outlets let me clear my mind and focus better on the song.

We'll start out informally this afternoon. They'll pick up the tune, I'll add the words. We'll go for a bit, then someone, usually me, will speak up, "Stop. That didn't work. Try again, but this time, with this bit . . ."

Maybe it's my attention deficit tendency, but I'm always working on several projects at the same time. I'd love to do an album of duets with different singers. I want to collaborate and stretch myself musically, and as a writer. I love the energy I get from working with other songwriters.

Working on the producer side brings out a slightly different strand of my creativity. I've been doing a bit more of it for others. Being able to take a song and create great music from it is a thrill.

The writer and the performers already have the general outline, sure, but the producer gets to the nuances of the music. He or she may hear the potential in the phrasing or the instrument selection that can take a song to another level. They pick out songs that aren't just good; they're good for the performer and band.

They can also be psychologists and coaches. Take Philbilly. I love working with him not only because of his music sense; he's also able to figure me out as a person. He'll have me in the studio early—7:00 a.m., say—and we'll work for a few hours until he picks up something that tells him I'm done for the day. I can't tell, but he can.

Lately I've been working as a producer for a young lady whom I've known since she was a child. It's been amazing to see how much she's grown. The challenge for me is to help her get the most out of her songs, whether it's how a certain arrangement works or maybe phrasing. But I also have to be like a coach—encouraging while gently pushing her to keep growing her talent.

You don't think of that as a military skill, but you know what? It's the same sort of leadership a good NCO exercises working with his unit. So maybe there's a lot more army in my music than it seems.

The part of producing that I don't like? Producing my own singing. I always feel it can be better. The musicians get tired of me. Worse, I don't want to hear me anymore.

People are always asking, what do you think when you hear yourself on the radio? What I'm thinking is: *Isn't there something else on the radio?* Seriously. I check the other channels when I come on.

As for other people singing something I wrote, God bless them. I want them to sing it. And I want them to sing it their way. They have to put their artistic impression on it, so it becomes theirs.

When I first started writing songs, I wrote all the time. In the late '90s and the early 2000s, I would go and write all day in between jobs. When I started writing full-time, I'd have two or three writing sessions a day, do demo sessions at night, and writers' events on the weekends. It was just nonstop, trying to chase that dream.

Now I know that I can write when I want to write. I don't force it like I used to have to. But you know, I think forcing it helped me develop the skill set that's necessary for songwriting. The time I had to spend doing that took time from my family and a lot of other things. I have no regrets, and if someone were starting out, my advice would be to write as much as possible—don't wait for the emotion or the melody to pop into your head.

There are two kinds of albums that I haven't done, I guess because I've always seen them as things you do after your career has plateaued—a live album, and an album of gospel music. OK, plenty of performers have done both on the way up. To me, a live album isn't going to increase my platform as a performer. Live albums are usually a way of looking back at a career, at least in country music. Nothing wrong with that, just not my style.

Forward.

Offense, rather than defense. That's the head you have as a Ranger or paratrooper.

As I've said, if I get to the point where people aren't listening to me anymore, then I won't stay in the music business as a performer. And if I had so much money that I knew I'd never have to worry about anything for the rest of my life and my kids wouldn't either—would I quit?

I'd still write and sing. I'd still do the Grand Ole Opry. I might not be doing it to generate income; I wouldn't be doing it as a job. But I'd be doing it.

For fun. And because it's who I am. It's just that there's just a lot more to me than that.

Leaving the military was one of the hardest decisions I've ever made.

Singing at the Grand Ole Opry

We loved that life, the friendships, the families, the lifestyle of living on base with our friends and the kids doing their thing.

Do I miss it? Yes. There are days. I still feel like I might reenlist. Fortunately, some of it is still part of my life. During the dark days of the Afghanistan withdrawal, I was talking constantly with friends there—and, to be honest, wishing I was there to help. I did what I could back in the States, but, you know . . . once a soldier, always a soldier.

It's just, like music, that there's a lot more to me.

Neil McCoy is one of the greatest entertainers ever. He's a country music superstar, but more than that, he's the entertainers' entertainer. He's that good.

Back some years ago, Neil and I had a show where I was scheduled to be the headliner. I walked up on his bus and said, I'm not going on after you. You're gonna have to go on last.

He looked at me very seriously and said, "Now listen, young man. That ain't the way it works. We all got our day, and today is yours."

Someday, I'll be saying that to someone myself.

EPILOGUE:
ALASKA

You haven't heard anything until you've heard a wolf.

I sit outside by the lake in the morning, too early to really call it morning, and the sound comes just off the water. Five hundred yards away.

Owhww-owhww-owwwww.

Endless. Not spooky. Not a warning either. A call. Whether to other wolves or to action, or to whatever your imagination wants to hear.

That's Alaska.

There are other animals. Lots. We've found brown bear scat on the property, but luckily nothing close enough to give concern. Bad things happen when you get close. I do have a moose that's calved nearby three years in a row. We give her room too.

What you feel out here—the cold, the wild—are the things at the core of our being, of mankind's being. There are echoes of it in war, in the birth of your children, in the death of loved ones. The things that make you exist. It's not one man against Nature, but that man in Nature.

The music doesn't stop. The click track, though, is Nature's. Your creativity is set against rougher, even purer things. You're creative to survive, to simply exist.

In Alaska I'm away from the demands and distractions. It's not a retreat. It's a confrontation with my soul. The things that are important are truly important—caring for my family and the people with me.

The many threads of my life—the military, music, my family, hunting, the adrenaline and rush of motorcycles and adventure—to an outsider, even to me, they appear distinct and separate. But in Alaska they are together at a deep level. The mysteries of faith and everyday life don't need to be consciously examined or debated; they need simply to be. The Holy Spirit touches you chopping wood or putting a hole in the ice to catch dinner.

We've carried that with us as we've progressed. We've found new ways to express it, whether in art or at home. We haven't turned away from it, but found new ways to live, to be human.

You can feel it in a song, when the night is right and the music is right. When your lover kisses you and the kids give you a hug. When you hear the wolves howl.

I have been so privileged to find it in my life.

Me with my grandchildren, Winnie Fox and Cruze, Florida, 2020

Kyle, Ryan, Alexandra, Cruze, and me in Dickson, Tennessee

NOTES & THANKS

I wrote this book hoping to share my story in a way that inspires people to pursue life with love and kindness for others, living to the fullest with appreciation for all of God's blessings, while attempting to glorify our Lord and Savior. At the same time, we have to accept that hardships are a part of life and don't define us; rather, it's how we deal with the hardships that truly makes us.

This life I've lived thus far is thanks to the blessings from God. Those blessings include my angel here on earth, my biggest fan and critic, my one true love, my wife, Karen; my children, Marisa, Alexandra, Kyle, Jerry, and Wyatt, each unique and loving and kind and each a part of me. My blessings include all of my family, especially Mom, Dad, Pebbles, Joey, and Gina, who have each influenced and encouraged me along the way. I credit my military family as well, especially Davis, Parris, Kerns, Steele, and Carlin, with added thanks for sharing their perspectives of my story; I'm grateful for the time we shared. My good friends Bill and Karen have always been there for me. Thanks, too, to all the folks at the record labels and country radio and my fellow songwriters, who've supported and helped me to become the artist I am today, especially Benny, Jon, Lilly, Lana, Shelly, Jo Jamie, Buddy, and Philbilly; my managers, past and present, Ralph, Christy, Faith, Bryan, Gaines, and Julie, who have helped to coordinate the chaos. To the publishers and editors at Blackstone who have supported this endeavor patiently with upmost class. Lastly to my cowriter and friend

Jim DeFelice, whose ability to articulate and translate the voice of my life to paper has been a blessing beyond words, and I look forward to our future projects together.

I pray God will bless you all and hope that collectively and individually we have made this temporary life better in preparation for our eternal life in heaven and hope we encourage others to live for God, Family, and Country.

COLLABORATOR'S NOTE

We worked on a lot of this book during the worst of the COVID pandemic. At one point I was with Craig in Florida while he did a live remote on Zoom for a virtual convention. The performance itself was everything you'd expect—totally entertaining, foot-stomping at points, inspirational at others. But it was what happened before the "show" that provides a real insight into who Craig is.

It was a small cramped studio with very high-tech equipment. While Craig was waiting for the virtual sound check, he started riffing on a melody he had in his head. His accompanist joined in.

Words began pouring from Craig as if he'd memorized them in childhood. The song was polished, upbeat, a lot of fun.

It wasn't a piece I recognized. I asked what song it was later on.

He shrugged. "I just made it up while we were playing."

I don't remember the words now, and I couldn't come close to humming the tune. What I do remember, though, is the smile on his face. The absolute joy he felt as he composed on the fly was something that could only have come from deep in his soul.

Not all artists are like that. Craig's not always like that either—if you see him perform "The Father, My Son, and the Holy Ghost," you'll see enough pain to haunt your nights forever. But it was obvious how deeply ingrained the impulse to create is in him, how much a part of him songwriting is. And how much joy it brings to him.

Most people have trouble reconciling their idea of warrior with songwriter, and not just because the roles of soldier and artist are so badly stereotyped in modern media. Achilles didn't bother documenting his fight with Ajax, and Odysseus left it to a blind troubadour to sing of his journey through the known and unknown worlds. But those two occupations have more in common than people think. Certain kinds of soldiers—paratroopers, commandoes—rely not just on their training, but their ability to improvise under fire. Many Special Operations soldiers are specifically chosen for their creativity; their "entrance exams" often have no set solution, and sometimes no solution at all.

To get anywhere at all today, musicians and artists must soldier on through all manner of difficulties, very often alone against the world, armed only with gifts and the sometimes shaky belief that they can succeed if they only fight hard enough.

So I don't think the fact that Craig Morgan is both a soldier and a creator is all that surprising. It may be unusual these days for someone to be successful at both occupations, but we have only to look back to World War II to find artists in every field who served their country with distinction on the battlefield. What's hard is adding a third role—*family man.*

Those two words can make his role as son, husband, and father seem trite, like a line out of a Father's Day card. But even with his kids grown up, he's a full-time dad and grandfather, who calls one of his kids after a late-night gig at the Grand Ole Opry to say hi and offer advice on a personal situation. One who'll rearrange professional commitments so he can put up a trampoline for the grandkids on a weekend afternoon.

Ask Craig why he does so many things, and he'll say he suffers from adult attention deficit syndrome. I'm not a doctor; I can't touch that diagnosis. To my mind, he's both curious and creative, and those two things drive him to write great music and to launch, or at least investigate, projects as varied as reality TV shows and coffee shops. Being creative makes him joyful. But what makes him whole—and what grounds that creativity and makes it more purposeful—is his family.

You can see it in his interaction with his wife, Karen. He's not a music star at home; he's a dad and husband who works in the entertainment field—the difference is the priorities. Family first.

Some people think that's old-fashioned. I think it's the way it ought to be.

—JIM DEFELICE

APPENDIX A:
SELECTED AWARDS & MEDALS FROM CRAIG'S MILITARY SERVICE

Army Service Ribbon

3 Meritorious Service Medals

5 Army Commendation Medals

7 Army Achievement Medals

Armed Forces Expeditionary Medal with Spearhead Device

Army Overseas Service Medal

3 Army Good Conduct Medals

National Defense Service Medal

Global War on Terrorism Medal

Master Parachutist Badge with Combat Jump Device

Air Assault Badge

US Army Marksman Shooting Badge (highest of three grades)

Expert Drivers Badge

APPENDIX B:
SELECTED HIGHLIGHTS FROM
CRAIG'S CIVILIAN CAREERS

May 3, 2000—

Craig Morgan (self-titled debut album) releases

2002—

"Almost Home" wins Song of the Year award from BMI and a Songwriter's Achievement Award from the Nashville Songwriters' Association International

March 3, 2003—

I Love It album releases

March 8, 2005—

My Kind of Living album releases

2005—

Scores his first number-one single with "That's What I Love About Sunday"

2006—

Receives the USO Merit Award

October 31, 2006—

Little Bit of Life album releases

September 18, 2008—

Invited by John Conlee to become a member of the Grand Ole Opry

September 30, 2008—

Greatest Hits album releases

October 21, 2008—

That's Why album releases

October 25, 2008—

Inducted into the Grand Ole Opry

June 29, 2010—

Craig Morgan: All Access Outdoors debuts on the Outdoor Channel (runs for eight seasons)

January 27, 2011—

Embarks on Not Alone tour, performing for service members stationed in Iraq and Kuwait

March 21, 2011—

Honored by the Tennessee City Volunteer Fire Department for his heroics in rescuing two small children from a house fire in Charlotte, TN

April 2, 2011—

Performs during The Academy of Country Music Awards and USO concert for troops and their families stationed at Nellis Air Force Base

October 18, 2011—

This Ole Boy EP releases

January 18, 2012—

Winner Best Deer Golden Moose Award for *Craig Morgan: All Access Outdoors*

Winner Best Turkey Golden Moose Award for *Craig Morgan: All Access Outdoors*

February 28, 2012—

This Ole Boy album releases

March 18, 2012—

Appears on Lifetime's hit drama *Army Wives*

July 4, 2012—

Performs as part of Nashville's Let Freedom Sing celebration

July 17, 2012—

Appears on TNT's *Rizzoli & Isles*

January 17, 2013—

Receives first-ever humanitarian accolade at the 13th Annual Golden Moose Awards

March 28, 2013—

108th General Assembly of the State of Tennessee honors Craig with a reading of House Joint Resolution No. 540, acknowledging him for his notable service to our country and his many musical contributions

April 9–13, 2013—

Participates in Fjällräven Polar, a thrilling 200-mile dogsled excursion above the Arctic Circle

September 3, 2013—

The Journey (Livin' Hits) album releases

January 15, 2014—

Appears on A&E's *Crazy Hearts: Nashville*

May 20, 2014—

Presents at *ACM Presents: An All-Star Salute to the Troops* on CBS

2015—

Winner Best Comedy Golden Moose Award for *Craig Morgan: All Access Outdoors*

July 21, 2015—

Makes 200th appearance at the Grand Ole Opry

January 1, 2016—

Receives AutoZone Liberty Bowl's 2015 Outstanding Achievement Award

March 15, 2016—

Joins Vice Chairman of the Joint Chiefs of Staff General Paul J. Selva for eight-day, seven-country USO Tour celebrating the USO's 75th Anniversary (the first of four annual trips)

June 3, 2016—

A Whole Lot More to Me album releases

October 20, 2016—

Attends USO's 75th Anniversary Gala: Honoring Those Who Serve

September 28, 2017—

Officially launches the Gallery at Morgan Farms, family-owned-and-operated farm-to-table business in downtown Dickson, Tennessee

March 1, 2018—

UPtv premieres the docuseries *Morgan Family Strong*

June 23, 2018—

Awarded the army's Outstanding Civilian Service Medal

June 8, 2019—

Appears on UPtv's *After the Storm*

September 12, 2019—

"The Father, My Son, and the Holy Ghost" hits number one on the iTunes All Genres Top Songs chart in addition to the Top Country Songs chart

November 13, 2019—

Presents at the CMA Awards on ABC

March 5, 2020—

Circle network premieres *Craig's World*

May 22, 2020—

God, Family, Country album releases

October 25, 2020—

Receives the Legacy Award from the Clement Railroad Hotel Museum

November 2020—

Plays Colonel Doug Cole in the TV movie *A Welcome Home Christmas*, premiering first in the US and then Europe

February 20, 2021—

Joins Monster Energy ProClass Riders for an exhibition on the final day of the Iron Dog Snowmobile Race in Alaska

Spring 2022—

One of the featured "survivors" in *Beyond the Edge* on CBS